# MORE PRAISE FOR ACCIDENTAL JOURNEY

"A grandly entertaining, picaresque tale, with the twist that it is not a novel, but the ironic, wittily observed report of actual events during World War II. Among the colorful characters Mark Lynton meets are many of the headline figures of the time, including George VI, the Archbishop of Canterbury, Clement Attlee, the last Kaiser's grandson, Dr. Werner Best, Himmler, Hoess, and Ed Murrow. *Accidental Journey* is a not-to-be-put-down book, the best read I've encountered all year."

—ANDRÉ EMMERICH

"This elegantly written, very personal account of the author's adventures during World War II is both fascinating and exciting from beginning to end. A book of great interest to young and old, it is surely one of the very best written about World War II."

—GENE R. LA ROCQUE, Rear Admiral. USN (Ret.)

"*Accidental Journey* is a great read, chronicling a most remarkable rite of passage. Millions of young men went to war in the 1940s but few had such an extraordinary story to tell, and fewer still could have told it so well. Literate, understated and loaded with a constant parade of famous people who step in and out of Mark Lynton's wartime experiences, this exhilarating book provides a wild ride across western Europe from D-Day to V-E Day!"

—JOSEPH P. HOAR, General, USMC (Ret)

"Mark Lynton is as amusing as he is modest—though in fact he was heroic. This is the story of a refugee from Hitler interned by the British in 1940, who returns to command a lead tank in an armored division fighting in the Normandy bocage, and finds his true home in America."

—NOEL ANNAN, (Lord Annan)

# ACCIDENTAL
# JOURNEY

# ACCIDENTAL JOURNEY

## A CAMBRIDGE INTERNEE'S MEMOIR OF WORLD WAR II

## MARK LYNTON

THE OVERLOOK PRESS
WOODSTOCK · NEW YORK

First published in paperback in 1998 by
The Overlook Press, Peter Mayer Publishers, Inc.
Lewis Hollow Road
Woodstock, New York 12498

Library of Congress Cataloging-in-Publications Data

Lynton, Mark
Accidental Journey : a Cambridge internee's memoir
of World War II / Mark Lynton.
p. cm..
1. Lynton, Mark. 2. Deportations—Great Britain—History—
20th century. 3. World War, 1939–45—Personal narratives, Jewish.
4. Aliens—Great Britain—History—20th century. 5. World War,
1935–45—Prisoners and prisons, British. 6. German students—
Great Britain— Biography. 7. Students and war. I. Title.
D801.G7L96    940.53'17'041—dc20    [B] 94-36769

BOOK DESIGN BY BERNARD SCHLEIFER

Manufactured in the United States of America

ISBN 0-87951-848-0
1 3 5 7 9 8 6 4 2

# CONTENTS

TO MARION, LILI AND MICHAEL, WHO HAVE READ
IT ALL BEFORE, AND TO CLAIRE, NINA AND ELOISE
WHO ONE DAY HOPEFULLY WILL.

# FOREWORD

P. G. Wodehouse once spoke of an author who told all about how and why he wrote his book, when a simple apology would have been sufficient. I therefore intend to be brief.

A memoir written fifty years after the events, must necessarily be suspect.

However, wars in general—and mine in particular—consist of brief spells of high excitement and even higher anxiety, alternating with very long stretches of just waiting around. I thus had much time to make copious and irreverent notes, which—being of a packrat disposition rather than having any specific intent—I have kept all these years.

This story is the result, and the events described are all based on facts as I then noted them. It is, of course, true that distance lends enchantment, and so my war, as here described, may not always have seemed quite so entertaining to me at the time.

It may surprise some readers and offend others that, throughout that period, I felt no hostility towards Germans in general; I did not then and I certainly do not now. My feeling towards the Germans I fought against I have tried to describe, and my views towards Germans in general are influenced by the fact that I have never believed in the concept of collective guilt. I do believe in the concept of collective responsibility, but there the past fifty years have shown that the Germans are both aware of such responsibility and shoulder it. Overall, my German roots go deep and remain so.

I am greatly beholden to my publisher, Peter Mayer, who, I suspect, let kindness take precedence over critical acumen. I am truly grateful to my editor Tracy Carns, whose guidance, encouragement, support and criticism gave shape to a jumbled heap of disjointed facts.

I had a lot of fun writing this book and do hope that you will too, in reading it.

Mark Lynton
Larchmont, New York
1994

# PROLOGUE

IT'S JUNE 1945 and the Grand
Place in Brussels lies in brilliant sunshine.

Several hundred British officers, members of Montgomery's victorious Twenty-first Army Group, are being inspected by King George VI.

Wearing full field marshall's regalia, he slowly walks along the ranks of rigidly still figures and, every so often, pauses and speaks briefly to officers whom he appears to recognize.

Thus he stops in front of Captain Lynton, Third Royal Tanks, and says—haltingly, as was his fashion—"I have seen you before, have I not?"

Stock-still and looking straight ahead as prescribed in the manual, Captain Lynton replies, ". . . With respect, no Sir!" The king looks at me for a very long moment and then moves on down the line.

It so happens that he was right, and how and why we met before and all that occurred before and since make up this story.

# I

# ONCE UPON A TIME...

I WAS BORN Max-Otto Ludwig Loewenstein, in Stuttgart, Germany. Both sides of my family had lived in or near Stuttgart for ten generations or more—a documented fact—and claimed earlier antecedents from Jews who had fled the Spanish Inquisition, which, if not necessarily fiction, remains unverified.

The Loewensteins had first settled in the principality of Loewenstein Fuerstenberg-Wertheim, whose Catholic rulers were tolerant of Jews, which explains why these three names were often adopted among German Jewry. The family subsequently moved to Hechingen, a small town some thirty miles south of Stuttgart and the ancestral home of the imperial Hohenzollern family. The Hohenzollern had left Hechingen centuries before, which may not be the only reason why the Loewensteins never met them.

Moving to Stuttgart in the early 1800s, they evolved from a succession of rabbis and money lenders to repeated generations of lawyers and bankers, a logical progression. Much the same thing happened to my mother's family, the Kiefes, who, for a number of generations, lived in Baissingen—a small hamlet southeast of Stuttgart—as the local *kueffen* (barrel makers), which led to the family name. They, too, discovered banking as a more promising profession and moved to Stuttgart. My grandparents were enthusiastic supporters of the king of Wuerttemberg, his overlord, the emperor of Germany, and of all things German; both my father and uncle won Iron Crosses in World War I, and my other uncle was killed in it as an eighteen-year-old volunteer recruit. My father, with both Law and Economics degrees from Heidelberg University, had spent some years in London before 1914 to learn to be a banker. My mother had attended finishing school in England, having been brought up bilingually in French and German. (The same Swiss governess responsible for this remained with the family for almost seventy years, so that my brother and I were equally at ease in both languages.)

In all, I came from a background of comfortably situated and convinced Germans, with a somewhat cosmopolitan outlook, who just happened to be of Jewish faith—or so we thought at the time.

My father was named head of a major German car manufacturer in 1922, when I was two years old, and we moved to Berlin, where my brother was born some years later. I had a very warm, happy, affluent and sheltered childhood, and I have equally happy memories of my high school years, which began in 1929 at the Franzoesisches Gymnasium. The school had been founded in the 1640s by and for immigrant French Huguenots, and was unusual in continuing to teach all subjects in French; it thus tended to attract a varied and mostly international body of pupils.

Subsequent events led to my being exposed to school systems in three different countries; I still believe the German system to have been the most balanced and well rounded.

Although no particular event precipitated my departure from Germany (my family remained in Berlin until 1935), my parents decided that—given my familiarity with the language—I should continue my schooling in France, and so I moved to Paris in the autumn of 1933. Living as a boarder with a German refugee family, I attended Lycée Pasteur in Neuilly for the following three years, academically the most taxing time of my life. Most French citizens believe that culture is a French discovery, and all of them are convinced they are its most articulate exponents; so they are, and their school system reflects it. It is intense, highly competitive, very cerebral, highly fact-oriented, wholly impersonal, and only marginally related to practical aspects of life. It will, however, leave you with abiding respect and encyclopedic knowledge of the language and its literature. There has not been a time since when I could not readily and almost reflexively recall a French quotation to fit whatever situation I found myself in. Having passed my

French Baccalauréat in the summer of 1936, further education in another language and environment was deemed the appropriate step, and so I headed for England. My parents had, a year earlier, moved from Berlin to Amsterdam.

My going to Cheltenham College in Gloucestershire, an English public school of indifferent academic reputation, sterling social standing, and towering military distinction, was an unlikely but very happy accident, which will be dealt with later in this story.

Three years of the French lycée were more than sufficient to allow me to concentrate exclusively on rugby, cricket, and similar Anglo-Saxon pursuits while at Cheltenham. My French academic baggage similarly allowed me to be named a Major Scholar of St. John's College, Cambridge, without making much noticeable effort. I look back on my two years in Cheltenham with lasting pleasure; it was an academic wasteland, but it taught me a great deal about relationships, team spirit, and camaraderie, concepts that the French might view as the hackneyed platitudes that they are, but which, as I was to find out, have their uses.

I moved to Cambridge in the fall of 1938 to read law, with the intention of eventually becoming a London barrister. Although this did require a modicum of application, I found that even at English university level, French lycée standards left me with enough academic reserves to enjoy my first Cambridge year in a wholly *Brideshead Revisited* ambiance and setting. It was and remains the most lotus-eating period of my life. In August 1939, however, things changed.

## II

---

# "NOT FORGOTTEN, JUST MISLAID: 1939–1941

# A

BSOLUTELY EVERYTHING changed over the next seven years, even my name; but not just yet. . . .

## 1

If Stanford-on-Soar did not exist, Trollope would have invented it.

Five miles from Loughborough, a county seat of dim distinction, Stanford was a tiny village in the very heart of England's hunting shires, where foxes, dogs, and horses not merely outnumber humans, but regularly outsmart them. Stanford consisted of a large stone church, reputedly Saxon in origin and sufficiently lichen-covered to back up such an unlikely boast, a much-frequented pub, a much-maligned all-purpose store-cum-post office, a single village street lined with thatched farmhouses on either side, a graveyard predictably larger than the village, and Stanford Rectory, a memorably ugly, infinitely cozy Victorian pile and home to the Reverend and Mrs. Briggs, my hosts for the summer in 1939.

John Briggs, their only offspring, was an Old Cheltonian as well as a St. John's undergraduate, and we had become friends, even though John was a dedicated medical student and a cricket nut; two addictions that I view with great suspicion to this day. John, when I last heard of him, was a respected doctor, family man, cricketer, and local dignitary in Nottingham.

The Reverend Briggs, looking just like Punch with a dog collar, owned a halo of white hair, a high-pitched, rather querulous voice, button-bright eyes, a perpetual pipe perpetually being relit, and was a bustling, opinionated, stubborn, nosy, thoroughly decent, and deeply kind little man.

Having spent some forty years in the Royal Navy, he had retired as chief chaplain of the Mediterranean Fleet and was now looking after his roses, his lawns, his dogs, his golf game, and the souls of a couple of hundred villagers, mostly in that order.

His naval antecedents had left him with an awesome capacity for absorbing alcohol of any kind and the unshakable belief that constant exercise, the British Navy, and occasional, rather cursory, invocations of the Deity would, in combination, deal with any conceivable problem. Color, race, or creed meant nothing to him; you either were British or you were not. If you were not, whether you came from Toulouse or Tibet did not matter to the Reverend Briggs. He loved anything that was four-legged or floated. Hitler was a "silly man" and should war occur, the British would, of course, beat him, even though burdened with the French and other superfluous allies.

His Sunday sermons were sparse, usually no more than reading out the lead article of that week's *Church Times*, but they would be followed by some incisive comments on matters local and international (Chamberlain was being a silly ass again; don't miss the Nottingham Cattle Fair, last day tomorrow) and then—breathlessly anticipated by Stanford all agog—came the weekly reckoning.

"Mary Bardsley, I heard about you and Jim Feathers over at Braithwaite's lower field. I won't have that, Mary! I want you to act properly, and I don't want to have to talk to you about this again!"

There would be about half a dozen such quarter-deck episodes, and, though the culprits seemed neither too penitent nor about to reform, it amused Pa Briggs and enthralled the village.

Ma Briggs shared her husband's innate decency and kindliness and was almost ludicrously British in a tweedy, horse-faced sort of way. As tall as he was short, she was as frighteningly capable as he, but where he fussed, bustled, and scurried, she displayed the nervous system of a stone and just "got things done." Moving in a perpetual cloud of cigarette smoke, Mrs. B. had a hoarse, rasping voice that with dismaying suddenness, would switch to a high cackling laugh, usually ending in a coughing fit.

A paragon of calm competence, whether chairing a committee or driving a golf ball, she had a distressing attachment to the AGA cooker, a fiendish invention intended for people who did not like to cook or who did not like to eat. Mrs. B. liked neither.

A cross between a wardrobe, a multilevel stove, and a rabbit warren, the AGA operated on the principle that cooking once a week was ample. You just cooked up various messes on one day and then popped them into different shelves and holes in the AGA, where they would harden and dessicate at constant temperatures until ready to be consumed—or at least wondered at. Eating an omelette on Thursday that had been concocted on Monday and maintained in the AGA with embalming fluid or whatever, made you agree with Mrs. B. that food was something best forgotten.

It was an absurdly beautiful summer, warm, lazy, timeless, filled with golf, tennis, dances, drives, girls, cucumber sandwiches, and other Bertie Wooster follies. Although you could not wholly ignore the gathering storm, you had that firm and insane conviction that lightning could not strike in Leicestershire.

Certainly not in Stanford Hall, the "house next door," where we spent most of our time. A vast, pseudo-Palladian pile, set among four thousand acres, which included the entire parish of Stanford-on-Soar, as well as a private golf course, indoor and outdoor pools, tennis courts by the handful, horses by the score, and servants in battalion strength, it was owned by Sir Julian Kahn, a saturnine, impeccably tailored figure, and reputedly one of England's wealthiest men. He certainly lived up to that reputation and, until I saw San Simeon twenty-five years later, Stanford Hall was my ultimate concept of self-indulgent opulence.

It had its own stage and theater, and the Kahns regularly entertained about eighty overnight guests on weekends, who would be ferried to and from Loughborough station by a fleet of black Rolls Royces with the Kahn crest on the doors. John and his parents had permanent visiting rights, and we spent most of our time golfing, swimming, or playing tennis there, and would occasionally be asked to stay for tea.

Lady Kahn—a nice, gemütlich Jewish Mama, much more Kahn than Lady—would frequently ask us to make up a tennis foursome, in which she would usually be joined by the senior butler, a figure quite as admirable and twice as daunting as the original Crichton. Perfect butlers do everything perfectly and hence he was obviously a fine tennis player; however even he had moments of mortality. On the rare occasions when he would lose a point, he would turn to Ma Kahn, bow slightly, and state in a stage baritone, "I deeply regret this, your Ladyship." Court manners have changed somewhat since then, I guess.

We did try to respond to the gathering gloom by offering to help Farmer Braithwaite bring in the harvest; a backbreaking endeavor in which, blinded by sweat, heat, and bugs, we pitched never-diminishing stacks of hay into seemingly ever-higher wagons. We were occasionally sustained in these worthy efforts by Mrs. Braith-waite producing lukewarm beer to be slurped out of buckets (if you go rural, you might as well go truly rural) and slabs of bread spread with salmon paste, which looked like blood plasma.

This agony ended in late August with a great Harvest Festival service in Stanford Church, the place awash in flowers, sheaves of corn, fruit, and vegetables, the entire village all assembled and scrubbed gleamingly clean, and the Reverend Briggs, for once, fore-going his recital of Stanford's *chronique scandaleuse*. It fell to me, a German Jew in a High Anglican church, to read the First Lesson from the pulpit, the wondrously and somberly appropriate Corinthian text of St. Paul's, "When I was a child . . ."

The war, of course, started with the invasion of Poland on September 1, and no one truly believed that the subsequent forty-eight hours would change the course of events. Gas masks had been issued to all civilians in funny little cardboard containers, which made passable lunch boxes—till they got wet. How good the masks were, no one fortunately ever had to find out.

Evacuation of city children had begun, and the rectory had been informed that we could expect a dozen or more from Sheffield. Since nothing was known about ages or sex, Mrs. B. had made contingency plans for any bisexual delinquency from nought to eighteen. The AGA cooker was obviously going to act as the great leveller, certain eventually to discourage even the most indiscriminate feeders.

On the other hand, the Munich episode, not even a year past, had seen such strange turns of events, and even now Chamberlain and his appeasement supporters were still acting so ambivalently, that war could not wholly be taken for granted.

And so, on September 3, a simply gorgeous Indian Summer Sunday, we all waited for that 11 A.M. Chamberlain announcement, for which we had been asked to stand by.

The Reverend Briggs, secure in his particular relationship to God, had cancelled the morning service, telling the villagers that "there were more important things to think about this morning," and so we all sat and listened to Chamberlain's tired, quavering voice explaining the situation and inviting us to "imagine what a bitter disappointment this is to me." The Reverend B. glared at the radio, snorted, "Well, old boy, we're not exactly pleased, either," and switched off the set. None of us actually heard the war being declared.

## 2

The Sheffield evacuees duly arrived that Sunday and, with them, an aura of unrelenting chaos. There were about a dozen of them, boys and girls, in their very early teens, and all of them little monsters. They were not just scruffy, they were verminous, and even a lifetime among sailors had left the Briggs couple unprepared for the range and variety of those kids' profanity. Some had come from broken homes, some from no homes at all; if there was an identifiable mother, she frequently turned out to be "on the game" (her kid's bland statement). In such case, her offspring usually visited her in pubs, to be fed broken biscuits and leftovers in the glasses on the bar; the rest of the time, the kids lived on the street.

They consistently avoided bathrooms, toilets, or indoor plumbing, since they had none of these in Sheffield and such contrivances scared them. There is the frequently quoted story of one of the mothers coming to visit her offspring in a home such as Stanford, seeing her child in the living room, and yelling, "You dirty little bastard; doing it on the lady's carpet! Go, do it in the corner, you nasty little sod." Believe it! They carved their initials or dirty words into every reachable piece of furniture. They only wanted to drink beer or gin—they were a nightmare, and a very sad one. None of them had ever seen a cow or milk that did not come in bottles; most of them had never seen a stand of trees or a patch of lawn.

Little by little, over the next few weeks, Mrs. B. and her household staff (in 1939 even a village rectory could afford three maids) cajoled or threatened them into a semblance of civilized living.

The Briggs family, like hosts of slum evacuees all over England, were genuinely horrified at the discovery that such conditions existed, and there was much talk about postwar priorities to set matters right.

It may have been that the war lasted a very long time, but somehow nothing ever came of those good intentions. In fact, the reverse took place; once places like Sheffield appeared to be spared German bombings (which concentrated on London and RAF airfields), kids were encouraged to "go home and visit mother for the weekend" and frequently did not return. Instead, in several cases, the Briggs received ill-spelt and abusive letters, accusing them of teaching the kids "things that ain't good for them"; culture shock existed long before it became a fashionable concept!

Later that month, John and I returned to Cambridge. Within a thousand-year-old institution, news of an occasional war hardly gets around, and where it had, it was treated with faintly irritated indifference. Since there was no likelihood of a Cromwellian confiscation of college plate to finance such an enterprise, Cambridge did not seem to feel any cause for concern. My tutor, C. W. Guillebaud, who had the twin distinction of looking like his own death mask and of being a renowned economist, typified Cambridge's sense of relevance by publishing a lengthy eulogy of Hitler's economic policies on Christmas Day 1939, three months after the war broke out.

My suggestion—based on Officer Training Corps at Cheltenham and the relentlessly patriotic outlook of that most martial of public schools—that I should volunteer right away was met with faint amusement and fatherly condescension by Guillebaud, who suggested that

Cicero was more in my line than Clausewitz. He pointed out that generally wars had a tendency to outlast their forecast duration, and that in all likelihood, the war would still be around after I finished my studies. He was of course right on both counts.

The upshot was that I resumed my prewar Cambridge routine; some lectures, much talk and beer, lots of movies and sherry parties, squash, golf, and bull sessions lasting through the night, solving the problems of the universe, occasionally and tangentially including the war. There was some rationing, but it did not include Stilton cheese, college-brewed stout, sherry, and similarly vital staples.

The only passing, and barely noticed, hint of events "outside," was the brief guest appearance of an Alien Tribunal, an extraordinary notion even by Home Office standards. The War Office, a bureaucratic Laocoön of infinitely tangled notions, had decreed that certain areas in England were "restricted," and the Home Office promptly felt called upon to complicate matters further. All aliens living in such areas were to be interviewed and classified, though no brief was ever issued to the investigators on what basis they should classify these people, or what to do with them once they had sorted them into categories. This benign neglect, bordering on outright idiocy, generally acclaimed as the British way of "muddling through," was well in line with the War Office's asinine efforts in the first place. London was never declared a "restricted area," nor was any major English city or even Oxford. Coastal areas fell under the category, which made some casual sense, but no one ever found out how Cambridge got to be considered near the coast. It is just conceivable that Sandringham had something to do with it; it is fairly close to Cambridge and the royal family spent occasional weekends there. But in that case, why expose George VI to all kinds of potentially murderous aliens during weekdays at Buckingham Palace? Classifying Cambridge as a "restricted" area only made sense to the War Office, which is itself an opaque mystery to ordinary people.

Undeterred by the fact that any alien wishing to avoid scrutiny merely had to make sure he lived in an unrestricted area (next to Whitehall, for instance), the Alien Tribunals set to work. Once again I contacted Guillebaud and once again his advice was sound. The important issue was to be able to produce credentials from a well-known, preferably titled, personage. It occurred to me that my father, as a member of the parent board of Michelin in Clermont-Ferrand, had, some years ago, "loaded" the board of the British Michelin operations with some aged dignitaries, who were to lend their names and stay well away, in return for a small yearly stipend. In that context I had heard of General Sir Ernest Swinton, a military historian and the originator of tank warfare in World War I.

Since the entire enterprise had a decidedly *opéra bouffe* air about it, why not write Sir Ernest whom, needless to say, I had never met?

I recall every word of his reply. "Dear Loewenstein," he wrote, "If you are the son of Dr. Arthur Loewenstein, I have no objection to being named as a reference, though I should have to point out that we have never met. Should you contact me again, please type the letter, as your handwriting is difficult to read. Sincerely yours, Ernest D. Swinton."

Since I was the son of Arthur L. and having been assured by Guillebaud that Swinton's "testimonial" was more than adequate, I duly took it with me before the Alien Tribunal. This was made up of half a dozen reserve officers, all decked out in faded World War I uniforms, and presided over by Judge Thesinger, a reasonably well-regarded judge and brother of a much better known actor. This geriatric gaggle set to in the finest Colonel Blimp tradition: what school had I been to (Cheltenham; very sound), did I play soccer or rugby there (rugby, of course; very good), did I play squash (I did; splendid), was I member of the Officer Training Corps (forgot it was Cheltenham; silly question, of course, ha-ha) what was I studying in Cambridge (law; bit odd that, brainy chap, what? never mind—).

It went on in that vein until it came to references, and I handed over Swinton's little note. Just as Guillebaud had forecast, it was reverently passed from hand to hand ("Sir Ernest? Why, I met him once near Cambrai in 1917—"), and I was promptly certified as a "friendly alien."

It should perhaps have occurred to me then that a screening process that would theoretically have allowed me to have long telephone chats with Hitler that very night might create problems at some later stage. It did not occur to me, and I carried on, undisturbed by the world outside Cambridge and bolstered by frequent and reassurring news from Holland. It was a period of phony war to the rest of the world—in Cambridge, there just was no war at all.

Except for McDougall. Just as Oxford has "scouts" who look after undergraduates living in college and who are a permanent monument to arthritis and inexhaustible memory, so Cambridge has "bedmakers" who fulfill the same functions. The only difference is that scouts are males, generally looking like a Cockney version of Quasimodo, and bedmakers are ancient crones who act like fugitives from a road company of *Macbeth*. Mrs. McDougall, who was "doing" for me, was, unlikely as it may sound to anyone not knowing Cambridge, the fifth generation of bedmakers looking after the same set of rooms! Her recall for gossip, mired in the oral history of a century, was encyclopedic, and like all members of her ilk, she was never without a hat, a cigarette, or a piece of unasked-for advice. She also had a husband, known widely and simply as "McDougall says . . ."

No one had never met McDougall, who was permanently bedridden after an industrial accident and evidently an insomniac to boot. McDougall read every single newspaper published every single day, and did so well before dawn, so that, when Mrs. McD. would appear around 9 A.M., the unvarying query was "What does McDougall say?" Mrs. McDougall would then embark upon a brief synopsis of the world at large, always prefaced by "McDougall says . . ." Thanks to McDougall we were not merely fully informed, but comforted by the knowledge that someone was watching events, even if we were not.

# 3

Friday, May 10, was another matchlessly sunny day in a summer that will long be remembered—and not merely for its fabulous weather.

Mrs. McDougall suddenly stood in the middle of my bedroom to state that "McDougall says, you'll never see your family again."

"Oh come on, Mrs. McD., it's much too early for jokes. What are you talking about?"

"The Germans invaded Holland this morning."

First I had heard about it—and that's how my war started.

In the end, McDougall proved an inaccurate prophet, but it did take almost a year and a half before I had news of my family, and more than six years before I saw them again.

Two days later, on Whit-Sunday, yet another cloudless day, the rumors were rife. SS troops were parachuting somewhere disguised as nuns, or they were parachuting nuns, it was never clear who was doing what or where. The Dutch were holding; they were not; the Belgians were either attacking or surrendering or both; the French were doing something; Chamberlain was distressed.

Since the war was clearly too confusing to retain our total attention, about a dozen of us decided to go punting over to Grantchester and get bibulously beatific in the process. We were the usual motley assembly of budding Indian revolutionaries, sufficiently unathletic to be likely to twist an ankle in their sleep, and hulking colonial toughs (including the United States in that geographic sweep) who rowed for Cambridge, and could both lift and empty beer kegs with equal nonchalance. St. John's College had always attracted Brahmins and oarsmen, and while there is no explanation for this, it becomes self-fulfilling after a while. In my time, the place was full of people who fifteen years later literally ran India and Pakistan, and awash with gigantic South Africans and Ivy Leaguers, whose entire universe centered on beer and boats.

Back from the river, feeling suitably unsteady and as chaotic but obviously happier than the war situation, some of us decided to round off the day by imbibing some more up in my rooms. At the head of the stairs we were met by a person whose outsize boots, bowler hat, and stern demeanor conveyed that we were dealing with "authority." Since that did not seem to fit the mood of the hour, one of the larger South Africans immediately and loudly volunteered to throw the man down the stairwell, which clearly rattled our bowler-hatted visitor. The next ten minutes were vintage Marx Brothers. Bowler hat, having identified himself as a police constable, diffidently conveyed the message that the chief constable wished to see me, whereupon I indicated that I would come to see him next day, which led to some rather pained whisperings about the chief constable wanting to see me urgently, which I then agreed to do right after dinner, which led to some further entreaty to "do so right away, please, Sir."

All this on the stairs, to the accompaniment of the rowing contingent, inflamed by anger and alcohol, trying to get physical, while my Indian friends, budding lawyers all, were loudly invoking unlawful arrest, habeas corpus, and other irrelevancies.

Amidst this pandemonium, I had caught another apologetic whisper about a civilian car waiting outside and so slipped out of the melée at the top of the stairs to pack an overnight case with a pair of pajamas, a couple of shirts, and some toiletries.

Nothing that had been said prompted me to do so, and I do not know to this day why I did; just as well, though, since I was not to return to Cambridge or to any of my belongings for nine months.

On reaching the main police station, it was quite obvious that something drastic was going on. I had had practically no contact with other Germans or Austrians while at Cambridge but knew that quite a number attended the university or lived in the area. It seemed as if every one of them had already been collected that afternoon and that, depending on their own intuition or possibly the information of a less-harassed escort than mine, they all seemed far better equipped than I. Each one had at least two suitcases, some had brought in full-size trunks, and I was clearly the only Spartan present. I have sometimes wondered since whether my notorious tendency to overpack for trips dates back to feeling a trifle unprepared that day. No one knew anything, rumors were rampant, tea and biscuits were offered at frequent intervals, no one ever saw the chief constable or anyone else, and, at nightfall, we were suddenly and hastily stowed into waiting buses and driven off. Not very far, actually; the buses stopped next to a large, partly ploughed field, obviously only recently surrounded by some flimsy strands of barbed wire, and dotted with a couple of dozen canvas tents. It had begun to rain, and a few damp and disconsolate-looking soldiers were wandering around the wire perimeter. They, like all our subsequent English guarding troops, were both incurious and utterly ignorant of who we might be, and proved to be friendly, indifferent, quite courteous, and staggeringly incompetent. By contrast, the soldiers who later watched over us in Canada were tough, smart, very efficient, and generally rather hostile.

We found out from our guards that we were somewhere near Bury St. Edmunds, thus just up the road from Cambridge; no one knew why, for what, or for how long. There were no lights, since there was a war on, and, aside from our soggy watchmen hanging about outside the wire, there was no one at all present, probably for the same reason. Any one of us could have walked back to Cambridge, and perhaps I should have done that. As it was, about a hundred of us started squelching around in the gloom, until someone stumbled across a tent full of straw pallets.

Looking back, it seems one of the Pythagorean given for any internment camp that, no matter what else may be lacking, there will be straw pallets tucked away somewhere. And once you have a straw pallet, you can start bitching in relative comfort. There was no food, but none of us were hungry; there were no latrines, but it was a pretty large field. The tents had duckboards, we had about run out of rumors, it was pitch dark and sogging wet, and so everyone just burrowed into a tent and under some pallets and went to sleep. Some of the better-organized inmates had of course brought along flashlights, and I recall one of the people in my tent opening three separate suitcases before finding the pajamas deemed suitable to the circumstances. I had no such problem.

Things began to happen at dawn—they always do, where the military are concerned; a most deplorable habit.

We were presented with vast mugs of tea, slabs of bread, and chunks of margarine, and having cursorily demired ourselves at the solitary water tap available, ate a hearty breakfast. A word about army tea, since it was to sustain me for many years to come. It is an almost syrup-like concoction, made up of black tea, sweetened tinned milk, and vast amounts of sugar. It has no relation whatever to ordinary tea and, when scaldingly hot and first thing in the morning, is the best beverage on the earth. Except for army cocoa.

While still munching away, we were suddenly faced with the splendid sight of a Rifle Brigade lieutenant, all in dark green, braided cord, and gleaming leather, and all of about nineteen years old.

He seemed delighted to see us, particularly since, as he explained, he was "so pleased that all you chaps have decided to join us." It remains a mystery to this day what chaps he had in mind or whom we were supposed to join, but it did get us onto another set of buses and off we went, this time on a full day's journey.

Except for the drivers, there was no one about, and again we could just have walked away at any one of the various maintenance halts during the day. No one even suggested it; my own guess is that it had nothing to do with lethargy, submissiveness, or reluctance to lug heavy suitcases. I believe we were all just curious; I know I was.

It was dusk again before we reached our destination—Liverpool City Hall, of all places. This time, by way of contrast, they had assembled enough troops and armaments to repel several invading armies. Judging by the way they looked and acted, our new guards did not seem too capable of handling all that hardware, nor at all inclined to try. They were positively welcoming, until the apparition of their sergeant major who, in the tradition of his genre, first bawled them out and then started bawling us out. He was getting remarkably frenzied and quite interesting to listen to when it suddenly and clearly dawned on him that he was dealing with people so far removed from martial matters that he might as well be speaking Mandarin. He literally stopped in mid-bellow, shrugged, and said, "Follow me, please, gentlemen!"

Which we did, to end up in a vast hall somewhere within that very large building, and there met other internees, several hundreds of them, coming from other parts of the country. They were all Germans and Austrians (I met no other nationalities during my internment), and some had been arrested as early as May 10, but no one knew any more about our status or the events outside than we did—and we, of course, knew nothing. Things seemed reasonably organized, with camp beds, double-decker bunks, latrines, washing facilities, and blankets all available, and since there were no windows and only one access door, surveillance was unobtrusive and presumably simple. By the time I got through being interned, I had been an inmate of six camps (not counting the initial muddy interlude), and there was a weird "heads or tails" alternation to them. Invariably you struck one where there was absolutely nothing, followed by one that was quite lavishly appointed, only to get involved with a "ground zero" situation again.

We stayed in Liverpool City Hall for two or three days, just generally milling about, but it was there that the "Cambridge Gang" emerged, a bunch of about a dozen of us, which became widely known, if mostly only by hearsay, among most English and Canadian internment camps.

There were around thirty people who, like myself, were Cambridge undergraduate or graduate students; generally from comfortable middle-class, mostly Jewish backgrounds; *jeunes fils de bonnes familles*. There were probably another thirty who had no connection with the university, but who lived in and around Cambridge, were involved in business or farming, were mostly somewhat older than we, and who, in quite some cases, were political rather than ethnic refugees. Most of that entire crowd I do not recall at all, and some, like Bondi and Gold, who later became illustrious mathematicians and astronomers, are just names to me now, but I have very vivid memories of the Cambridge Gang.

Two "gang members" in particular require some comment, not merely because they were the unquestioned leaders, both of the Cambridge Gang, and of any camp in which we found ourselves, but also because, in diametrically opposite fashion, they were unusual— to put it mildly.

Hans Kahle had little to do with Cambridge and nothing to do with the university, but as an ardent antiNazi, he had fled Germany in the 1930s and was working on a farm near Cambridge. He was a balding, raw-boned Raymond Massey–type of person in his late forties, thus much older than most of us—and not merely in years.

Frederick the Great had instituted new decorations for sheer personal bravery and, francophile that he was, named the highest *Pour le Mérite*. For two hundred years, Pour le Mérite was Germany's highest award for courage, until Hitler replaced it with an escalation of Knight's Cross, Knight's Cross with Oak Leaves, Knight's Cross with Oak Leaves and Swords, and (awarded only three times, I believe) Knight's Cross with Oak Leaves, Swords, and Diamonds. (I had dealings with an "Oak Leaves and Swords" bearer some five years later, and he was a pretty overwhelming specimen.)

Kahle had won the Pour le Mérite in 1918, one of just a few hundred in that entire war to do so. Having turned into a soldier of fortune, he then fought in China under Sun Yat-sen and, in the process, became a fanatic and doctrinaire communist. During the

Spanish Civil War, he had been chief of staff of the International Brigades for several years and was the legendary "General Hans," who had planned, fought, and won the battle of Guadalajara.

Later, in 1945, Kahle predictably moved to East Germany and was police chief of the state of Mecklenburg until his death in the 1960s.

Fritz Lingen was the utter antithesis to Kahle, aside from being a Cambridge undergraduate as we were. Born the ex-crown prince's third son, and grandson of the kaiser, he was registered at birth as Friedrich Wilhelm, Prince of Prussia, followed by a dozen ducal and princely titles in descending order, with Count Lingen at the tail end. In Cambridge and in camp, he went by that name, and, even though officially he only became a Prussian prince again after 1945, he was not too plebeian when we knew him. You looked at him and at any English coin and saw a mirror image—not all that surprising since George VI and he were cousins.

In the late 1940s, he married a Guinness heiress and became part of England's landed gentry, and twenty years later, he drowned himself in the Rhine, a suicide that remains both inexplicable and strange. People of his background use guns, not rivers.

Fritz was very tall, very thin, very blond, and very handsome, in an almost ludicrously Teutonic way. He was not too bright, had immense presence and poise, boundless energy, an attractive sense of humor, unfailing manners, and not a snobbish bone in him. We respected Kahle, we liked Fritz. Until we left for Canada some six weeks later, Fritz regularly received food hampers sent by Fortnum & Mason at the behest of some august and frequently royal personages, to the utter bemusement of our guards, who, on such occasions, appeared dubious as to which side of the wire they should be on.

Neither Fritz nor anyone else ever discovered how that lofty grapevine worked and how his blue-blooded benefactors always knew where he was, when we did not even know that ourselves. But they did know and kept on feeding him and us, since the Cambridge Gang shared everything. Aside from the hampers, nothing was ever done from the outside to have Fritz treated differently from internees, nor did Fritz ever seek such support.

**4**

As long as we were in Liverpool, we were living in the isolation of a diving bell. Hitler could have been in Manchester or the French in Leipzig, though the latter seemed less likely. Things changed when, about three days after our arrival, we got back into buses and were driven out to Huyton, a large and rather distressing suburb of Liverpool where we found a true Matthew Arnold setting; drab-looking council houses with peeling paint, which were jammed against each other, with only a postage-stamp-sized yard front and back. The authorities had merely cordoned off several streets with barbed wire, thus creating a compound, and then added a kind of "no man's land" by putting a wide layer of barbed wire coil all around the compound. Beyond that area, they had further requisitioned a concentric ring of houses to be inhabited by guards and official personnel. We never heard what happened to the original inhabitants, but they had left with absolutely everything that could be lifted, unscrewed, or pried off—and that included floor boards in some instances. The place was bare!

Throughout that day more buses and internees arrived and by late afternoon there were at least five hundred people in the compound waiting for someone to tell them something.

The man who told them was Kahle. Since there clearly was no one around who was either interested or authorized to take matters in hand, we got to know "General Hans." He never raised his voice; he just took charge. People were split up in groups of twenty or so, each group was allocated to one house and told whom to send off to find straw pallets (which, predictably, were located somewhere), whom to detail to clean up the place as much as possible and ready it for the night, whom to dispatch to check out cooking and washing facilities—things just fell into place.

The Cambridge Gang became effective that evening. Kahle naturally viewed us as his delegates, and we were responsible for his orders being carried out. So we raced around, helping here, shoving there, and generally making ourselves unpopular, since most of that Huyton crowd was much older and more frightened than we were— and just as confused. Given our age and physical condition, we were prone to "do something" and were tearing about like demented terriers, whereas they would probably have preferred just to be left alone—except that Kahle and we would not let them.

Meanwhile, Kahle and Lingen walked to the barbed wire fence, and Kahle, with his Eric von Stroheim accent and in a voice that had obviously made people jump for the past twenty years, shouted, "Sergeant, get the Orderly Officer." The sergeant found time to yell, "Yes, Sir," and ran—Kahle had that kind of effect on people. The orderly officer, a pleasant-looking child, duly arrived and, within a matter of minutes, was clearly putty in Kahle's and Lingen's hands. We were much too busy herding our fellow internees around or filling pallets to follow details of the conversation, but once, while running past the threesome, I heard Lingen explain something in his high-pitched, barely-accented BBC English, with the orderly officer re-peating, "Of course, Sir, rely on me. Yes, Sir," and being suitably obedient.

The upshot of these "negotiations" was that we would imme-diately be issued cooking and eating utensils, would get benches and tables so as to be able to organize communal cooking and eating facilities, would draw rations for everybody every second day, and would get two blankets each, as well as soap, towel, and four nails per man (to be hammered into the wall to act as a wardrobe).

Given the sparsity of my wardrobe, I had three nails to spare, the only surplus I had.

The main problem was to persuade this uniformed infant to let us have some light bulbs. We had of course found none, and Lingen and Kahle finally talked him into disgorging three or four, as well as some blackout material for windows, since the blackout was being strictly enforced (Liverpool being a major potential bombing target). We could then at least turn one of the houses into a combination of mess hall, central kitchen, and community center. It took another two weeks, though, to convince our jailers to supply additional bulbs; in the meanwhile, we had to rely on clear nights and continent blad-ders, not always an assured combination. Those initial arrangements also included permission to write one weekly letter (which would, of course, be censored), for each street to get at least one newspaper every day, and, most important of all, "someone from Intelligence" to come by that very evening to tell us what all this was about. I do not recall whether we had not been allowed to bring any radios or whether, in those pre-transistorized days, large suitcases would have accommodated them, in any event there were none around, nor had anyone read or heard any news for a week.

Our guards were perfectly willing to be informative, but it is a long and unshakable tradition for the English in general and English soldiery in particular to be profoundly uninterested in anything happening on the other side of the channel. Major wars are no reason to interfere with such embedded philosophy, so what little news we heard was invariably garbled and almost certainly inaccurate. The only certainty appeared to be that the French were having a very bad time, which seemed to fill our informants with profound satisfaction.

Kahle and Lingen completed arrangements for that night by decreeing that each house should elect a "house father," that the assembly of such worthies should elect respective "street fathers," and that this reassuringly paternal structure should culminate in a "camp father," who would represent us all. Typically, neither Kahle nor Lingen, then or later, ever accepted nominations to any of these functions; equally predictably, no other "father" at any level ever made any important decision before clearing it first with one of our two "godfathers."

Choosing "fathers" to speak for us had no filial or jesuitic implications; it was simply that even a remote translation of any kind of "fuehrer" was clearly anathema, and no one came up with a better appellation.

The Cambridge Gang set to, that evening, to scour and scrub the designated "community house," install bulbs, blacken out windows, get some tables and benches set up, and shoehorn the entire crowd under one roof, in anticipation of the "man from Intelligence."

The "man from Intelligence" was certainly a novel specimen to us; a Maigret-like figure, paunchy, balding, looking both benevolent and distracted, and wearing a uniform unpressed since the day they wove the cloth; with no insignia, but with 1914–1918 ribbons.

Having fussed with his glasses and pipe for a while, he briefly, but quite clearly, sketched out the situation. The Home Office's original attempt to screen aliens had been "simply cretinous," a judgment I would not have argued with. The war was going badly: Benelux had been overrun, France was being lost, England might be invaded. German successes had been aided by Fifth Column activities or so his "masters" believed; personally, he thought it "arrant nonsense." However, given that perception, the Home Office and the War Office ("for once working together, a sure recipe for utter chaos," according to our friend) had decided to intern all aliens living in "restricted areas," and hold them in camps until the authorities had time to sort everyone out. Since the assumption was that most of us would turn out to be "friendly aliens," the powers-that-be hoped that we would understand and bear with their predicament. As a matter of fact, we did; most of us did not bear the slightest grudge then, nor oddly enough, ever afterwards. More fussing with glasses and pipe and then, switching into accentless German, our strange friend indicated that he was well aware that just about all of us were Jews or political refugees, and that he thought all this to be wholly absurd. Back into English, he briefly referred to "my masters' tendency to act like idiots whenever they can," and then lumbered out of our lives. We all thought what he had said was both treasonous and most encouraging. We, of course, never learned his name; Smiley, probably.

And so we settled in Huyton.

Less by design than through sheer excess energy, the Cambridge Gang fell into an "encouragement through exasperation" pattern. We did everything and did everything first; cook, clean, carpenting, any plumbing or electrician's chore, garbage disposal, whatever. None of us had either aptitude or skill in any such endeavor, but someone had to do it and our almost invariably justified assumption was that someone more qualified would be sufficiently distressed by our pathetic display eventually to take over. Predictably, the first such hand-over occurred in the communal kitchen; even Escoffier might have had some problems with powdered eggs, but what we did to them brought out some real cooks in a hurry. We never found anyone who thought he could collect garbage better than we could, but then you can't win them all.

By now, internment was bringing home some lessons to us, or at least to me:

☐ when a lot of people are forced to live within a restricted space, everyone's physical actions and psychological moods impinge on everyone else's. Their interrelation is extraordinary and it is essential to remember it constantly;

☐ in that context, both dignity and privacy become very dominant realities, or at least they did to me. It is a "turf" not to be
invaded unless absolutely unavoidable;

☐ someone has to take the initiative and lead and keep on doing
it. Left to themselves, most people tend to mill about and get
discouraged; activity makes for optimism.

These are brash generalizations, but I found them to be true, both
in internment camps and in the army.

Over the next couple of weeks, while the war went from bad to
worse, our situation improved steadily. The houses became livable,
the food edible, we had newspapers (which admittedly made terrible
reading), our surveillance was casual and friendly, and, except for the
barbed wire (and the dismal look of Huyton itself), we might have
been in a holiday camp.

All of us were busily writing the first of an endless chain of letters,
all addressed to the Home Office, all repeating the "It's me, I'm
innocent" message. Most of us assumed that, given the traditional fog
of war, the Home Office had just mislaid us and would be pleased to be
reminded. As subsequent events proved, we were very right in this
assumption, though the Home Office managed to contain its enthusiasm about locating us.

The only unfailing radar track led to Fritz Lingen, whose Fortnum
& Mason parcels continued with gratifying regularity and to the
increasing mystification of our guards. I remember a gnome of a
Welshman, unhappily disguised as a soldier, dumping a parcel almost
his own height at Lingen's feet and, wishing to be helpful, proceeding
to read out the accompanying card. Having read aloud, "By Command of her Majesty, the Queen Mother . . ." he hastily dropped
the card and shuffled back to more democratic environs.

## 5

The war news continued to worsen, and just when we had Huyton in
livable shape, in the last days of May, our Intelligence guru turned up
once more. Having complimented us on what we had done to that

wired-off shambles, he informed us casually that we would be moved to the Isle of Man in a day or two.

The danger of invasion was apparently imminent and the authorities therefore wanted all internees to be assembled in one place. The concept appeared to entertain our friend considerably, and he was quite ready to share his amusement. The fact that we were interned would indicate that at least some of his masters had doubts about our loyalty. If they were right, concentrating us in one place would make it much easier for any invading Germans to add additional manpower. Putting us on the Isle of Man would make it easier for them still, since one of the logical German invasion routes would be through neutral Ireland, and from there to the Isle of Man. If we felt that this was sheer idiocy, all he could tell us is that he was used to idiots, and to this day, I am unable to think of any logical reason for sending us to the Isle of Man. All I knew about it was that it hosted motorcycle races and housed cats without tails; not exactly premier tourist attractions. In postwar years, they have added tax evasion as an inducement, but I still think of the Isle of Man as a rather deplorable spot.

We duly arrived there two days later, via buses, Liverpool, and a very antique and asthmatic excursion steamer, and settled in Douglas, right on the cliffs overlooking the Irish Sea. For all I know, the purpose was to make it that much easier for the Germans to spot and collect us; anyway the view was nice.

The island's climate at that time of year is bracing, in the traditional English sense in that it rains all the time. Douglas, to the extent that we discovered it, consisted of a serried row of tawdry boarding houses hugging the cliff top and was vacation heaven to generations of English holiday makers before they discovered Torremolinos and Benidorm, places just as lamentable, but where it rains less. As for Douglas, we probably did everybody (except ourselves) a favor by taking it out of the vacation circuit.

Here again a compound had been created by wiring off a large part of the cliff area, but it was a much larger camp than Huyton, as internees from all over the country were being assembled, several thousands of them. Since we were being housed in boarding houses and the like, there was much more furniture and other fittings available, and the whole place was quite comfortable right from the start.

Two distinct and rather intriguing trends developed almost immediately. Even though the Huyton people had barely been together for more than a couple of weeks, and, in most cases, did not know each other, the "Huyton Camp Group" very much kept to itself, and so, it turned out, did the crowds from various other camps. People also started being and acting acquisitive or rather tending to "nest;" you heard someone arguing about "his" chair or of "his" cardboard box having been moved. As I had been busily rotating two shirts over three weeks, that squirreling instinct passed me by.

We gradually started exchanging and lending items to each other—raincoats were in acute demand, but of course not more so than cigarettes. Everybody seemed to smoke in those days (I was a pack-a-day man myself until the Surgeon General scared me in 1962), and everybody was trading or begging cigarettes all over the place; postwar Germany was going to have a déjà vu quality for some of us. A great deal of time was again spent composing letters to the Home Office and, in the case of the Cambridge Gang, asking to join the armed forces, a suggestion viewed with derision or suspicion by most fellow internees.

Although no one was released in all the time we were in Huyton or Douglas, we kept on hearing rumors that the great majority of Germans had not been interned, simply because they lived in "unrestricted" areas, and so we felt that somebody, somewhere could surely resolve this Lewis Carroll situation. Well, we never found him—even though these rumors turned out to be quite true. In later years I was often asked just how the days were spent in various internment and army camps, when we were not actually busy clearing a latrine, firing a tank, hanging out laundry, parachuting from a plane, or engaging in similarly trivial pursuits. The answer lies with whom you ask; La Rochefoucauld felt that misery stemmed from never being left alone. He would not have made a good internee. My answer is that, as long as you have a tight schedule or set one for yourself, then, no matter what the activity, the day will be neither long nor dull. It never was for me in all those seven years, and my almost manic need for structure and generally slow and poor response to totally impromptu situations almost certainly goes back all the way to Huyton.

Even though we spent a month in Douglas, I recall little of that period; it was just another internment camp, without the trauma of the first or the drama of later ones. We were dealt with correctly, or mostly not at all, and in any event, this was June 1940 and the military events totally overshadowed anything that happened in Douglas or my memory of it.

Taking stock of my situation at the time, things seemed both complicated and simple. First, the complicated parts:

I was wholly out of touch with everyone, everywhere. My weekly allowance of one letter was taken up by my weekly plea to the Home Office; hence, no one else knew where I was and so no one wrote to me.

I had been about to complete my second year at Cambridge, but it seemed very problematical whether I could pursue my studies, since I had fifty pounds in the bank and knew of no immediate way to raise more funds. (Cambridge did grant me a BA and, subsequently and *ex officio*, an MA, as it did to all undergraduates during the war who had completed five terms and one tripos (honors exam) with respectable grades; but I did not know that then.)

I had no notion how long I might be interned or what might eventually happen. For all we knew, the British might ship us back to Germany, if the Germans did not collect us where we now were.

In September 1939, all Germans living abroad, regardless of religion or other disqualifications, had received German call-up papers, and all those who did not comply, as people like me obviously would not, had been deprived of German nationality by due decree, published in the *Staatsanzeiger*, a government publication. As far as the Germans were concerned, someone like me was stateless.

The British, by some weird legal boondoggle that in essence usurped the rights of another sovereign power, blandly maintained that we remained German, and that "Hitler laws" were not valid in that respect. Since, in addition, the Home Office suspended all naturalization proceedings for the duration of the war, this was to lead to the Mad Hatter anomaly that I remained a German for British officialdom until March 1947, while in the meantime I became a major in the British army while technically an "enemy alien." I know of a dozen or more similar cases in the army; there were just a few in the RAF, though none in the navy, but I'm not sure whether they even took Welshmen there! With impeccable Alice-in-Wonderland logic, the British never suggested, let alone insisted, that any alien should join the armed forces; in turn, they felt no obligation to grant citizenship to anyone who did, a somewhat distressingly liberal interpretation of freedom of choice.

Those were the complicated bits. The simple part was that I had been interned with ten shillings and two packets of cigarettes (both long gone), one each of jacket, pants, and tie, two each of shirts, socks, and underwear, one pair of pajamas, and some toiletries, all stowed away in the forefather to an airline bag, and those were my sole possessions in June 1940.

I remember wondering how many Nazis there might be among the significant number of non-Jewish internees. In all my months in internment, I never heard anyone express pro-Hitler sentiments. In that environment that would have been tantamount to a death wish, so it was hard to tell.

People like Kahle were clearly anti-Nazi; he was a dedicated revolutionary communist, a Maoist in today's terms, and once he was released and Russia entered the war, he became a War Office adviser on guerilla warfare, parachute drops, and similarly esoteric capers.

Lingen was just as vehemently opposed to Hitler, but for totally different reasons. He, like all Hohenzollern, was favorably inclined toward Jews, but that was not his objection to Nazis, any more than was the fact that he, again like the rest of his family, considered every German government after 1918 to be vaguely invalid. What truly upset him about Hitler and his gang was that they were proletarian yokels, unmannered upstarts, people no gentleman could possibly have dealings with. They were dishonorable scoundrels, real lumpen, no style, no class. It really was more a matter of embarrassment than anger with Fritz.

# 6

In the last days of June, with the war news sounding truly desperate, several hundred Douglas internees were ordered to "be ready to move within the hour." There had been no prior indication or warning and, except that it appeared to include only younger and unmarried people, there seemed to be no discernible logic to the selection process.

The Cambridge Gang left together, and back we went to Liverpool City Hall and from there, that same evening, to the SS *Ettrick*, a fifteen-thousand-ton freighter converted into a semblance of a troopship.

Only about half the people who left Douglas ended up on the *Ettrick*; a couple of hundred all told, including all of us Cantabrians. The remainder (again selected by osmosis or some similarly occult process) stayed behind in Liverpool. Some subsequently never left England; others left on other ships to other destinations that same day or the day following. The Home Office, without accurate records to start with and keeping no records while these migrations were in process, did not even bother to be confused. They just had no clue at all—with variable sequels, as will appear.

The *Ettrick* (which was torpedoed and sunk in a convoy two or three years later) had two huge air shafts running down through five or six layers of decks, and each deck, about a quarter of an acre in size with seven-foot-high ceilings, held lots of bolted-down tables and benches and masses of hammocks and ceiling hooks to fasten them on.

Since we were the first bunch to enter the ship, we were allocated to the lowest deck, well below the waterline and without portholes or other natural ventilation. We tried to console ourselves with the old Berlin adage, Besser warmer Mief als kalte Luft,† but on a hot June evening that did not sound too convincing.

We could figure out why the four lowest decks were separated by barbed-wire fencing from the remainder of the ship above, but we were puzzled by yet another wire barrier dividing the lower decks down the middle. It seemed more like a trip wire than an actual obstacle; it would have been easy to climb over it, and since no guard ever ventured into our bowels of the ship throughout the journey, no one would have prevented it. There was no need for any guards to

---

†Better a smelly fug than a cold draft.

descend to our levels; wherever there were portholes, those had been welded shut, and the only access to our decks was through the two airshafts, and the wire barricade installed above effectively guarded that. Food stuffs and other supplies were deposited every morning at the wire gate up top, a fatigue party from each deck would go and collect them—or rather, such was the plan.

We found that sleeping in hammocks is a very agreeable way to get through the night and awoke full of Nelsonian optimism. Not for long, though; by midday all four decks had been crammed with other internees, the ailing ventilation system was getting really sick, and the place was like a furnace and smelt worse. The other half of all four decks, divided by that wire strand, remained empty and speculation about them ranged from recreation area to temporary morgue, depending on one's state of mind. There was actually not much time to speculate. We, the Cambridge Gang, led as always by Kahle and Lingen, had again swung into action. Clambering up and down those four decks, we got people to get out of their hammocks and roll and stow them; we set up several teams of cooks to handle the communal kitchen on the third deck, arranged for working parties to collect food, sweep decks, and altogether tried to get that whole crowd (probably close to five hundred) into some semblance of order. It hardly made us popular among our shipmates, but if there is a large bunch of people who do not know what to do and what they want being harassed by a small group of people who do, in the end, they will go along with the small group, and we sure harassed them. Both Huyton and Douglas had convinced us that being interned was sufficiently disorienting without the additional hassle of being disorganized, and all this bullying on our part was not an unselfish exercise.

The prime focus of our attention, even while still in harbor, were the toilets, or "heads," as they are called on a ship, all located on the highest deck accessible to us. Eight wash basins and four toilet stalls in one tiled compartment clearly required some roster arrangement to cope with hundreds of people spread over four decks.

The *Ettrick* heads would become the site and origin of the enduring Cambridge Gang legend.

During that afternoon, the mystery of the empty deck spaces was resolved in spectacular and scary fashion. Suddenly all four "half decks" were crowded by extraordinarily fit and tough-looking German soldiers, all with paratrooper wings, who got done and squared away in a matter of minutes what it had taken us half a day to do. We quickly established that these were prisoners from the original German assault waves on Holland and Belgium, thus considered particularly aggressive and dangerous by the authorities, and hence, with a German invasion threatening, they were to be shipped away as quickly and as far as possible. It took them even less time to identify us as a bunch of German Jews, which led to their totally ignoring us for the entire time we spent together on that ship. To be separated by a thin strand of wire from hundreds of highly trained, effective, and obviously fanatic Nazis for almost ten days was distinctly unnerving and not the least of our *Ettrick* traumas, but to them we were just not there. It surprised us then (even though Kahle, based on experience, had foretold it), but I found it confirmed time and again in later years: When you face combat troops, you will almost never have to deal with "atrocities" or even any inclination to commit them. When you deal with support troops, let alone with police or civilian "authorities" who show up even later, then conquest often becomes criminality and the most horrible things can happen.

However, now we were just plain scared. Our guards were no help, since to them we were all just a bunch of Germans, some in uniform, some out of it, and our concern was utterly beyond their interest, let alone their comprehension. The fact is that not one of those German paratroopers ever threatened any of us by word or gesture at any time, and also, while it was to be a memorably wretched voyage for us internees, none of them ever seemed so much as indisposed throughout the trip. It later led to endless conjectures that they might have "got to our food"; they did no such thing. They did nothing to us, except scare us; not that we needed that under the circumstances.

The *Ettrick* sailed that night, July 2, and for the following nine days and nights we had absolutely no idea where we were heading, nor how long it would take to get there. We seemed unescorted, which meant either a fast ship or expendable cargo, probably the latter. Some people were seasick going through what we later identified as the Irish Sea, a notoriously rough stretch of water, but there was little to complain about, except overcrowding. Captain Bligh's crews would have had no problems with our sardine-tin hammock arrangements, but we felt a bit cramped.

Then quite suddenly, around noon of the second day, the situation became catastrophic. From one moment to the next the hundreds of internees started acute and sustained leaks, from both top and bottom. In no time a line to the heads had formed stretching right through all four decks, and the line never diminished over the next five days and nights. Matters rapidly and progressively got worse. People who an hour earlier had at least attempted to join the line just took to leaning over the side of their hammock, and sometimes not even that. I have a ghastly and unforgettable memory of an elderly man, lined up at least one deck away from the heads and clearly convinced that he would not reach them in time, grabbing the nearest suitcase (clearly not his own) and relieving himself into it. All the time he remained in the line, doubtlessly on the assumption that he would be in need again by the time he eventually reached the heads.

Things got worse, hour by hour. It was obviously some kind of bug or food poisoning, and by early afternoon, all the heads were blocked, backing up and beginning to overflow, while that line just kept on pushing towards them. The guards on the top decks never came near us throughout the entire episode, and aside from the stench that enveloped us all, the paratroopers beyond the wire remained equally uninvolved. This was where the Cambridge Gang came into its own. As usual, Kahle and Lingen made the decisions; for ten minutes every two hours around the clock some of us had to physically restrain the line from moving forward, while the others, armed with brooms, brushes, buckets, and rubber boots (all of which we had originally been given to scrub the decks) would literally wade into the heads and clean them out. For some unexplained reason, none of us ever caught whatever bug it was, so we set up two teams, led by Lingen and Kahle respectively; each team would work on a four-hour shift around the clock. We ended up doing that for five full days and nights!

From the start, we decided to work stark naked (except for those rubber boots); it was stiflingly hot and it seemed the simplest and most hygienic way to go.

It all became a blur of manhandling sick people, of vomit, excrement, cleaning out toilet bowls with bare hands (we had rubber boots but no rubber gloves), of snatching a sandwich or some tea (our appetites never left us), of sleeping like the dead, and then starting all over again.

Ten minutes every two hours just was not enough, and we had to extend the "curfew" to half an hour every two hours, which made it really tough on people (the suitcase incident occurred then). But even then we were fighting a losing battle, until someone discovered a pressure hose on one of the decks. That must have been around the third day, and we started blasting the heads clear, both of occupants and of "deposits," which, at times, were inches up the wall. It was simply indescribable, and there seemed no end to it. You elbowed your way through the shuffling line, fought your way up several decks and into the heads, threw everyone out of them, started cleaning up, then hosed yourself down, went back to your deck and some sleep, then back up again to start all over.

On the fourth day or so matters reached a climax when some poor soul cut his wrists while in the heads, and there was blood all over in addition to everything else. I happened to be on duty since I was on Kahle's shift, and he very quickly got the would-be suicide topside and seen to, and used these dramatic circumstances to insist on seeing "someone in charge," since matters were clearly getting out of hand. That feeling must finally have percolated to the upper decks, and Kahle returned with the promise of more hoses, Lysol, and above all, lots of paregoric, all of which were delivered within the hour. That was the turning point; we kept on cleaning the heads on a round-the-clock basis right up to the end of the voyage, but we were now gaining on the situation, and the last two or three days of the trip were really just routine—not least, because it had become so to us. Kahle had also persuaded the powers-that-be, none of whom we ever saw, that all hatches should be opened one hour in every three during daytime and we should be allowed, in small groups, to come up on deck for an hour every day. It made a huge difference, and we didn't even mind that— fair play being a British invention—such groups would be evenly divided between internees, who looked and felt like the wrath of God, and those German paratroopers who seemed to impersonate it.

Being on deck, we obviously noticed that we were on the high seas, but we had no idea where until, on the tenth day out of Liverpool, the *Ettrick* entered the St. Lawrence estuary and started sailing upriver, one of the world's truly stunning sights. Rumor had it that we would land in Quebec the next day and would be distributed over several camps, and for once, rumor had it right. We moored in Quebec, a most attractive, faintly eighteenth-century vision coming up the river, but were kept well below decks once we had landed to allow disembarkation of the "other lot." They were collected by a whole slew of Canadian Mounties, considerably less flashily dressed than Nelson Eddy and, for all I know, in less good voice, but looking rather less vapid and more competent than he. Though there had been no contact whatever between us, the brooding presence of those Aryan supermen had not added to the pleasures of the trip, and we were happy to see the last of them. Another bunch of Mounties then dealt with us, and we should have been forewarned when one of them asked a colleague, "Where on earth did Jerry use this scruffy lot?" It did not register at the time, particularly since our group was busy trying to keep together while the Mounties arbitrarily divided us all into three lots to be sent to different camps. We did stick together and were the first to go down the gangway when someone among those hundreds of internees on deck shouted, "Let's hear it for the lavatory gang," and they cheered us all the way to the buses! Aside from eventually being released, it was one of the two best moments of the entire internment.

## 7

The other memorable event occurred later that same day. We had been driven through Quebec, a charming-looking city, and glowered at by a surprising number of pedestrians, surprising both in number and in the evident hostility displayed. Who on earth did they think we were? There certainly were more guards than we had in England, and they seemed both fiercer and more alert than our previous protectors.

We ended up just outside Quebec in a fenced compound in the very heart of the Heights of Abraham, with the memorial marking the spot of General Wolfe's death right next to one of our huts, and with a simply glorious view of the St. Lawrence and the many-gabled folly of the Chateau Frontenac.

Quebec itself, about three miles away, was hidden behind a small range of hills. Camp L, which this was, had originally been constructed as an army camp and was destined to hold far more people than we were. The huts were numerous and spacious, all built on short stilts off the ground and superbly insulated, fitted with double bunks, showers, wash basins, cupboards—all luxuries that lay at least two months past and seemed like years ago. We were a mere ten people to each hut, and the mess was large enough to accommodate all of us, about 150 men all told; the adjoining kitchen and storage rooms had every gadget known in the Western Hemisphere, some of which, I suspect, may not have reached England to this day. In short, absolute bliss; except for a very high and dense double barbed-wire enclosure, with guards patrolling between the two enclosures, and watch towers at intervals manned by soldiers with machine guns. We were as impressed as we were mystified.

We were enlightened soon enough, when, called into the mess hall, we were addressed by the commandant and his security officer. The commandant was an endearing little man and the only camp commandant whom I remember at all. He was small, pink, round, and short-sighted, a successful local builder and the Canadian addition to Dad's army. His name was Wiggs, but he was known affectionately as Piggy-Wiggy, and not always behind his back. He was a most amiable and friendly soul, and appeared justifiably apologetic whenever he attempted to be martial. On this, his first time out, he gave up the attempt very quickly and handed us over to his security officer who, to the amazement of the Cambridge crowd, turned out to be one Freddie McKenzie an undergraduate a year or two older than most of us. Freddie was a vastly athletic, exceptionally handsome, and exceptionally stupid Canadian but was well known as having been very much a social lion and trendsetter in his day. He evidently had been commissioned into some fancy Scottish-Canadian regiment and, equally obviously, was as handsome and stupid as ever. The fact that he almost certainly had no files on us was not material, since many of us doubted whether Freddie could read, but he certainly knew a number of us personally and should have been able to guess whom he had before him. Boneheaded as ever, our Freddie ploughed through an absolutely amazing little address, invoking the Geneva Convention and the rights and duties of lawful prisoners of war, promising us to be strict but fair, with Piggy nodding in the background trying all the while to look as strict and fair as that gentle little guy was capable of.

The upshot of all that was that we were marched off to a hut outside the compound and there issued with a plethora of clothing, everything from socks and underwear to caps, earmuffs, and mackinaws, all outer garments in dark blue wool with a large red circle painted on the back and the letters *P.O.W.* stenciled across the circle.

Throughout our stay in Canada, that POW delusion was never cleared up, nor was the public amazement that so motley a crowd could ever have had any military impact—the conquest of France, no less!

The new clothing, however ludicrous, suited me just fine. The *Ettrick* interlude had retarded the disintegration of my own stuff, but it was irreversible. I threw everything away and wore POW clothing from that day until I came back to England. We were then marched back to camp and left in the care of Sergeant-Major Fritze and Sergeant Parry, virtually the only people whom we dealt with while at Camp L, and, aside from Piggy, the only two people I remember from my Canadian outing. Fritze was tall, painfully thin, with a gaunt, desiccated face and a very reluctant smile, mostly because he had badly fitting teeth which tended to slip when least expected. He had the voice and mannerism of the late Walter Brennan and was a thoroughly decent man who tried, quite unsuccessfully, not to appear so.

Parry was a joy; a fur trapper from the northern tip of Canada, he was huge and self-reliant. Everything about him was enormous; his drinking, laughing, or swearing was gargantuan, but he could also be as silent as a cat. On occasion, you might be sitting near the window quietly reading, only to have a throwing-knife, the size of a small machete, thudding into the wall right next to your head; that would be Parry, having glided through the door and down the hut, checking whether he could still hit a pin at twenty paces. It used to give him so much pleasure that it would have been positively churlish to have a cardiac arrest, but some of us came close. He was as friendly as a puppy, always helpful, easy to get along with, and ever-ready to bend a rule.

After the *Ettrick*, it seemed quite natural for the Cambridge dozen to take charge, which here and now meant drawing rations and arranging for a meal—the first meal in nine days or so for almost everybody. We therefore felt due restraint should be exercised, and while we quickly relinquished that nursemaid attitude and adopted a "suspended animation" posture till we moved camp again, the Cambridge gang was very much in charge that night. It is just possible that there has been better white bread, stronger coffee, thicker bacon, or sweeter honey somewhere than there was that evening at Camp L, but none of us thought so then, and some of us doubt it to this day.

We made sure that everyone ate enough but not too much, and that everyone had been fed before we ate ourselves. At 10 P.M. or so that night (Fritze having, typically, bent a curfew rule for the "kitchen crowd") came that second magic moment of the day and of the entire internment. We sat down, ten or twelve of us, in the empty mess hall, and there was white bread and bacon and honey and coffee—it is more than fifty years ago and I can taste it still; I have never, ever had a better meal in all my life!

The next day we started settling in once more, by now almost a routine activity, made much easier by all the facilities available and after the *Ettrick*, anything was a breeze.

The very first day brought a *coup de théatre*. Lingen was summoned to see Piggy urgently and returned having been named Camp Spokesman, which seemed a perfectly reasonable move. But this elevation had evidently been preceded by "Piggy's incoherent babblings about a phone call and cousin Alice." Princess Alice, Princess Royal in her own right, sister to the late King George V, wife to the Earl of Athlone, Governor-General of Canada, in other words cousin Alice, had indeed called. Fritz's unfailing bush telegraph had been operating again, and Major Wiggs had had an early morning call from Government House in Ottawa to tell Lingen that "cousin Alice had called," which totally unnerved our Piggy.

Clearly she had not suggested that Lingen be made spokesman, nor did she later exert "influence" of any kind; she did send a lot of useful parcels though. As for Piggy-Wiggy, he basked in reflected glory, and some of us suspected that he never again washed the hand that held the phone receiver that morning.

Settling in meant setting up working parties, batches of twenty people each who would leave camp for Quebec after breakfast and would spend the day, heavily guarded, doing things in and to the streets of Quebec, ranging from laying drain pipes to clearing snow, later that year. This to the accompaniment of some pretty picturesque and uniformly offensive language on the part of the watching populace, but since almost all of it was in French, the true flavor was wasted on most recipients. The Battle of Britain was at its height, the U-boat war was gathering impetus, and German prisoners of war, such as we, were obviously winning no popularity contests in Quebec. We were told much later that Quebec had strong separatist leanings during the war; you could have fooled us. Looking back, it seems like a Feydeau farce and pretty funny; at the time, we were bewildered at first but after a while, it just became an accompanying noise, a kind of digging-and-be-damned chorus and part of the scene.

Settling in also meant organizing quite a few activities within the camp. We laid out a rather complicated obstacle course, an ankle-twisting, lung-bursting exercise that some of us attempted at least once a day, just to keep in shape. For real health nuts, there were judo courses given by a diminutive Austrian who looked like a matchstick below the waist but like King Kong above it, and who tried to convince some of us that elegance was the key to killing.

Most of the activities, however, tended to be more cerebral; we had a bewildering variety of activities going on and an equally astonishing number of people interested in them. I assiduously attended courses in Spanish and shorthand, and ended up remaining ignorant of both, and led a very well-attended seminar on seventeenth- and eighteenth-century French literature, which left my listeners none the wiser. I also recall one Klaus Fuchs teaching a Physics course with as much finesse as he used teaching the Russians how to build an A-bomb some six years later.

We also, for the first time, re-established contacts with the outside world. We were now allowed two letters a week (to be written on specially issued and singularly unattractive notepaper, supposedly impervious to invisible ink; and in fact impervious to just about any ink), and since only one was needed for the weekly bleat to the Home Office, based on custom rather than expectations, we could now try and reach someone else. Quite a few of us did know people in the United States, so parcels started to come in as well, mostly cigarettes, which were in perennially short supply despite the Canadians issuing each of us with two packs of Sweet Caporals a week. It was then I developed a weakness for Camel cigarettes, which stuck with me for the next twenty years.

We established a camp newspaper under the aegis of an art critic for the paper in King's Lynn (they cannot have been very critical of art in King's Lynn—a town in Norfolk) who, in return for a "private course" on the writings of La Bruyère, the seventeenth-century French moralist (who can guess the whims of an art critic?), agreed to let me play deputy editor. The Geneva Convention denies daily newspapers to POW's and Piggy-Wiggy's amiable solution to that was to let the camp paper editors read everything and have them con-dense the news in our intramural outpourings. Being even then the newspaper maven I have remained, that had been my sole incentive in getting involved in the camp paper, not exactly a publication that would have kept Pulitzer awake at night.

Catching up on back news, I learned that SS *Arandora Star*, apparently loaded with internees and heading for Australia, had been torpedoed and sunk in the Irish Sea around the same time that the *Ettrick* sailed in that area, and there had been great loss of life. At the time it did not occur to me that this might affect me in any way.

Settling in meant sleeping like logs, eating well, being weirdly detached from a war going on thousands of miles away, and witness-ing the leaves changing color up and down the St. Lawrence, surely one of the world's most beautiful sights. Settling in, finally, meant feeling sufficiently established to think of entertainment, to wit a "mock trial." We held it in mid-September, and it apparently became the talk of every internee camp in Canada. Wherever you get more than three law students together, someone is bound to suggest a mock trial; most of the Cambridge bunch were aspiring legal eagles, and there were some practicing and successful barristers among the re-mainder of the inmates.

A mock trial is a simple and enjoyable theatrical concept; you set up a panel of judges, a counsel for the defense, a counsel for the prosecution, and a person accused. The facts of the "crime" are predetermined, but who will be called as witness and how prosecution and defense will interrogate such witnesses is wholly impromptu as the trial progresses. The jury is made up of the entire audience who, on a majority vote and after briefing by the judges, will render its verdict. A mock trial might take anywhere up to six or seven hours, but we were in no rush.

Thus, we had Chief Justice Sir Monotony Redtape presiding and Internee Ladislaus Schlemmer was the person accused, having been apprehended by Lieutenant Eustace Blimp on the doorstep of '69, rue Blondel in downtown Quebec (internment makes for reminiscing rather than inspiration, and our name choices showed it). The prosecution's case, made by Sir Hector Blount-Rapier, KC, was that Schlemmer was trying to escape. The defense, by Mr. Moderate Waffles, KC, was that, far from wishing to escape, Schlemmer had merely broken out of camp to spend the night with one Yvonne de Bonne Nuit, whose expertise, as described by one of the guards, had been an irresistible lure.

Schlemmer, when arrested, was actually on his way back to camp and clearly looking forward to similar sorties in the future. Among the whole crowd of internees, we had a goodly number of people involved in stage and fashion, so that costumes and makeup presented no problems, and Werner Hinze, an original member of the *Threepenny Opera* cast and a well-known postwar movie actor, took charge of the "production" and did so handsomely.

I have no notion, then or now, why they picked on me as Yvonne, but there I was on the witness stand, with a skin-tight skirt slit to the waist, two grapefruits sown into a silk blouse, a blond Veronica Lake wig, hamming it up with a potpourri of squeals, French innuendos, and bellydancer motions. Waffles, KC, did a perfectly splendid job for Schlemmer and for me, and the evening ended with Piggy and Fritze (our *ex officio* guests of honor) both on their feet and leading the assembled jury in shouting for acquittal by acclamation.

It was terrific fun, and I still have the designer's sketch of Yvonne's dress and makeup, signed by all the participants in the trial.

It is the only document I own that hints at my ever having been interned.

# 8

Sometime in October, with a lot of snow already on the ground, we got word that Camp L was to be disbanded and we would be moved within twenty-four hours. These abrupt and absurd moves appear to be the hallmark of the military mind, such as it is, just about anywhere and presumably are supposed to demonstrate decisiveness. At the time it just amazed and annoyed us. It still does when I think about it, since Camp L was without doubt the coziest and most bucolic camp I occupied in nearly seven years of exposure to such habitats.

An additional irritation was that the authorities insisted on splitting up the Cambridge Gang, though no one ever gave us a reason for doing so. Some of us thought that Freddie McKenzie did it just to pay us back for the evident contempt in which we held him, and it is as plausible an explanation as any.

Split us up they did, and only Lingen and a few others remained together in a contingent of about a hundred people to be shipped out that afternoon, with Freddie M. continuing to be our security body for the next camp, which improved no one's mood, least of all his, which was some compensation. The remainder of the Camp L inmates also left that day, divided into several groups and sent to other camps. I did not meet any of them again while interned, and though I heard about one or the other in later years, there really never was any further contact. I wish I could say differently; we had some memorable times together.

We set off by train from some unidentified station in the middle of the snows, and the train stopped once in a while, seemingly to add more carriages. As we were not allowed to walk through the train, we could not tell how many so we just watched a wintry countryside and acted like extras in a trailer for *Dr. Zhivago.*

Just before dark, the train turned off the main track and ran for a mile or so along a secondary spur to fetch up before a most impressive barbed wire enclosure, at least fifteen feet high, complete with watch towers, search lights, even baying dogs. It was all getting a little too Hollywood for comfort.

The track continued for another fifty yards beyond the wire enclosure, and so did the train, until track, train, and we ran right into a vast hangar, long enough to accommodate the entire train, six carriages by now, of which only one had come out of Camp L.

Everybody detrained to discover that the track actually ended at two big buffers at the end of the hangar. While we were trying to puzzle this out, the now-empty train reversed, rumbled out of the hangar, out of the enclosure, and out of our lives. The hangar doors were slid shut and locked, and by the light of half a dozen naked light bulbs swinging from the rafters, we could survey what would turn out to be Camp N. The shed was enormous, easily the size of a football field, as you might expect from a repair shed of the Canadian Pacific Railway, which we subsequently discovered it to be. The light was miserable, but there was not that much to see. There was one enormous expanse of concrete floor bisected by the railroad track, a large pile of rather grubby looking blankets, and that was it. No beds, tables, toilets, utensils of any kind, just one great big empty shed. Some further exploration yielded a couple of iron staircases in the gloom at the rear, which lead to an iron-grill gallery about fifteen feet wide, running right round the hangar at about twenty-five foot height. That gallery in turn had stairs leading to a similar gallery of similar width almost underneath the roof and virtually at nosebleed height. Neither gallery contained anything except an echo.

Having established with dismaying certainty that this was no Camp L, we started looking around to see with whom we were sharing this wasteland. The six or seven hundred men now assembled appeared to have come from about eight different camps, and none of them knew any more than we did—why we were here or where here was. However it became quickly apparent that the other camps had been much less club-like and attractive than Camp L and our new fellow-inmates had very different backgrounds and skills. Although the Cambridge University component had always been a minority in Huyton, Douglas, and Camp L, the bulk of internees in those camps had been businessmen, scientists, lawyers, engineers—"intellectuals" supposedly (giving the businessmen the benefit of the doubt)—whereas this bunch here had a strong artisan and "manual" flavor.

We had now been joined by butchers, pipelayers, masons, electricians, and bartenders—all Germans who had lived in large cities such as Manchester and Glasgow and who had been detained during the second arrest wave later in May, when almost every major English city (always excepting London) had been declared "restricted." Our original "country squire" milieu was thus being leavened by an "artisan" element that would turn out greatly to our advantage.

The first thing to do was to make a nuisance of ourselves, to find out what the hell was going on, and where it was taking place. A considerable amount of screaming and banging of doors and walls produced Freddie McKenzie, complete with megaphone, spotlight, and some rather ferocious-looking armed guards, presumably in case we would rush him, which we were certainly bad-tempered enough to attempt.

It turned out that Camp N was in Sherbrooke, a township very close to Trois-Rivières, which lies upstream on the St. Lawrence River about halfway between Quebec and Montreal. The camp compound, we were told, consisted of the shed we were in, an earthen yard about twice the size of the hangar, and at its other end, a smaller shed, supposedly housing washing facilities, toilets, kitchen, and mess space. The whole compound, all of it surrounded by wire, towers, guards, and dogs, would be open during daylight, but at night the yard would be lit up and anyone wishing to go from the "living" shed to the "washing" shed would have to step out into the light and be challenged by the guards before being allowed to proceed. When returning from the washing shed, the procedure was to be reversed; clearly Freddie was discounting *Ettrick*-like emergencies. In actual fact, this asinine procedure got torpedoed that very night; the first internee emerging and gingerly waiting to be challenged by the guards heard, "You don't think we'll waste all night playing games—you want a pee, you go have a pee; don't bother us." And that's what we did from then on.

However that was the only bit of good news for the night; the other shed turned out to be as bare as the first. It did however have a mind-boggling installation mounted on a similarly elevated platform as the one in our living shed—nothing Rube Goldberg ever thought of could have been funnier or more effective. An immense cast-iron pipe, about four feet in diameter, ran the entire length of the platform. Every three feet or so, a foot-wide hole had been drilled into the pipe, clearly intended to fit a medium-sized posterior—about a dozen holes in all. There were chest-high wooden slats separating these "nests," but no closure, front or rear. Flushing had the simplicity of genius. Every ten seconds or so, a burst of water reaching almost, but never quite, to seating level swept through the pipe, starting at one end and rushing to the other. If you looked up at the platform, you could see a dozen perchers side by side; first the guy on the extreme left would bob up quickly, and then his neighbor, and so on right down the line, by which time the first sitter would be ready to bob again. It threw an entirely new light on the principles of toilet training and "motion with motion" became part of our lives. The full potential of the scene did not dawn on us that first night, but later on, if you had nothing better to amuse you, you could always hang out and watch the "late" bobbers. Who invented this astonishing installation, or who had used it before us, was never revealed.

That first evening, all we noticed was that, except for that bird perch, everything else was missing, and October in those parts is no time of year to hang out, certainly not with a bare end. Freddie had never seen Camp N before either and, to his credit, seemed as taken aback as we. For want of a more inspirational thought, he bellowed, "Wait here," (where else?) and charged off in search of the commandant (a wholly mythical figure, whom none of us ever saw in all those weeks). In the meantime, Lingen and his shrunken band of minions— there were about five of us—took over one last time to try and sort out people by skills and professions, so that we would know, as Churchill later said in a more pregnant context, how, given the tools, we could do just about any job. In the process, we also discovered that, to many of our new fellow-internees, English was not their second or even third language, but a kind of homemade invention of their own.

Words and their usage assumed a distinctly baroque flavor, and as again Churchill would have said, it was the sort of English up with which one should not put.

That situation required long-term solutions to which we could not address ourselves, but the job part turned out to be providentially simple. It appeared we had not been expected for another two weeks and all the materials were at hand, though not yet installed. Literally within minutes, trucks, hand carts, even wheel barrows started pouring into the shed, depositing wood, nails, insulating materials, piping, beds, wash basins, cupboards, lights, boilers, cables, wires, kitchen fittings—an absolute avalanche of stuff that abruptly stopped when it got really dark and they locked us up for the night. However, there had been a soup kitchen coming and going among all this activity, and there we were, reasonably fed, rolled into our scruffy blankets on a very cold concrete floor, but with the prospect of making something out of the mountains of material surrounding us, and so this ambiance of hardware store and building site made for a pretty happy night. Next morning at dawn, the stream of supplies resumed. By noon we had just about everything "in house," and for the next eight weeks we built! There were some Tower of Babel aspects to the undertaking, but we were faced with a Canadian winter and had no time for trivia.

Since it was clearly impossible to heat the shed, the solution was to build forty "bungalows" within it, each with walls, rooms, and roof of its own, but connected to each other by enclosed walkways. The bungalows were to be lit and heated, and elaborate washing and showering facilities would be installed at each of the sheds. The galleries running around the walls would get wood enclosures, light, and heating and be turned into a selfcontained hospital unit.

We had at least a dozen doctors among the crowd, some of international reputation, and while we did not feel grandiose enough to include a surgical unit, we would have been competent enough to handle it.

We stretched asbestos insulation sheets under the hangar roof to withstand winter temperatures (asbestos was thought a very "consumer friendly" material then), and since we could not install canalization pipes under the concrete floor, and the ground outside had already frozen hard, we decided to stick to the original concept of having the other shed as a cooking-cum-toilet facility. That extraordinary perching contraption remained, simply because there was no way to get rid of it, but we put some additional and less-entertaining installations alongside. We put insulation walls between the entire toilet complex and the remainder of the shed, which in turn, was subdivided into various bungalow constructions housing kitchens, store rooms, eating halls, and reading rooms. Every single bit of all this was assembled and installed by internees: chairs, bunks, boilers, pipes, electrical lines, stoves, door handles, refrigerators—everything. The Canadians supplied us with all we needed in the way of materials, including welding equipment (the likelihood of our tunnelling our way to the United States border seemed remote, and it was getting much too chilly to escape anyway), but every single item that was ultimately installed in Camp N we put together. Naturally all this took weeks, and one of the genuine satisfactions of each day was to check on how far things had progressed at the end of it.

Eventually Camp N became an extraordinarily sophisticated "living unit," with such esoteric goodies as a chess room, card room (there was a lot of bridge being played, not all of it bad; just those games I participated in), even a "gift shop," which dealt in complex but well-regulated barter. You would receive a parcel and did not fancy the salami in it; Joe did not like the socks in his—the gift shop was the answer, though the charitable connotation was pure fancy. No one gave anything away. The whole camp finally turned into a troglodyte exhibit, with those beehives packed inside each shed and a two-hundred-foot heated and lit wooden tunnel linking them, with the snow packed ten feet high on either side. There came a time in December when virtually no one went out in the open air, except the isolated fitness maniac or a working party to collect supplies. We even cut back on that by building cold storage facilities that allowed for twice-weekly supplies only. Admiral Byrd and his Little America settlement was better known at the time, but not more comfortable.

This "we" is purely editorial. Being the possessor of ten left thumbs, my involvement in all this was mainly as a "gofer"—be that fetching this plank or holding that nail, the latter already falling under skilled and certainly risky occupation, in my view.

One of the first organized items was a Central Notice Board, where each evening before curfew the next day's requirements would be posted ("Kitchen needs six"; "Four to electricians") and you would put your name down on a first-come basis and report there the next morning. There never was a work division in any formal sense, but there was always something for everyone to do, and almost invariably people did what they liked to do. There were, of course, heated and lengthy discussions among electrical or plumbing experts but never any overall plan, yet in the end everything just meshed together. Lots of planned housing projects that I can think of could not touch Camp N!

It was both fun and immensely constructive in every sense. On a mundane level, it certainly brought home to me how much pride and satisfaction there is in mastering a skill and having the hands to implement it. In a more metaphysical vein, Goethe had it right: "Erst muss man es glauben, dann muss man es wollen dann wird es geschehen."†

We had, on arrival, been issued with winter clothing, expectedly dark blue with red POW circles, but also with some lovely red flannel BVD's, which I kept for years afterward. None too soon, because it was getting really brisk, particularly at night. At first we thought that our guards occasionally fired weapons, just for the fun of it; there was a sound like pistol shots, and it happened almost every night. But we found that the cold was literally popping nails out of the insulating asbestos!

Contact with the outside world was more sparse and complicated than it had been at Camp L, which led to our considerably expanding the daily camp newspaper and naming it *Das Nebengleis* (The Side Track), which, given our location and status, seemed clever and appropriate to us at the time. The railroad track, though now invisible, was of course still there, and some of our more imaginative nightmares involved a wrongly thrown switch and the Quebec-Montreal local.

One of the few skills I managed to acquire was to "recycle" cigarette butts by rolling my own cigarettes. All our guards displayed almost magical dexterity in going through the entire operation, some using one hand only, which to me is on a level with the fourth somersault on the flying trapeze. Some internees did reach such

---

†"First you must want it, then you must believe in it, then it will come about." It sounds much better when Goethe says it.

black-belt levels, but most of us contented ourselves with a home-made rubber-and-tin box device, which looked like a mouse trap for a very small mouse and produced tiny, fat cigarettes, much derided by the experts showing off their stringy, crooked, but handmade variety.

Looking back, this real sense of isolation, emphasized of course by the Canadian winter, was largely of our own making. We apparently could write anything we wanted in our two weekly letters; the Home Office did not answer anyway, and if Freddie could in fact read, he clearly did not care to. Our guards were lax and for good reason; all they had to do was casually watch the wire. You could not have gone underground with dynamite.

## 9

We were increasingly hunkering down in hibernation in our burrows; our comforts were extending to homemade lamp shades and napkins, the inclusion of crossword puzzles in the camp newspaper, and some inflammatory though supposedly non-alcoholic concoctions devised by an internee who had previously tended bar at the Adelphi Hotel in Liverpool, a nationally notorious waterhole.

Close to Christmas, the first rumors about the "man from the Home Office" started, some individual who was supposedly touring the Canadian camps and had discretion to detain or release. True enough, in the first days of January, we were informed that such a plenipotentiary had arrived and would stay about two weeks to interview all of us. We were issued a form to be filled out indicating who we were, where we had been interned, and what we had been doing at the time we were interned; the first time, I suspected then and know now, that anything about any of us had been recorded by anybody.

The first interviews started next day, and within minutes, the whole camp knew that "the man" was Alec Paterson, His Majesty's Principal Commissioner for Prisons, a somewhat derogatory but obviously apt choice.

It so happened that I knew Alec P. reasonably well. While at Cheltenham, I had attended several of his talks and seminars. Since he was not an Old Cheltonian, I can only imagine that Paterson picked on Cheltenham as clearly housing delinquent potential, since I had not heard of his visiting other schools. Whatever the reason, we had had several spirited exchanges on matters of crime and punishment; I remembered these well and just hoped that he did too.

It was time to "review the bidding" and that I tried to do. I had now been interned for some seven months, five of them in Canada. Except for knowing nothing about my family's fate or whereabouts, I was reasonably well informed about the world at large. Aside from wanting to be released, I was not too sure what I wanted to do. One option was to go back to England and join the army. While it did not seem likely that my somewhat haphazard participation in the Cheltenham OTC would lead to an immediate commission in the Guards, it was one way to go. Another would be to let the war look after itself for a while longer and go back to Cambridge. If I did, I would not only finish my Law Tripos, but also complete a personal project, in which vanity chased futility and which therefore seemed important to me. I had always hankered after a Ph.D., if for no other reason than that my dad, the quintessential German university product, had two of them! The only Ph.D. I could remotely aspire to would be in French or German, neither of which had any bearing on law. But, strictly on an ego trip, I had induced the French faculty to accept me as an "off course" Ph.D. candidate, so to speak. They had even provided me with a thesis subject, "The Influence of English Aristocracy on the French Theatre of the Eighteenth Century," a topic of truly theatrical lack of appeal or interest. Nevertheless, I had managed to put together about fifty pages of notes, cribbed and plagiarized from all over and almost certainly sufficient to put up a thesis of sorts within a few weeks.

There also were rumors that one might be allowed to stay in Canada, and possibly even move to the United States, to resume and conclude one's studies. It seemed a somewhat brusque reversal from the "enemy alien" concept, but subsequently I did hear of about a dozen or so internees who did just that, with Paterson's blessings.

I never seriously considered that choice, since I had a lemming-like urge to return to England without, just like any good lemming, being able to explain why. Clearly the war was not going to make significant progress by my being involved in it, but I was quite convinced that I ought to go "home."

It is something I believed in very firmly at the time and as long as the war lasted, but never really before or after. To the extent that I have any sense of "belonging," I feel, in all candor, as much German as I ever did before 1933, and since such admission is rightly viewed askance by many, I am perfectly content to settle for *ubi bene, ibi patria.*

Nationalities and passports are a convenience, if I am to be truthful, and when it comes to being British, well, I feel I have paid my dues, as this entire tale should manifest. Neither side owes the other anything.

My interview with Alec Paterson was one of the great moments of farce in all those years. I had expected to see him, but clearly the reverse was not so. "Good God, what the hell are you doing here?" was the first thing he said. He then started rummaging through his files, muttering in growing disbelief, and this, reciprocal expletives suitably deleted, was the story.

Just about all the Cambridge University people, including Lingen and I, had been released in early June, except that by that time the Home Office had no idea which camp we were in. Other war issues being more pressing, enquiries had been cursory, and had come to a total halt when some official convinced himself and his entourage that we had all been shipped out on the *Arandora Star* and thus drowned in the Irish Sea. The Home Office thereupon duly informed the "next of kin" (Guillebaud, the nearest kin they seemed to be able to locate) and closed the file.

By the time we left Douglas, possibly even by the time we left Huyton, we had actually been released and the Canadian journey had been most emphatically unnecessary!

Just as Zola once said, "qui est absent, a toujours tort."† If he had been around, he would have really made a fuss!

---

†"He who is absent, is always at fault."

Obviously Guillebaud, Briggs, or anyone else had had no call to try to write to a drowned corpse, and our U.S. friends in turn had had no reason to start corresponding with the Home Office. As to our letters to that majestic and messed-up organization, either someone there believed in the occult or, more likely, no one read our letters. The whole story is much too absurd to have been invented, so you had better believe it. In fact it was retold and confirmed several years later when, wholly by accident, I ran into Alec Paterson once more. I was then a captain in Tanks and on leave in London, and he was now Sir Alec Paterson and hosted me for dinner at his club, the Oxford & Cambridge, where we were joined by Clement Attlee and Dr. Temple, evidently old friends of his. Attlee was then deputy prime minister and leader of the Labor Party and Temple was Archbishop of Canterbury. I was duly mute, faced by such eminences, but Alec, in introducing me, went on at some length about just how and why we last met. And who would lie to an archbishop? I might, but not Alec.

That, however, was in the future; right now, in Sherbrooke, we hit another snag. Since I was not supposed to be there, there were clearly no government funds available to get me back to where I should never have left from. So what did Alec suggest? Well, all he could suggest was free train fare to Halifax, which he really was not authorized to offer either, and once there, I would have to make my own arrangements. Such as which? Well, there were regular North Atlantic convoys leaving from Halifax to Liverpool and other ports, and they were chronically short of crews. If I really insisted on going back, he would arrange for some "unmarked" clothing and get me some funds to see me through a couple of days in Halifax. Was I quite sure I wanted to go back? Well then, he was truly terribly sorry about all this mix-up and maybe our paths would cross again, and now he really had to get on with other matters. And there I was, out in the snow—a belatedly free man.

In the end there were five of us, all in the same boat, literally, setting out for Halifax that same afternoon, and I never saw or heard anything of Camp N again.

None of us had any papers (my German passport, invalid according to Berlin, wholly authentic according to London, was in my desk at Cambridge; I had not anticipated foreign travel on that May evening), but Alec Paterson had supplied us with an improvised *laissez-passer* that served us well all the way to Liverpool.

Wedged on a Halifax-bound train among merchant seamen, draftees, soldiers on leave, and other patriotic folk, we were the happy and indiscriminate recipients of coffee and doughnuts distributed at every stop to all us worthy heroes. We arrived in Halifax to find the docks awash with ships of every size, all of which, on enquiry, appeared to be short of crews. Since no one seemed interested in who we were or where we came from, security evidently would be no problem, nor the fact that our collective seafaring experience consisted of Lingen having once sailed in a Cowes Regatta.

## 10

There remained the procedural detail of becoming a unionized body. There may have been times when being a member of the Canadian Seamen's Union (or whatever convoluted and allegorical name it went by) was restricted to a selected elite, but 1941 in Halifax was not one of them. No one even asked us our names (just as well, since Loewenstein rather lacks that Anglo-Saxon ring) they just asked for five dollars, which nearly bankrupted us, and off we went, with our yellow membership card, to sign on on the nearest ship. We had decided to split up (whether to spread or minimize the risk I do not recall; nor which risk), and my choice fell on SS *Thysville*. It was the vessel moored nearest to union headquarters and was listed as Belgian, which, in my view, held out the twin advantage of good cuisine and sloppy seamanship.

She turned out to be a freighter of about six thousand tons, part of a private shipping line that had served the coastal and river routes around the Belgian Congo, and hence she had more and larger fans than any other ship I have ever seen, a rather superfluous amenity in January on the North Atlantic.

She was a venerable old thing, fitted out with some rudimentary passenger accommodations, and together with her sister ships, she had left Africa in 1940 to put herself at the disposal of the British Admiralty, which had allocated her to convoy duty.

The original crew had been Chinese, Malayan, and African, whereas all the officers were Belgian, including the line's owner, who had fled with his ships and, quite arbitrarily, had declared himself a supernumerary third officer on the *Thysville*. His knowledge of matters nautical was about on par with mine, but since he inhabited the bar throughout the trip, he interfered as little as I.

To attempt some semblance of seaworthiness, the admiralty had allocated a British captain to sort out this floating shambles, a grizzled sea-bear of uncertain age, even more uncertain temper, and really awesome language. A native of Liverpool speaking barely intelligible English and no other language, most of his more flowery imprecations were wholly lost on his Belgian colleagues, whom he held in utter contempt and with whom he never attempted to communicate. He ran the ship single-handedly, making himself understood to the engine room and other vital parts of the ship by sheer decibel count, or by such explosive swearing that it transcended any language barrier. The Belgian officers, in turn, seemed perfectly content to abdicate all nautical functions to the *vieux salaud*, since it liberated them to devote themselves to drink and bridge.

The reference to "dirty old man" was not so much a reference to age or unbridled language but to the baffling fact that he had acquired a lady steward, a remarkably pretty, utterly silent Malayan, whose exact functions were never clear or revealed, and who was a constant topic of conversation and envy. Since the captain was either on the bridge or in his cabin, and never talked to anyone except her, and since she never talked to anyone at all, she remains one of the mini-mysteries of the North Atlantic.

I learned all this within the first hour of being aboard, as well as the reason for the crew shortage. The *Thysville* had been carrying freight between Halifax and the Caribbean for the past six months, and had only been told a day or so before that the next trip would involve a North Atlantic convoy. Predictably this news had not thrilled the crew, quite a few of whom had decided to skip both trip and ship. The essential engine crew had not done so, merely because the captain, clearly canny in the ways of the sea, had not told them. He kept them busy, incommunicado and below decks till we were three days out of Halifax. For the rest, we were decidedly shorthanded, although the crew remnants included two Chinese laundry men operating out of an astounding little wooden contraption on the ship's stern that looked like an outsize outhouse, but was in fact the only seagoing Chinese laundry I ever saw. Regardless of gales and assorted perils of the deep, those two turned out gleamingly clean laundry at all hours.

Despite clearly more pressing crew needs, I was named a deck steward, since it was evident that any more responsible involvement on my part would endanger the ship. However, since there were no passengers, my responsibilities merely extended to looking after the three officers (the captain having clearly and enviably made his own arrangements), which in turn mostly involved making sure their glasses were never empty. In return for being an ambulant bartender, I was to draw the princely sum of five pounds a week and have the use of one of the passenger's cabins; after the past seven months, it felt like being given the run of Blenheim Palace.

Scuttlebutt had it that we would be a part of a large convoy (more than forty ships, as it ultimately turned out), which would form up within the next twenty-four hours, and it would take anything up to three weeks to get to Liverpool. I do not know why the Germans bothered to employ high-priced help to spy out Allied plans or whether they even did. They could have asked anyone wandering about the deck on the *Thysville* and gotten all the correct answers for free.

In any event, it all turned out to be wholly accurate; we got under way the next day, accompanied by the rumor that a German raider, or even a pocket battleship, was sailing around in the North Atlantic and that our convoy was intended as a stalking horse to allow the British Navy to bring it to battle. Since we assumed that similar rumors accompanied every convoy, we did not take that one very seriously. Everyone assiduously practiced boat-drill, however, and by the time we ultimately reached Liverpool, I could get out of bed, into my boots, and onto the allocated boat station in about fifteen seconds flat. We fortunately never had to test whether the boats were seaworthy. The first day at sea was still in coastal waters, with the entire convoy forming up over several square miles, ships of all sizes and types, including some huge oil tankers, all being herded into formation by four or five accompanying destroyers. Destroyers going at flank speed look fabulous and know it, to the point that I doubt whether destroyer captains ever order any speed below forty knots. Throwing up a huge bow wave, with one side of the ship practically submerged, and with those shrill, frenetic sirens going, a destroyer must be to sailors what bagpipes are to charging Highlanders, or maybe they're just a nuisance, as bagpipes tend to be.

We duly set off, and aside from encountering even more gales and high seas than is usual in January in the North Atlantic, it was a fairly uneventful trip. After a night of howling winds and high waters, morning would find the convoy all over the place, with the destroyers charging about like sheepdogs to get it back into formation. There would be the recurrent signals during the day from the convoy commander, a stately and elderly armed merchant ship, blinking out a change of course, and those miles and miles of ships would duly execute the required turns to adopt the new required pattern. Invariably one or two ships would be slow to respond, which would result immediately in furiously blinking lamp signals from one of the destroyers, followed frequently by the destroyer setting off at headlong speed and clearly on a collision course, only to sheer off at the last moment, masses of white water cascading from the bow—talk about showboating! We also had a submarine escorting us that had the heart-stopping habit of crash-surfacing at odd intervals and places, which was, I supposed, good practice for them and never failed to scare us silly. They do not fly flags on those things and conning towers all look alike to landlubbers like me. To get us even closer to cardiac arrest, one or another destroyer would frequently enter into the spirit of the thing by taking a tight turn and come charging down at the surfacing submarine, with all depth charge crews at the ready, presumably just to keep everyone alert. We saw a couple of possibly German reconnaissance planes on several occasions but were never molested in any way. A day or so out of Liverpool, just after dawn, we were overtaken by an enormous British battleship, with its attendant cruisers and destroyers, about eight ships in all, all going at top speed, with our destroyer's sirens "yup-yupping" away in salute and the battleship blowing a deep bass in reply. An absolutely gorgeous sight; maybe there was something to that decoy rumor, after all, if so, it had not worked.

The really memorable part about the voyage was getting involved in a marathon bridge game, which evidently had been going for months but had been interrupted by one of the participants finding pressing reasons to remain in Halifax. That left the ship's owner and the other two Belgians with the need for someone who was familiar with both French and bridge. Familiarity in some cases breeds contempt and in others is no cure for ignorance; I liked the game but there was no indication (nor has there been, to this day) that this favor was reciprocated.

Nevertheless, there I was every night and a good part of the day trying to guess my partner's hand; just bidding is not enough of a clue for the likes of me. Since an early and very casual reference to "usual stakes" had meant absolutely nothing to me, being paid winnings of nearly one hundred pounds at the end of the trip was just another crazy incident in a wholly crazy period.

I left *Thysville* in Liverpool in mid-February 1941, with about one hundred and twenty pounds in winnings and wages, having been interned with ten shillings nine months earlier. Financially speaking, the internment had been a success.

The Germans promptly bombed Liverpool on the night we docked, and since this was the first time for me, I thought it to be much more spectacular than scary; I learned better later.

My problem was not bombs, but *bona fides*; the local military police viewed my identity papers with understandable skepticism and suggested that I take a bus out to Huyton to get the internment camp commandant there to furnish me with some official release document. It seemed both preposterous and entirely reasonable, so I went out to Huyton to get myself readmitted in order to get released. Since nothing is that simple where official channels are concerned, all this took almost three days, during which I found out that the current Huyton inmates (none of whom I recognized) had evidently settled in for the duration, complete with geraniums on the window sills and notice boards announcing seminars on "Mittel-Hochdeutsch and its impact on Goethe."

Three days later I left, duly documented, and headed for Stanford and the Briggs household, just to catch my breath. Getting to Stanford by train, bus, and hitchhiking the last mile or so, I walked straight into the living room, where the Reverend Briggs sat reading his paper. Here I was, after nine months of total silence, at least partly explained by my having drowned on the *Arandora Star*, and there he was, looking up from his paper. So he said "Hello, Max. You staying for dinner?" Sang-froid is an enviable quality.

# LABOR OMNIA VINCIT: 1941–1943

**W**E DID, in the next couple of days, fill in the past nine months, but we never again achieved the stage effect of that opening remark.

## 1

My next stop was Cambridge, where the gate porters at St. John's treated me as if I had just been out for a stroll. They treated me exactly the same way eight years later and twenty years after that; time is not a dimension Cambridge is familiar with.

Everything in my rooms seemed precisely as I had left it; clothes in the wardrobe, sherry in the cupboard, but I could not locate a single piece of paper in my desk or anywhere else, and most alarmingly, not a single note for my nearly completed thesis. Mrs. McDougall appeared, uncharacteristically burst into tears, and, much more in character, was quickly comforted by a glass of sherry. Another glass produced the solution to the missing papers.

She had obviously informed her husband of my being collected by the police, and McDougall, in turn, had assured her that in England only wrongdoers were so treated and not just taken away without reason. ("Not like in your country, Sir.") "My country," for these comparisons of justice, evidently being Germany, she had then asked McDougall how she might be of help to me, despite such sinister origins and since I was such a nice gentleman. McDougall felt that chances were that I was, if not spying, at least busily corresponding with unsavory people, and that her best course would be to locate and burn anything in my handwriting. She would be breaking the law in doing so, but it just might be helpful to me. So we had another sherry, and I thanked Mrs. McDougall for having taken such risks on my behalf (and taken care of my Ph.D. thesis notes in the process). As I had always planned to get martially involved once I had been academically certified, Mrs. McDougall had just accelerated the process. So off I went to join the army.

Since I was now officially a "friendly enemy alien," my induction had to be preceded by appearing before two delightful, grandfatherly, World War I officers, delegated to deal with "special cases," who informed me that my particular species would only be allowed to join either the Pioneer Corps or the Land Army, a euphemism for being a conscripted farm laborer. Of course, I could also drop the whole idea and sensibly remain a civilian. They suggested I sit down and think it over while they dealt with the next case.

That, to my amazement, turned out to be Fritz Lingen, last seen on the dockside in Halifax, and so we first caught up with each other before Lingen faced those two ancients and was put before the same choice. I should add that Lingen, before going to Cambridge, had been working in the city for a while and was some seven years older than I. Hence his reaction, after listening politely to the choices at hand and declining to take time out to think them over. He explained quite matter-of-factly that, at the age of five, he had been named Colonel-in-Chief of the Seventh Prussian Foot Guards and that becoming a private in the Pioneer Corps would not be compatible with his family's military tradition. The two old gentlemen looked as if someone had addressed them in Sanskrit and, though visibly relieved that this obvious mental case had turned down the army, seemed somewhat apprehensive when he opted for the Land Army. Clearly they would have preferred Fritz to walk out altogether and rejoin a world with which they did not even have a notional involvement. Fritz did in fact work on the land for the remainder of the war.

Having witnessed this splendid bit of nonsense (one would have thought that, in 1918, Fritz's grandfather had more pressing appointments to make), it was my turn to inform them that my family tradition would not even inhibit my joining the Boy Scouts, whom, at the time, I considered even less martial than the Pioneer Corps—erroneously, as it turned out.

I knew nothing at all about the Pioneer Corps except that someone had mentioned that they did not bear arms. Well, neither did the German Pioneer Corps, a formidable body of people much quoted in the press as constantly in the thick of things, building or blowing up bridges, invariably surrounded by shot and shell. So why wouldn't their British counterpart?

I was duly sworn in and given the king's shilling (a delightfully archaic and pre-inflationary tradition—by taking the shilling, you are in the king's debt. Not for long, I guess, nowadays) and medically examined for the first of perhaps a hundred occasions over the next few years. When not dealing with people wounded in action, military doctors act along long-established and, on the whole, surprisingly sound principles. If any ailment is above the waist, aspirin will do the trick; if below, then laxatives will provide relief. Complicated complaints are generally classified as malingering and dismissed; the overall mortality rate is lower than among civilians, so there must be something to it.

I was duly sworn in and became No. 13805532 Private Max-Otto Ludwig Loewenstein, 251st Company, Pioneer Corps. Over the next six years, every single part of that label changed, including the number.

The "somewhere in England" security blanket never applied to the Pioneer Corps; they could have put the various locations on the front page of the *Times*, without jeopardizing the safety of the realm. 251st Company was a brand new company, being formed in Ilfracombe in Cornwall, and it said so right on a poster in the recruiting office. I was duly issued a railway warrant, since a private's pay in those days (two shilling and six pence a day; just about $2.00 a week) made private travel a bit arduous.

*Un peu d'histoire,* as they say in the green Michelin guides—the Pioneer Corps is a sufficiently arcane body to justify a short pit stop.

# 2

Though somewhat more fully dressed, the Pioneer Corps was the Gunga Din of the British Army, when it came to pecking order.

Its emblem was the crossed pick and shovel and the legend *labor omnia vincit* ("work conquers all"—which I have always held to be an absurd assumption), and there are few airports, roads, and probably not a single public toilet built in the west of England between 1941 and 1943 where I did not participate in the construction. Except for a brief and disastrous foray to France in 1940, from which few returned, no Pioneers were ever sent overseas, and the government viewed it as a cheap though inefficient labor force, and it was both. There were a great number of Pioneer companies. Probably as many as two hundred, representing about fifty thousand men, were made up exclusively of 1914–18 veterans who, in the years since, had not risen beyond garbage collecting and road sweeping and felt, justifiably, that their talents would flourish equally well as licentious soldiers. They were of course all British subjects, as were the inmates (literally) of another half dozen Pioneer companies whose complement was made up of mentally defective men, with afflictions ranging from epilepsy to being mildly mongoloid (better known today as Down's Syndrome), obviously unable to fight but certainly employable as unskilled labor. The indifference to mental illness when not violent or criminal was really quite horrifying, and there is of course no telling how much these poor men were further impaired by being used as beasts of burden.

These companies were generally kept well isolated from other Pioneer outfits, but just occasionally you would be involved on the same work site, and it was both eerie and very sad to see someone digging while weeping silently for no obvious reason, or hear another at night literally howling at the moon.

Finally, there were about ten "alien" companies, of about three thousand people altogether, overwhelmingly made up of Germans and Austrians, but with a sprinkling of other nationalities whose identity the authorities found apparently too esoteric to define. Italians, though clearly "aliens," were never put into uniform; they wore them well but were thought to be inept in them, so Italians in England had been organized into civilian labor gangs.

Alien companies had little or no contact with the remainder of the Pioneer Corps, but just about everybody knew of everybody else within the foreign component; it was a very gossipy little army. 251st

Company, the most recent and, as it would turn out, the last alien company to be formed, harbored a surprising number of various nationalities, all long-term Foreign Legion members and as tough and battle-hardened as the rest of us were not. Foreign Legion elements had fought valiantly in northern Norway in May 1940 and had been evacuated to England. Some of them had evidently then expressed some doubts as to whether the Free French could either use or pay them. Rather than argue the matter, de Gaulle had turned them over to the British who, ever pragmatic and ever clueless, shoved them into the Pioneer Corps. They stayed around until late 1941 when, predictably, they joined the Commandos en masse. Until then they added a tough and truly alien leavening to about as unsoldierly a bunch of people as have been seen since the Children's Crusade.

The noncommissioned officers in alien companies (though that has an extraterrestrial sound nowadays, we were pretty earthbound) were, at first, all British veterans of World War I who were mostly arthritic and fond of expletives, but rarely mean.

The private soldiers in these companies came from a vastly different world. The corporals would discuss women and beer, which are very acceptable army topics, while in the lower ranks, you might hear heated arguments as to whether Catullus wrote in decadent or merely sophisticated Latin; a subject not usually a preoccupation of the military mind.

We had, at one time, six Nobel laureates serving in 251st Company, one Nobel for every sixty men—even Athenian levies would be hard put to match that!

Now, back to Ilfracombe, base depot of the Pioneer Corps, and to Private Loewenstein, shambling into the war—

Ilfracombe has much in common with Brittany, both in terms of landscape and the fact that an earlier and thriving livelihood based on smuggling and piracy had been replaced by an equally flourishing tourist trade—presumably since it often involves comparable talents and endeavors.

Just about all of Ilfracombe's hotels and boarding houses had been requisitioned by the army, with the earnest but futile aim to make soldiers out of the likes of us. The uniforms issued for that purpose were no help. Quartermasters the world over invariably have stuff two sizes too large or two sizes too small, but even a Savile Row tailor would have been defeated by the basic concepts. The British forage cap served no purpose, except to fall off, since it had been designed only for people with pear-shaped heads or who had been trepanned. The battle jacket, a recent and lamentable innovation, made you look pregnant in front and hunchbacked in the rear. The collar was variably cut either to cause apoplexy or to allow inspection of your rib cage; its shovel-sized lapels extended to the arm pits. The accompanying trousers, made of concrete-reinforced felt starting at the shoulder blades and ending well ahead of your toes, were cut for Oliver Hardy posteriors carried at knee level. Puttees—the glory of Cheltenham OTC, where we had been endlessly taught to roll them into shapes otherwise known only to pastry cooks—had, to my distress, been discarded altogether by the army on the arguable assumption that snake bites and rock cuts, so prevalent on the Khyber Pass, were not primary threats in western Europe. The varicose-vein bandage of the early puttee had now been replaced by some shorter contraption of unmanageable canvas and mystifying purpose, which in turn led to boots, weighing ten pounds when dry and about thirty when wet, and looking like black canoes.

A belt, made of the same intractable material, acted as anchor for the webbing, a filigree of pouches, pockets, hooks, and crevasses, all attached to the belt and worn over both shoulders. The purpose of this assembly of hooks, latches, and holes has always remained a mystery to me. Its use in stowing away cartridges, hand grenades, or similarly martial trivia would presuppose an enemy army of arthritics; nothing could be recovered from that canvas rabbit warren in less than three minutes.

Shirts dyed in khaki, and underwear and socks in their original gray excrement shades, all felt like inquisitional hairshirts, without their concomitant purifying effect; the "great-coat" for cold weather both looked and felt like a pup tent left over from the Crimean War; and all of these manmade disasters could, with some difficulty, be rammed into one large duffel bag—and then best be forgotten.

In addition, we were issued a washing kit, a towel (a piece of grey wood, which could be bent when very wet), a "housewife" (pronounced "hassiv," and having no culinary or sexual connotations; it was a rather cute assembly of thread and needles to allow some to darn socks and others to draw blood), and a mess kit.

For design failure so total as to be truly memorable, the World War II British Army mess kit is equalled only by the British jerry can.

Picture two vaguely rectangular tin containers, about six-by-four inches, with fold-out handles. Since tin is a fine heat conductor, any really hot content like soup made the handles impossible to touch. Once you could touch them, the soup was cold. Thus, the impossibility of drinking out of a rectangular container became an academic issue.

We were issued a gas mask, no longer in a cardboard box but now in a rather elegant khaki shoulder bag—forerunner of the fashion of the 1970s—and since the masks were never used and even gas drills were abandoned by 1942, they ultimately made quite handy overnight cases.

As to helmets, it had taken the War Office just over twenty years to discover that the German World War I version afforded better protection than its British barber-basin variety. The British Army was being equipped with new "coal scuttle" helmets, but they were still in short supply, and the Pioneer Corps, understandably, was not on the priority list. So we kept on wandering about the old-fashioned way, looking like Sergeant York with flat feet. When not actively fighting someone, the greater part of the British soldier's day is taken up by inexplicable parades and roll calls and by unending cleaning of boots, buttons, and equipment. Cleaning buttons as to be visible in the dark at fifty paces (a somewhat outdated military advantage) is a pointless but achievable skill, but things get more complex when cleaning belts and webbing. Some officers like them white, some khaki, some green or yellow, and depending on which officer is in charge, you might have to go through these chameleon changes several times a day, which is wearisome and not funny.

Only while at Sandhurst did I ever come across absolute conformity of color, but then the commandant of Sandhurst was a man of notoriously firm views, whose dislike of indecision reputedly led him to decree that, in Sandhurst at least, electricity ran from negative to positive and no other way; thereby resolving an issue that has puzzled scientists since Faraday.

I have little recollection of my stay in Ilfracombe, a typical base depot and, like all such places, a center of institutionalized boredom and petty crime, but I do recall some of the activities and characters that typified 251st Company, then and subsequently.

## 3

Sergeant-Major Machin was a small, sly, efficient, and venal man who ran the company with very little fuss and, in return for regular though very minor favors (five-shilling loans, fated to go the way of subsequent Third World Debt), was easy to get along with. I have vivid memories of Major McKay, Military Cross and Bar, commanding 251st Company, and who, like Machin, was going to be around for a couple of years. He was a huge man, with a ferocious ginger mustache and side whiskers to match, a crimson hawk's nose that had braved battles and bottles without number, several generous and wattled chins, and the bearing of a Roman emperor. He had clearly been a hero in World War I (Military Crosses were not uncommon; bars to them were), during which he had been shot through the throat. This had left him with a deep, permanently hoarse, and peculiarly carrying voice, a male counter to Tallulah Bankhead; add a monocle and you had the very caricature of the Victorian Empire Builder. This part he had frequently and successfully played on stage and screen between the wars, as well as other character roles dealing with choleric denizens of clubs and Turkish baths. Hiding behind this absurd Colonel Blimp apparition was a keen wit, a lively and well-educated mind, and an extensive knowledge of places and people well beyond the British borders. He was the only officer I met during the war who understood and was interested in the complexities of being a German refugee and an enemy alien; he liked us all and that affection was certainly returned. Since our destined purpose was to disport ourselves with picks and shovels, our actual military training was cursory at best, but even so it was well beyond the capabilities of some 251'ers. This was partly due to the Pioneer Corps taking people into their sixties, not exactly prime assault course material (it was rumored that one Heinrichs, a dear old dodderer, was in his eighties, and

Machin wisely relegated him to the mailroom, where he misread addresses), and partly to the educational level of the instruction personnel. Being mostly over-age and unemployed WWI veterans, literacy or articulateness was not their forté, and as many of them had considerable difficulties distinguishing left from right, taking instruction from them was often akin to a mind-reading exercise.

However, after a couple of weeks, we had mastered the rudiments of saluting and whom to do it to, and on being ordered to "Halt," the company would manage to straggle to a standstill within the next couple of minutes; thus we were deemed ready to venture forth and do our bit.

I knew a few fellow recruits by sight from various internment camps, but no one personally, and I have no recollection of any of them today.

I do, however, distinctly remember a gargantuan and saturnine Greek legionnaire, who looked like Anthony Quinn's twin and who was steadily and successfully working his way out of the army. He was a man of almost no speech, immense strength, and marvelous speed and economy of movement; our bunks were next to each other and I spoke French, which seemed to make him comfortable. I do not recall ever knowing his name. He had been in the Foreign Legion for nearly twenty years, had been awarded the Legion d'Honneur and the Médaille Militaire several times over, and to see him mend a sock, lay out his kit, pick up a girl, or empty a bar of its occupants was a lesson in neatness and efficiency.

His succinct outline of the situation, "Why wait for old friend? Here is new friend!" appeared to convince perfectly respectable young ladies, clearly waiting for someone else (respectable being a relative term in a base depot, in wartime, and perhaps even in Cornwall). Once I saw him respond to the shout of "La Legion! A Moi," a distress signal that I had previously only read about in *Beau Geste*. He waded into the pub whence the call came, and within a few minutes, the entire pub was laid out on the street: occupants, chairs, fittings, the lot. Whereupon he and the legionnaire previously in need, solemnly shook hands and went their respective ways. James Cagney would have loved it. My Greek friend had heard that civilian life in England offered considerably better financial prospects than the Pioneers (being a nightclub bouncer, for which he was predestined, would make him rich), and he was determined to abandon the army. If you are well over six feet and look as strong as you are, this is not easy.

However, within a week, my friend's urine was turning blue. Medical tests showed nothing, but the urine was getting bluer, and when we left Ilfracombe, he stayed behind. We heard some months later from a fellow Greek, that he had been discharged, had instantly recovered, and settled in London. They teach you lots of things in the Foreign Legion.

We, on the other hand, close to three hundred men, left Ilfracombe on our first assignment: Avonmouth, the main harbor area of Bristol. At that time the Luftwaffe concentrated night attacks on London and various English ports, and Avonmouth, a key oil storage area, was high on the German target list. There were miles of storage tanks in the harbor area, and 251st Company's first task was to construct "decoy installations."

The Germans bombed almost every night and regularly hit a few tanks, so the thought was (if thought fits such an asinine concept) to build some storage tank simulation out in the countryside, which would induce some astigmatic German pilot to unload his bombs among the cows. We were to fashion a circular outline in clay, even "crumpling" one side to indicate a semi-collapsed storage tank, then feed oil into this clay ring, and with German bombers approaching, set the oil alight. The Germans would see a burning, collapsing storage tank and would bomb the area to set off more tanks.

It took about twenty of us several days to construct such an outline, since the resident engineer insisted on calipers, theodolites, and other precision measurements, which, you would have thought, would not really have been a deciding factor at twenty thousand feet. We built about thirty of these decoys, which were lit every time the Germans approached, and every time the Germans serenely flew by them to drop their bombs on Avonmouth; it is reasonable to assume that they used our handiwork as directional beacons.

Our actual billets were on a small hillside overlooking the harbor installations, and on the first night, among the noise and confusion of a first exposure to carpet bombing, we were wondering what those hailstones and general bangings on the roofs of our tin huts were all about. When a piece of anti-aircraft shrapnel sliced through the roof, breaking someone's arm, we had the answer; from then on we ducked into shelters, like good and scared little soldiers should. We did not often have the opportunity, though; German air attacks were getting so consistent and heavy, that the Avonmouth fire fighters needed all the help they could get. Fighting blazing oil tanks is not difficult to learn, but it is no fun. Years later, reading about Red Adair and his exploits, it really came home to me just how bloody dangerous it must have been; at the time we were too busy and too tired to notice. Besides, there is no question about the adrenalin factor: fight a blazing oil tank, get into a real confrontation with a combat tank, get set for a parachute drop, and every time some atavistic sense of excitement, almost exhilaration, comes into play and becomes uppermost—at least I found it so.

The real problem about fighting a blazing oil tank was that it gets so unbelievably hot and the protective clothing they gave us just could not cope with it. There were frequent occasions when you really had to work close to the burning tank, sometimes just fifty feet away, and the only way to do that was for others to keep hoses on you to keep you from being roasted—you tended to get a bit toasted anyway. Water is useless when dealing with oil, and all we ever used was foam; by the time the Germans broke off their attacks, usually around two A.M., everyone was wading around in about four feet of whipped cream. It was a rather spectacular way to be introduced to oil fires, air attacks, and the war in general.

There were less dramatic aspects, such as the "unfinished movie." The local movie theater was showing *Unfaithfully Yours* with Pat O'Brien. The movie started at nine o'clock, the Germans started bombing at 9:10, and we went racing off to fight fires. Next day, back to the movie, which started at nine, and the Germans started at 9:08. Third day the Luftwaffe, unaccountably delayed (maybe by our decoys?), started at 9:12; following day, regular as clockwork, back they were by 9:08. I saw the beginning of the movie four times, then I passed. Anyone know how that movie ended?

There was the Mauritania in Bristol, where you could imbibe limitless varieties of alcohol among endless settings. *Mauritania* had been a hallowed name in the tales of great ocean liners, and when

Cunard retired the ship shortly before the war, the Harvey sherry people bought every bar and lounge the ship held and re-housed them under one roof in the middle of Bristol. It had become a pilgrimage site for generations of *Mauritania* travelers or mere alcoholics, and the variety of locales and beverages was awesome. We used to repair there in our cleaned up togs, all shipshape and Bristol-fashion (when in Rome . . . ), and though the Mauritania was well beyond our means, we always found a kind-hearted or just bibulous soul, intent upon looking after "our boys in khaki," even though some of the "boys" might be older than the donor by twenty years or spoke English like Otto Preminger.

## 4

Three months after having moved to Avonmouth, 251st Company was ordered to Cheltenham, where we would be stationed for almost two years.

Adjacent to the Cotswolds in Gloucestershire and one of England's prettiest regions, Cheltenham became a popular spa in Napoleonic times and, like Bath and Leamington, adopted a gracious and spacious Regency air, with a good deal of attractive and affluent architecture in Beau Nash style. Where Cheltenham's healing waters were and what they healed seems no longer clear today, but it has always retained that somnolent, self-satisfied look of a fashionable spa. Until well into the 1960s, steeple-chasing races were the only events that focused national interest on Cheltenham; in recent years, spy scandals have overshadowed horses and hurdles.

Cheltenham has an unusually benign climate that supposedly is the nearest thing England has to offer to compare to a hill station in British India. However unlikely a meteorological theory that may be, Cheltenham, for over one hundred years, has been the final retirement haven for untold Indian Army colonels and their ladies. Hindustani had become a required language for local shopkeepers and other box-wallahs, and the customs of Poonah, Simla, and Peshawar are fondly remembered and rigidly observed. Soldiering was the only calling acceptable to such "ruling class" of Cheltenham, and soldiering meant being a pukkah cavalry officer defending remote empire outposts against riotously colored natives.

Serving in 251st Company, Pioneer Corps, did not quite fall under that definition.

By no coincidence, Cheltenham also houses Cheltenham College, not to be confused with Cheltenham Ladies' College, founded later but of much loftier reputation. Cheltenham College, then only for boys, but coeducational since the 1980s, is a well-regarded public school, not among the top half dozen, but certainly among the top twenty in the kingdom. The Ladies' College, on the other hand, is unquestionably the premier English boarding school for girls; there was no contact between the two schools, except once a year when we used to dance against each other-an event anticipated with justified dread by all participants.

In 1841, Queen Victoria had decreed the creation of public schools specifically intended to educate boys wishing to make the army, and more particularly the Indian Army, their career. Cheltenham is held to be preeminent among that newly created batch of schools, which also included Marlborough, Wellington, Clifton, Haileybury, and Westward Ho! (which Kipling attended and which has since folded).

People like the author John Masters (an Old Cliftonian) were typical of an intercontinental to-ing and fro-ing. He was the sixth generation in a series of father going to India to serve, son returning to England to be educated (sort of), before going back out to India, while father would return to England and retirement, just as the son would in due course, at a time when grandson was already in the circuit, and so on.

The sole reason I had attended Cheltenham was that my (by now) old friend Ernest Swinton had been an Old Cheltonian and had persuaded my dad, back in 1936, that it was the right school for any son of any friend of his. My father had no specific views on the matter and neither had I, and so I went.

I had a memorably good and enjoyable two years in Cheltenham, and when I left in 1938 to go up to Cambridge, I was one of two, in a class of more than twenty, who did not become a professional soldier. I was a foreigner, and the other guy had some other deficiency which I do not recall. However, a Cheltonian remains a Cheltonian and there never was any doubt in anyone's mind, that, should hostilities break out, I would immediately participate in them at a station commensurate with school tradition. Whether that should turn out to be as a cornet with Probyn's Horse or as an Uhlanen Hauptmann was not that relevant. In Paul Scott's wonderful *Raj Quartet*, the pivotal school constantly referred to is Chillingborough, clearly a contraction of Cheltenham, Wellington, and Marlborough; the *Raj Quartet* was what Cheltenham was all about.

I had met quite a number of these military fossils while at Cheltenham. They were forever tottering around the school's playing fields, and I was—on rare and unpredictable occasions—a reserve member of the Cheltenham Rugby XV, which meant freezing on the side lines waiting for one of my betters to break a leg or catch the flu. It was a spot to meet these old codgers, and now, while busily digging up assorted drains all over Cheltenham, I saw quite a few of them again. They may well have viewed me as a kind of urban Lawrence of Arabia, turning his back on his class and "going native" for some wildly eccentric and wholly unfathomable reason. Or perhaps I was a latter-day John Buchan character, doing nameless deeds in nameless places, all to be revealed in due time and full glory? Whatever such speculations, the general consensus of these decorated dinosaurs was aptly summed up by Colonel Fullerton, DSO and two bars, erstwhile commanding Fourth Poona Horse (I kid you not!), whose brick-red face hovered over me one fine morning, while some fellow Pioneers and I were doing something to a gas main in Cheltenham High Street. "You there, that German fella from Newick House," he rasped, "when are ye goin' to stop this confounded nonsense and take a commission in a decent regiment? Demn silly way of buggerin' about, this." Spoken like a true Cheltonian.

As it happened, outside the Pioneer Corps, no former "enemy alien" was ever considered for commission until late 1943, after which time army commissions were obtainable anywhere to those good or lucky enough to qualify. Perhaps a dozen or so "aliens" were commissioned as Pioneer Corps officers up to 1943, invariably people who had joined the corps quite early on. We hugely envied them, and their fellow Pioneer officers, all 1914–18 veterans, ignored them. In the end, they were left at the starting gate, since later, when some of us climbed to field rank in such vaunted outfits as Commandos, Paratroops, Tanks, or Gliders, they just continued to supervise a bunch of ditch diggers till the end of the war and never rose higher than captain in the process. So, being a tortoise was not all bad.

In the years up to 1943, the group of veteran English sergeants and corporals was increasingly replaced by "enemy alien" personnel; by the time I left the Pioneers in 1943, there were hardly any British NCO's left. From the beginning, lance-corporals had been aliens, since a lance-corporal is strictly a "gofer" and has a harassed and hapless existence. A private can goof off all over the place, if undetected, and a corporal is a body of some authority, but as a "Corporal, Lance, temporary, unpaid, acting" you were just a schmuck—except that you had to go that route to climb the promotion ladder.

During my two years with the Pioneer Corps, I made it to unpaid lance corporal three or four times and got busted just as often; I recall neither the reasons for promotion nor for degradation. I did leave the corps as a temporary acting unpaid L/C and my next step up the promotion ladder was officer cadet; I never made corporal or sergeant anywhere.

In Cheltenham we were housed in splendid, modern, and permanent barracks, and except for having bunk beds and sleeping twenty to a (very large) room, led an almost hotel-like existence; considerably more pleasant, I suspect, than any of those Douglas hotels, when still operating as such.

Although Cheltenham was to be our base, it became apparent that the majority of the company would be in varying detachments and on various projects all over the countryside; up to twenty people would form one detachment that might be gone for up to two months fifty miles away from Cheltenham. Petrol rationing was a much more serious consideration than mere inconvenience, and so we were spread all over the countryside. In all, I probably spent no more than three months in the town itself (to Fullerton & Co.'s relief, no doubt), and a good deal of that time I had the wonderfully relaxing job of being telephone operator to the local Civil Engineering Board. That meant cycling down to a delightful old Regency house at 9 A.M., sitting in front of a six-extension switchboard till 5 P.M., and then cycling back; averagely, there was about one call an hour. Either engineers do not talk much or they do not do much—in wartime Cheltenham, that is.

During that early summer of 1941, I also renewed many of my old Cheltenham contacts; it was, after all, less than three years ago that I had left Newick House. (Like most English public schools, Cheltenham divided its 450 or so boys into houses for rooming, study, and team sport purposes. There were nine houses and Newick was one of them.)

The people I remember most vividly were the Borchardts; he a quiet, dried prune of a little man who had taught mathematics and been housemaster of Hazelwood House; she very much like Mrs. Briggs. They had retired just when I left Cheltenham and, being independently wealthy, lived in a lovely Regency house, surrounded by about three acres of walled gardens, in the very middle of Cheltenham and amid a profusion of dogs, flower beds, and servants. They had had one son, the apple of their eye, who had been a very senior prefect at college in my day, and much too august a person for me to know, except very slightly. He had enlisted in the navy and, shortly after we arrived in Cheltenham, been killed on the battle cruiser *Hood,* when *Bismarck* blew it up. I spent quite some time with the Borchardts in their lovely home with beautifully laid tables and fine paintings, both of them almost maniacally active, utterly inconsolable, and just waiting for their lives to end. They were perhaps the saddest people I met during the entire war.

McKay, as a professional actor and a ham at all times, was much in favor of organized company entertainment and, during a period when most of the company was working within walking distance, this resulted in some memorable performances held in—of all places—Cheltenham College's main auditorium.

The concept started with our awareness of two Auxiliary Territorial Service, or ATS, companies (the British WAC equivalent) just down the road, and visually speaking, there seemed to be a good deal of talent there. Contacts of various kinds ensued—not all of us were over sixty—and McKay and his ATS opposite number may have come to the conclusion that a more formalized association might discourage all this licentious soldiering. It did not seem to serve that purpose, but it did lead to the production of *Aladdin,* the most time-honored name for any British pantomime (and therefore the only reason we picked it). Pantomime — traditionally only viewable at Christmas, but English tradition was not a particularly strong suit in 251st Company — is to art or theater, what burlesque is to Milton; except for a tangentially common language, there is no connection. Pantomime is an "anything goes" format geared to its audience: fairy tales for children, songs and pretty girls for their elders, off-color jokes and political satire for late performances, slapstick and balloons for matinées, just shove it all together and push it out on the stage.

Being quintessentially English, a pantomime has immutable and inexplicably Anglo-Saxon features; there is always a Principal Boy who, in fact, is always a pretty girl with exceedingly pretty legs, and there is always an unsavory elderly female, invariably played by a man in drag.

I do not recall my volunteering to write and produce this joint enterprise, but apparently I did. Ending up with a cast of about a hundred, half of them ATS and as scantily dressed as their looks and McKay's tolerance allowed, everything was based on ad-libbing, chutzpah, and hope. To my surprise, McKay had parlayed Cheltenham College as a venue, and we performed there for three successive August nights during school vacation, before massed Pioneer and ATS soldiery, assorted wives, sweethearts, and other appendages, and various civil and local luminaries. During the inevitable and almost incessant behind-the-curtain disasters (collapsing scenery or actors, assorted hysterics, mislaid props), I was in front of it, trying to distract the audience's attention by rambling tales, which had only two elements in common — they were all in dubious taste and the audience liked them. I like to think that I resembled Joel Grey in *Cabaret* — at least we had the stay-rite hairdo in common.

I had of course been in this auditorium many times before and on occasions when any of my present stories would have led to instant dismissal from the school. In addition, the Loewenstein now loping around the stage was the same Loewenstein featured frequently and quite prominently on various large wooden tablets all around the hall, commemorating sundry scholastic achievements. To be fair, to be a scholar at Cheltenham should not be confused with being so considered in a normal academic environment; if you could read, you had a head start. McKay may have known about this double identity; no one else in the audience did, and it tickled me—and still does. The show was so noisy a success that there was talk of going "on tour," but this was prevented by some insuperable logistics and by the fact that the leading lady turned out to be two months pregnant, which seemed to worry her considerably less than it did various male members of the cast. I organized some more shows while with 251, and later in Blackdown and Sandhurst, but none was ever as spontaneous, funny, successful, and downright dirty as *Aladdin*.

# 5

Most of my time in Cheltenham was spent "on detachment" and on a variety of jobs. We built various structures for the public weal: roads, runways, Nissen huts, and such. But our prime time and talent were devoted to latrines. We built them in Gloucestershire, Wiltshire, Shropshire, even in Hampshire, and well into Wales—a seat for every citizen, or almost. Constructing the operative part, so to speak, was repetitive and simple: dig a hole ten foot deep and about twice as wide, put down a layer of large stones, followed by a layer of gravel, followed by a layer of quicklime, and then repeat the process, starting with the large stones, until you reach the top. The creative part lay in the superstructures; we built them in wood, asbestos, corrugated iron, or concrete; we built them squared, rounded, with domes, or eaves; for single occupancy or massed retreat; we delivered them in light grey, medium grey, and even dark grey—the Mies van der Rohes of bowel motion.

Some of us in the process became "trade tested" concrete mixers, which carried threepence a day extra pay and was a backbreaking extension of a child's sandbox. You sloshed around in rubber boots, stirring gravel, water, sand, and cement into a wonderfully gooey gray syrup, which you then shovelled into wheelbarrows and, teetering precariously over assorted slanting planks, deposited where required. After a while, everything was gray and congealing, you included.

When assigned to roadwork or runways, we frequently joined civilian construction gangs, considerably more efficient and vastly better paid than we, who would usually handle the "difficult" part of the job. They would set up theodolites and such, which was deemed beyond our competence, and we would read out instructions to them, which saved them time and lip-reading.

On occasion, I handled a pneumatic drill and to be plainly and noisily destructive is splendid, but the drills were unbelievably heavy after a while and gave you the shakes, to the point of being unable to write anything for at least a day or so afterwards.

Building Nissen huts was another specialty. I do not know who or what the original Nissen was, but the hut of that name is one of the most practical and ugliest dwellings ever conceived, and rather like a snail carrying its own shell, we frequently began our "detached" existence by putting up the first Nissen hut for ourselves. You start out with two wooden half-moons, each containing a door and two windows and which will form either end of the hut, then connect and secure them with a floor of wooden planks to be nailed together and kept a couple of inches off the ground for insulation purposes. You then erect a framework of half-moon-shaped metal ribs between either end and finally, manhandle, clamp, and weld overlapping sheets of corrugated iron onto them. The finished hut (which it then is) can house about two dozen people and a small but very effective stove. It looks odd, ugly, compact, and indestructible, and it is all of those things.

Half a dozen men could put up such a hut in less then a day and, in 251 Company, that would include periods of contemplative construction, so to speak, involving arguments in how far Kant's categorical imperative applied to welding corrugated sheets or who among Xenophon's men actually spotted the sea first.

Some of those Nissen huts still stand today and are likely to do so till Armageddon or the Second Coming, whichever you think is to come first.

There were times when we were detached in considerable splendor, such as when we built a whole slew of toilets in the Lechdale region; doubtless a clairvoyant endeavor, since many years later Lechdale made world headlines as the site of "The Great Train

Robbery," and for weeks the place was overrun with press, investigators, and other inquisitive hordes requiring occasional relief. We were housed in a disused fourteenth-century chapel belonging to an equally ancient baronial hall nearby. It was very grand and impressive, Gothic vaulted ceilings, bats and all, and nowhere near as comfortable as a Nissen hut.

Incomparably the best job in any working party was to be "orderly," a much sought-after function, which we rotated every week. You would draw rations for your working party every morning; cocoa, tinned milk, sugar, bread, margarine, cream cheese, and Spam (if there were ever any deviation from those components, it must have been after I left the Pioneers). The trick was to persuade the issuing cook that your party was more numerous than it in fact was; you may consider that diet both uninteresting and unhealthy, and you would be right, but we were always ravenous.

All that stuff, together with two large buckets, would go into a wheelbarrow, which you would then manhandle to the working site, which might be all of a mile away. That was the only arduous part of the day, though a cinch after all that sloshing about with cement. Once arrived, while everyone else worked or went through the motions, all you had to do was to find a watertap, a few stray rocks to build a "table," some odds and ends to start a fire, and a sunny spot for yourself. At 10:30 A.M. you boiled up some cocoa (cocoa deserving of its name should hold a spoon at no less than seventy degrees angle!), cut and cover slabs of bread of approximately discus size and consistency, and wait for your mob to devour it all. This would happen between 10:45 and 11:00, after which time you washed out the buckets and went back into the sun. You went through the same procedure at 1 P.M. and again at 3:15 (cocoa only this time, a real cinch). Then a final washing up, buckets back into the barrow, final sunbathe, and back to barracks by 5 P.M.—lovely day!

Depending on location, evenings could be fun or just deadly. If near any inhabited locality, there would be pubs, possibly girls, and maybe even movies, and since we would almost invariably be putting something together that troops yet to arrive were to utilize later, we rarely if ever had to compete with other uniformed heroes. As we almost always hung out in areas previously only visited by poachers, land surveyors, and similar riff-raff, we frequently were the only supplement to the BBC news in keeping the locals abreast of how the war was really going. We may not have been the most accurate informants, but we certainly tried to be imaginative. Quite frequently, however, we would literally be working in the middle of nowhere (military airfields tend to be planned in lunar isolation), with just a ration truck visiting us every other day. On evenings in those parts you had the choice between watching socks dry, which is mildly entertaining and rather repetitive, or discussing Schopenhauer and such, which after a while was not so hilarious either.

Alien Pioneers were a spectacularly unmilitary bunch and what little military demeanor Ilfracombe had tried to inculcate had withered on the vine within months. Picture a newly detailed detachment in Cheltenham having managed to congregate in a heap of ill-fitting khaki and waiting to be told what to do next. The sergeant, new to both rank and entourage, clearly tries to find the *mot juste* that would both indicate martial intent and be comprehensible to the motley *mélange* before him. He takes a long look, shrugs, says, "Oh well, let's go," in a most conversational tone, and then sets off, hoping that those flat-footed stragglers would follow him in due course. So much for parade-ground displays in the Pioneer Corps.

Very occasionally some officer hit upon the extraordinary notion of having us mount guard at night over the site we were working at. Aside from the fact that the "two hours on, four hours off" routine was a nuisance when all you wanted to do was sleep and let things be, it was unclear how we should handle any incident. Yell for help presumably, since we carried no weapons of any kind. This charade came to an end when about fifty of us were building a huge Nissen hut camp somewhere in Wiltshire. There were at least a hundred huts when we arrived, and we were supposed to add that many more, and there was not a soul in any of them. The "guard hut" was set up at the perimeter of the camp and two of us lynx-eyed Pioneers were supposed to patrol all around for two hours, presumably to make sure that no one stole a Nissen hut. The solution to this asinine undertaking seemed very simple: the two guards would wander off, equipped with blankets and an alarm clock, pick any hut among the multitude around, and go to sleep. The alarm would ring after two hours, and the guards would go back to wake the next detail and now catch some legitimate sleep. With hundreds of huts, and officers notoriously reluctant to get up themselves to inspect us night owls, the odds were astronomically in favor of not being caught. So they were until one guard detail forgot to take the alarm clock with them and dozed off without it. By midmorning we were still scouring the entire camp, trying to find out just where those two guys had mislaid themselves. It discouraged our superiors from further burdening us with such responsibilities.

The Nobel laureate ingredient within 251st Company, as well as the lofty level and range of conversation, did not measurably add to our digging competence or our building skills, so as the archetypical idiots savants within a Pioneer Corps context, our sergeants and officers dealt with us in an aura of helpless exasperation. We were reasonably able to cope with the jobs, but it was those pauses, when half the ditch leaned on their shovels to listen to someone propound a variant on Hegel's concept of objective logic, that drove them crazy.

# 6

Much later that year, close to Christmas time, I had been "detached," singly and right across the country, to act as driver/telephone operator for an infantry battalion stationed near Cambridge. Pioneers did not pioneer much that I am aware of, except to popularize the "temporary help" concept.

The war going as poorly as it then did, any real soldier was supposed to be just that, which left the likes of alien Pioneers to perform as temporary waiters, drivers, kitchen help, and in other nonmartial arts. It made for a change and never lasted longer than a couple of weeks; a uniformed variant of the Kelly girls. My present and very temporary employer had the responsibility of providing a guard detachment to ensure the security of the king whenever he spent time at Sandringham Castle nearby, a small one as castles go in the middle of an immense park and the private property of the Windsor family. It appeared that the king came fairly frequently and that, once again, his arrival was expected.

True enough, during one of my first evenings at the switchboard (as somnolent an occupation as my previous Cheltenham exposure had led me to expect), the phone rang and some hyphenated-named colonel requested the duty officer to come to the castle to report to him, "as a certain personage has arrived." This kind of security talk might have deluded a tribal warrior on the Lower Congo, though I doubt it; anyway the duty officer duly departed and so, in my capacity as a driver, did I with him.

It had snowed and was still snowing, which made for a very pretty drive; it took about a quarter of an hour to reach the gates of Sandringham Park and another ten minutes or so to drive through the grounds and get to the main house, a quite cozy-looking Victorian monstrosity, all turrets, gables, and red brick. The duty officer's briefing did not take long, barely time for me to swap some dubious and unlikely stories with the resident guard troop, when we were off again through the swirling snow. The duty officer "knew a shortcut." I of course knew nothing, and after ten minutes driving into the gathering darkness, that made two of us; here we were lost in Sandringham Park. Not quite, though, since, silhouetted in the head-lights, we saw a figure in cloak and deerstalker hat walking towards a side path. My officer leaned over the windshield and yelled, "Hey, you! Come here," and the figure did.

There could not be the slightest doubt in either of our minds that it was King George! With the boldness of desperation, my superior left the king standing in the snow and merely said, "We seem to be lost. Which way is it to Cambridge?" King George slowly and care-fully explained the route, complete with the heart-stopping speech defect he had, and, really going for broke, my officer said, "Thank you, my good man," (chutzpah of such dimension is truly awesome!) and turning to me said "Driver, drive on," and believe you me, I did!

The last we saw of King George VI, he was standing in the swirling snow, looking benign and slightly puzzled; not quite the last I saw of him though.

On the drive home, my officer pledged me to eternal silence on pain of being immediately posted to the Outer Orkneys, and we both speculated what life in the Tower of London might be like and how soon we would find out.

In any event, absolutely nothing happened, and when I was sent back to 251st, two weeks later, I soon forgot about the whole episode.

Until sometime in mid-summer 1945 when the British Army held a Victory parade in Brussels . . .

The only other occasion when I hobnobbed with the Royals, was sometime in 1942, hitchhiking near Oxford. A vast and antique Daimler pulled up, and sitting in the back, ramrod-straight in gray silk, complete with parasol and toque hat, was Queen Mary, the Queen Mother. She sat in the rear, and I sat next to the driver; we were separated by a glass partition, and by two ladies-in-waiting sitting on the jump seats. When the car had stopped, I had saluted and Queen Mary had said nothing; when I got off ten minutes later, I saluted again and again the queen said nothing. We did not get to know each other very well.

# 7

The war in general in 1941 and 1942 did not directly affect us much. The air raids had greatly subsided, and the main military action was in North Africa and in Russia. Since the English have this absurd love affair with a "pukka" opponent, everyone thought Rommel a simply splendid fellow, and it seemed almost a pity that we could not let him have Cairo and Alexandria. The alternating British and German surges back and forth along the North African coast were known as the "Benghazi Handicap," which lent a cozy racetrack note to the whole endeavor. Until I joined 3rd Royal Tanks, a year or so hence, (which had participated in every tank engagement in the Western Desert), the war in North Africa had seemed rather like Fontenoy-with-sand ("Après vous, Messieurs les Anglais"; no fighting after dark; prisoners being let go; and so on), and even talking to participants later never quite erased that impression of knights in armor—literally, as it happened—and their idiosyncrasies.

Russia, of course, was a very different situation and awesome in every aspect: the size of the country, the scope of the battles, the numbers involved, the claims on either side. There were some convinced Communists among 251st members, and some of them had spent time in Russia; they were all totally certain that the Russians would ultimately halt and then defeat the Germans. Shortly after the Germans invaded Russia and had achieved some immense successes, I recall one of those hard-line communists, who had spent ten years in Moscow and subsequently just as many in Berlin as a Communist organizer, blandly dismissing those masses of captured Russians as "just frontier guards with funny green hats" and telling us to wait till winter when the Russians would start throwing in their Siberian assault divisions. He was, of course, right, but it sure was, like Waterloo, a "damn close-run thing." We, in the 251st, never thought that was so, being steadily brainwashed by these Moscow experts, who seemingly really knew, we always had total confidence in ultimate Russian victory, despite recurrent and very obvious evidence to the contrary.

Sometime in September 1941, I finally had news of my family. They had left Holland a month earlier with a small number of German Jews whom the Nazis had agreed to let leave, as a result of some complex negotiations and substantial financial sacrifices borne by the Warburg clan in New York. Travelling by sealed train through France, the group had boarded ship in Lisbon and had arrived in New York. It was the first news I had had of them in almost eighteen months, and we did not actually see each other again until August 1946, almost five years later. However, correspondence became possible after September 1941, though it was never very regular or frequent until May 1945, after which time letters, even phone calls, and—not least—CARE packages came pouring in, and were duly reciprocated or appreciated.

I do not recall getting any leaves, but we did get thirty-six- or forty-eight-hour passes, mostly at random and without advance warning. Most of these I spent in London, at times in places of poor repute with ladies of even lesser, but, after 1942, increasingly in and around Le Petit Club Francais in St. James, to which Arthur Wells had introduced me. I do not recall how we met, but I saw a good deal of Arthur over the next two years. I remember him looking like an overweight Robert McNamara and being in London for the Canadian Film Board. He kept an apartment in the Athenaeum Court, a slightly dubious but very fashionable service flat complex on

Piccadilly, and as different from the Athenaeum Club as go-go dancers are from Goethe. It was the scene of some epic gatherings, as Arthur had inexhaustible sources of everything: food, liquor, girls, rumors, news—one of the most resourceful men I ever met— nice guy, too.

Le Petit Club is still fondly remembered by all who knew it. Tucked away in a cul-de-sac just off St. James's, it consisted of a large bar full of ramshackle and very comfortable furniture, a small dining room and kitchen on the floor above, and below, in the cellar, a vast "playroom," as indeed it was, with more couches, chairs, booze, and papers and magazines from just about every allied nation. The club's owner and not-always-benevolent despot was a chain-smoking be-spectacled Welsh woman of indeterminate age, who had some con-nections with filmmaking. She was a rabid Welsh nationalist and Francophile, a combination rarely met outside of a production of *Henry V.*

The club had originally been intended for the relaxation of "special operatives" among the Free French, shadowy types who would disappear for months on end, presumably parachuted into France, and who would just as suddenly reappear, though sometimes not. When they did turn up, they were invariably in the company of attractive women; there never was any doubt that the prettiest girls in London were to be found at Le Petit Club. None of them were English; there were French, Poles, Canadians, Russians, even one ravishing full-blooded American Indian, and they were all pretty sensational. Since they were usually escorted by these *revenants*, whose trade it was to kill expertly and with speed and enjoyment, it was a "don't touch the merchandise" situation.

But by 1942, there was sufficient unattached talent around to have come to the notice of American and Canadian war correspon-dents. They had started to make Le Petit Club their London head-quarters, provided Bronwen, the owner, approved of them. If she liked you, you paid five shillings a year and were a member; if she did not, there was no way to become one. Fortunately, she approved of quite a few people, all of them got to know each other sufficiently well to have meals together at Le Club or go back from there "to my place" to hear a new record or poem or piece of music. In this way, I got to know Ed Murrow, who needs no introduction from anyone, nor does William Saroyan, who always looked and acted like a huge and petulant baby. There was Margaret Higgins, writing for her second or third Pulitzer, and Marc Blitzstein, the composer; Robert Capa and Eliot Elisofon were club regulars and so was Carl Mydans, all *Life* luminaries at the time. Hemingway dropped in once in a while, and Bill Mauldin, the great *Yank* cartoonist, did so all the time. Harry Brown wrote most of *A Walk in the Sun* there, which became an immediate best-seller and is still one of the best books written about the Anzio beachhead. The closest Harry ever came to Anzio, however, was the Italian porter at the Ritz, where he was staying, five minutes' walk away from Le Club's recreational and evidently inspirational facilities. Quentin Reynolds and Alan Moorehead use to be around a lot, and so was Alan Campbell, who read me letters from his wife and was enchanted when I suggested that she sounded like Dorothy Parker. As it turned out, she was! All these people, and of course Arthur Wells, seemed to be hanging out at Le Petit Club whenever I managed to get to London (about once a month on average), and, in a very casual now-you-see-it-now-you-don't way, all were friends and it was heady company to keep.

The great attraction of Le Club was its fabulous cuisine, the ladies attached to the Free French contingent taking turns in the kitchen, all of them notable cooks and wholly untroubled by any rationing inhibitions. To eat there was as memorable as it was reasonable; sometimes Bronwen did not bother to charge at all. She also showed sovereign contempt for licensing hours. Le Club was open twenty-four hours a day for food and drink, and the police, rather than tangle with unpredictably tempered and potentially lethal characters (those Free French; not us, we were just amiably smashed), preferred to have a quick snort themselves and then leave well enough alone. The only house rule was for the last person out to lock up and leave the key in a slot behind the second garbage can; whoever came to the club next would find it. Bronwen lived on the second floor and would appear or go when she saw fit; Le Petit Club Francais was as much home to me as any place I can think of throughout those years.

Spending the night in London, other than at someone's place, presented problems. Hotels were prohibitive to people of my salary level and, in any event, wholly booked out ever since U.S. personnel had come to London en masse. The best, though hardest-to-copy solution, had been found by one of those French buccaneers, who had managed, by means never discussed, to acquire a perfectly legitimate ambulance truck, complete with Free French markings and plates. He could park it anywhere and, since it held two stretchers and other useful space, even entertain in it. My choice was to head for the Turkish baths, either in Jermyn Street or Russell Square. The Jermyn baths were just round the corner from St. James, but Russell was two shillings less, a constant choice between being indulgent and insolvent. The routine was the same in both places; payment entitled you to a twelve hours-stay from the moment of entry, a bed, a chair, and a small cupboard, all of which were separated from similar assemblies by a hospital-like curtain arrangement all around. The fee also included a Turkish bath as such, which was well worthwhile if you had enough time to sleep it off afterwards. Turkish baths, with their population of retired Indian Army colonels, gays, health nuts, and just plain heat lovers, did not then have the furtive sex connotations they later acquired. They were a total novelty to me, and though I have not been near one since, I still remember them and their fauna fondly. My clearest memories are of the attendant masseurs, all Scandinavians, all huge and, because they were exposed to so much steam and heat and presumably to little fresh air, they all had dead-white complexions. These silent behemoths would knead and paddle you into sobriety, wrap you in a damp towel like a cocoon, and dump the parcel on your allocated bed. You were asleep before your head hit the pillow and stayed that way until one of them shook you, to tell you that your twelve hours were up. Never slept better anywhere—[mens was reasonably sana and corpore totally sano and the combination is hard to beat.]

# 8

During 1942, the War Office went into another of its unfathomable policy spins. Aliens could still stay out of the uniformed rabble altogether or join the Pioneers; a "regular" army regiment remained taboo. However, now all of a sudden, they were perfectly welcome to try and be admitted to "special units," whose name, purpose, routine, and locale all remained hidden in a shroud of either secrecy or chronic administrative inability to locate the right file.

Having built enough toilets for a while, quite a few of us volunteered our names to become human torpedoes for all we knew, and, over the next months, there was a small but steady exodus of people. Some we heard of later, some we never saw again, and some, like myself, would go into orbiting motion and reappear at intervals, until we, too, finally found a niche.

Some of my fellow 251st diggers ended up with No. 10 Commando, then being formed in the wilds of Scotland and later to become a renowned and much decorated outfit. I was never called to the Commandos, but instead was summoned to Oxford to be tested as a potential glider pilot. I had never seen a glider, except in the movies, and was wholly unaware of a Glider Regiment, one of the War Office's darkest secrets, nor what possible good it could do or where. Still, it seemed like a change, so I spent three days being tested. I was whirled, spun, centrifuged, compressed, and decompressed; it is of course all old hat to present-day NASA fans, but I thought it pretty exciting and thoroughly nauseating at the time. I was then told that I had been declared fit to be a glider pilot and I should return to Cheltenham to await further instructions. Those never materialized, and it was not until 1944 that I heard of any alien joining the Glider Regiment, by which time I was busy with other capers.

Shortly afterwards I was summoned to London and to so-secret a location that it had neither name nor address. It either had a map reference or I found it with a seeing-eye dog, I do not recall.

There, I was ushered into the presence of an unknown colonel (years later revealed to me as the notorious Colonel Buckmaster of Special Operations Executive fame, but at the same time I had no notion either of his or SOE's existence) who, together with two civilians present, addressed me in flawless French, clearly to find out whether mine matched theirs.

It evidently did, and upon being perfectly agreeable to "engage upon a hazardous mission" (why not?), I was that same evening dispatched to Ringway Airport, near Manchester, the main para-trooping training center in England, which again was news to me. I spent the following eight weeks there in absolute seclusion together with six other men, all of them French, and none of whom I ever saw again. None of us had any notion why we were there, nor did we ever find out. We were taught how to handle explosives (the plastic kind, which had just been invented; like noisy play-dough, rather fun), how to use a commando knife (messy), what to do with a strangling wire (most unattractive), how to creep, crawl, and either fire or dismantle submachine guns while doing so, how to handle a wireless set (and as an enemy alien, yet). Most of all, we were taught how to fold a parachute, how to stow it, and how to jump with it.

In the course of those weeks I twice jumped from a moored balloon and twelve times from a Dakota DC3. To be more accurate, I jumped once and was nudged out the next thirteen times. The first time I thought it would be fun, and on the following occasions I was properly panicked and not much comforted by the instructors' stan-dard jokes ("Don't worry if it doesn't open; we'll get you a new one" or "If it does not open, that's known as jumping to a conclusion").

However, eight jumps or more entitled you to paratrooper wings and *il faut souffrir pour être beau*, particularly with all that competition at Le Petit Club Francais. Intrepid was not my nickname at Ringway, but I did get those damn wings, and they did social wonders for me for years thereafter.

As to what it was all for, there was one persistent rumor, which sounded just mad enough to be close to the possible truth. We were supposed to drop somewhere upriver on the Rhone, then make our way downriver, blowing things up as we went and generally making a nuisance of ourselves until we reached the estuary, where a submarine would pick us up—or not, as the case may be. If this strikes you as cretinous beyond belief, rest assured that SOE actually implemented schemes far more outlandish than this one—which did not work either.

On completion of my time at Ringway, the local SOE body made me swear blood oaths that I would reveal nothing to anyone about what I had been up to; hardly a difficult promise, since I had been quite unable to figure it out.

Still, within that Alice-in-Wonderland logic warp, there was no objection to my wearing paratrooper wings, so I returned to the 251st and Cheltenham, lips sealed, chest prominent, and mystification all around. My coterie of Cheltenham colonels, though equally in the dark, were encouraged in the belief that whatever I had been up to, I had not been up to it in latrines, and hence I had behaved much more in the Cheltonian spirit. Yet, back to the toilets I went.

The next War Office caper in that period involved my name change. I was called in by McKay, whom the War Office had informed that, to "avoid unnecessary risks in case of capture" and in view of my "special service potential," I should be urged to change my name to something less Teutonic.

The news puzzled both of us. McKay, who was unaware of the exact nature of my Oxford and Ringway jaunts and only knew that I seemed incapable of holding on to my lance corporal's stripe in the 251st, clearly questioned the potential referred to. As for myself, I thought that capture was in itself an unnecessary risk and therefore viewed the entire message to be in poor taste and altogether redundant. We both agreed to ignore it.

Some weeks later, a second message came through giving me a deadline to comply, as otherwise the War Office would change my name for me. This, of course, was serious news; an imposed name change might either involve some nameless antisemite or some titled country squire, both of whom seemed to infest the War Office in unusually large numbers. In one case I might end up with a name like Muddytummy or Arseless, which would annoy me, or else I might reappear as Montmorency or de Vere, which would irritate others. Everybody gets a little on edge if you are introduced as de Courcy and someone says, "Oh, de Courcy from Wiltshire?" and your reply is, "Well, actually Stuttgart; my maiden name is Loewenstein." I therefore spent an evening in the canteen with the Cheltenham telephone book and a couple of beers and gave birth to Mark Oliver Lawrence Lynton, which I have been ever since. The purpose was to be both bland and "unrelated," and it took twenty years and a move to Scarsdale, New York, before I met another Lynton, who had been born and not invented.

The change led to considerable puzzlement and hilarity among my fellow Pioneers. "Loewenstein ist zwar nicht schoen, aber Lynton ist bloed"† was the general consensus. I always only intended Lynton to be a nom de guerre in the most literal sense, and to become a Loewenstein again when it was all over. The war just lasted too long and everyone, myself included, became used to Lynton. All this took place in the latter part of 1942; in early 1943 another policy somersault occurred and both army and air force declared aliens to be welcome whenever, wherever. The navy, Britain's senior service, of course did no such thing; Welshmen and Irishmen were foreign enough, as far as the admiralty was concerned.

As a result, the alien Pioneer Corps underwent rapid and profound changes; some people had already left during the "special units" phase, and now many more were moving out. The typical remaining alien Pioneer, from mid-1943 until the end of the war, would be a Viennese art historian, with hernia, beard, and glasses, vintage 1890, using his shovel more as a truss than a tool, and being most articulate about the salient differences between Veroccio and Veronese.

One of the 251st members at that time was Arthur Koestler, an incompetent soldier and a mean, egotistical, and resentful little man. Having survived the Spanish Civil War and barely escaped from France in 1940, he passionately resented the evident English indifference to his past and talents. He was much disliked, and he wrote a great deal. Most of *Darkness at Noon* was written while with 251st Company in Cheltenham and so much can be forgiven him.

Another feature of that period was the emergence of fancy uniforms. The War Office had, understandably, given up any thought that alien Pioneers might ever be mistaken for soldiers, and evidently did not care if we disguised ourselves to look like Vatican Guards. This had fired the imagination of a surprising number of tailors who appeared to have strayed into the 251st, and this, in turn, led to pleats, fancy buttons, and even colored stitching, so that 251st Company on parade became almost indistinguishable from a Graefin Maritza rehearsal.

---

†"Loewenstein ain't pretty, but Lynton is just dopey."

The whole atmosphere of amiable unreality was heightened by McKay being succeeded by Major Howard, former military governor of the Fiji Islands. Howard suffered from high blood pressure and the handicap of being pre-verbal. Since he virtually never said anything, it was hard to tell, but he seemed quite a nice man. "I understand natives," he once said, on a rare occasion when he got a sentence together; whether he was referring to the Fiji Islanders or to 251st Company, he did not say.

IV
_____

# FEAR NOUGHT†:
# 1943–1945

J OINING THE royal Armored
Corps was a poor way to repay Sir Ernest Swinton's support, but a
good choice by process of elimination. Commandos and Paratroops
were clearly dangerous occupations and the RAF barely less so. In the
infantry you walked all the time and could not count on warm meals.
Tanks, I had heard, offered shelter, warmth, pleasant immobility,
built-in cooking facilities, and came close to being a mobile rest
home. It turned out that I had misheard, but by then I was part of the
armored world.

## 1

Tanks were a British invention, intended to break the terrible stale-
mate of trench warfare in World War I and were first tried out in
Cambrai in 1917, under the command of Major Ernest Swinton. By
the end of the war, there were five Royal Tank regiments, which
together formed the Royal Tank Corps, which in subsequent years
was extended to ten regiments.

In the mid 1930s the Royal Armored Corps was created, which
absorbed the Royal Tank Corps as well as a number of illustrious

_____

†Motto of the Royal Tank Corps—not necessarily mine.

cavalry regiments who, with great reluctance, came off their saddles and into tanks. This unhorsed crowd was forever after viewed by Royal Tank Corps people as displaced jockeys and invariably referred to as "donkey wallopers." Though the social graces and military antecedents of the likes of ¹²⁄₁₇th Lancers or King's Own Dragoons were light years removed from the Tank Corps and made Royal Tank people look like fugitives from a reform school, that whole cavalry mob never quite lost its reputation for being skittish and unpredictable in action. There is no recorded instance of an ex-calvary regiment having set up a tank charge with drawn sabers, but possibly only because no one survived to tell about it. Tank people generally suspected them of doing just that kind of thing and viewed them with disdain, distrust, or both—with a few shining exceptions such as Eleventh Hussars, famed for their Western Desert exploits. I was unaware of these facts of life and would have thought them mere prejudices when I first joined a Royal Armored Corps training regiment in the spring of 1943. Just as well since there was no telling, nor could I in any way influence, whether I would end up among the donkey wallopers or among genuine tank people.

The unit I joined was stationed close to Aldershot and, Huyton style, had commandeered a whole housing development; in fact it was "déjà vu all over again" except for the toilets which, to my amazement, had been installed without my involvement. There were several hundred trainees at various levels of competence. Trainees spent three months learning all aspects of tanks and how to use them and were then sent off as reinforcements to whichever fighting unit was in need of them.

The average fighting tank had five inmates, of whom four were supposedly experts in what they were doing and the fifth, the tank commander, was deemed to know everything the other four did. In reality, he was usually in command merely by luck, by influence, by being an officer, or by having survived the other four.

A reconnaissance tank, incidentally, much faster and less well armed, only had a three-man crew and was not supposed to fight; most recce tanks I came across did not seem to care about that and fought anyway; donkey wallopers, most of them, as you would expect. The best tank driver would be a small gorilla; intelligence level was of no concern, but a low center of gravity, very strong arms, and the ability to live in a crouched position indefinitely were all key, as was very keen hearing, to distinguish the tank commander's babblings from the general panicking that went on over the radio most of the time.

The qualifications of a deputy driver were harder to define; his main purpose was to wait for the driver to get killed and to make tea meanwhile. He was supposed to fire the forward machine gun, but if the tank got close enough for that, it usually was in sufficient trouble for the crew to bail out, so that duty was rather notional. These two sit way down in front, separated from the tank turret and their three colleagues by half a foot of steel. It was very unusual for all five crew members to get blown up or burnt out simultaneously. Either the three in the turret caught it or the two below, more often the latter. The turret crew was made up of the gunner who, ideally, should have just one of everything, since space was at a premium. One cyclopean eye to peer through the gunsight, one hamlike fist to operate the gun, and an ostrich-sized foot to correct aim and elevation ("Elevate dem guns a little lower," as Andrew Jackson said at New Orleans). Sitting at the bottom of the turret, with the commander using his shoulders as a footrest, he never saw daylight. A lack of imagination was helpful to a gunner since he was constantly being told what to do anyway, and the chances of his ever getting out of a burning turret were remote.

The two good spots in the turret were occupied by the wireless operator and the commander; each one had his own hatch to look out from, watch the countryside, wave at girls, and generally enjoy the ride. The operator was supposed to take care of radio traffic, but since that was almost invariably snarled anyway, he could always blame his inattention on others. He was also supposed to load the gun, but unless he was cursed with a maniacally active gunner or a glory-hungry commander, that was not too taxing.

What a commander does and when was not clear to most people, least of all to him. Since his tank was invariably part of a troop of four, his safest bet was to watch the troop commander's tank, get the word from his operator, and not get underfoot too much.

The cavalry influx into armor, coupled with their lofty social eminence, resulted in the War Office agreeing to some archaic nomenclature. All British tank regiments were divided into four squadrons, each squadron was divided into four troops; it is not even horse sense, but there it is. Just to save you complex calculations, a regiment can field about sixty-four fighting tanks.

In training camp, you were supposed to learn how to be a driver, a gunner, and an operator, on the mind-boggling assumption that anyone within a tank could be switched around at any time. Everyone has read about the pilot getting a heart attack in midflight and his store clerk friend, on his first flight ever, managing to land the plane somehow; in similarly catastrophic circumstances someone might switch places in a tank, but otherwise, never.

For obvious reasons everyone hoped to become an operator; those incapable of mastering even rudimentary tank skills became dispatch riders, which meant racing about on high-powered motorcycles to deliver cryptic messages to various people, who mostly ignored them. Being a dispatch rider was quite a sought-after occupation, until the Germans took to stringing steel cables across roads at chest height, at which time it became less popular. A headless dispatch rider was sometimes the first indication that Germans were lurking about somewhere.

The purpose of a training regiment was also to spot potential officer material and to send such people to selection boards to be tested; Major Costerbadie, the man in charge here, fortunately had some unorthodox views on that subject.

They set out to make soldiers out of us; most people were raw recruits and thus much more malleable than former Pioneers, who had been corrupted by some very peripheral military exposure. We got well-fitting uniforms, which we wore, as opposed to uniforms wearing us, as had been the case in the 251st; we got to wear the famed black beret; and we got a haircut. No more flowing locks and other expressions of Austrian artistry; from two inches above the ear, everything came off. It left you looking like a cross between a shorn sheep and a Mohawk warrior, improved the looks of very few, but simplified matters. We were taught how to really shine boots: you should be able to read small print in their reflection until nightfall and ordinary print at any time. Most of all we were taught how to march, walk, run, and stand still as soldiers. Drill sergeants are a schizoid species; they have an uncanny ability to gauge the exact length of your step even when fifty yards away, but are otherwise incapable of counting up to twenty without taking their socks off. They are all leather-lunged, and while once in a while you discovered quite a pleasant person behind all these anguished howlings, they mostly tend to be bullies by nature. At the lower levels, that is; Regimental Sergeant Major Britton, of whom more later, was reputed to be able to stop a running train with one bellow at up to a mile and a half, yet he was basically a gentle person and most certainly a gentlemen. The guys in Aldershot were bastards, pure and simple.

After three or four weeks of being harried about, we began to look and act as we were supposed to and at about that time the injection incident occurred. In my years in the army I was injected endlessly, usually against diseases prevalent two continents away from where I was. The only logical explanation for these recurrent syringe frenzies was that the army occasionally found stocks of antibodies about to spoil and did not want to waste them; so whoever was in the neighborhood got shots. It was typhus and typhoid in this particular instance; no big deal, except when administered into the chest, a procedure usually reserved for horses, but followed by British army doctors until 1944. Subsequently, when they found that injecting horses' behinds worked as well, they switched, first for the horses, then for us. Since chest shots are really uncomfortable and since typhus injections routinely bring about high though very temporary fever, we were excused from duty for twenty-four hours, and I recall really not feeling too much like a happy warrior. The event coincided with an intercompany rugby match, an endeavor recurrently encouraged and organized by Major Costerbadie, an absolute rugby fanatic. I had turned out for these events on occasion because I happen to like the game and because there was a chronic shortage of players.

There is something splendidly ironic and doubtlessly deeply significant about the fact that rugby, an undertaking that involves a great deal of mud, swearing, and considerable physical violence, is an exclusive pursuit of public schools and the supposedly "better people" who attend them, whereas soccer, a game of considerable finesse and elegance and no body contact to speak of, is the domain of grammar schools and the reputedly lesser people who are found there.

I don't intend to get into a Danny Kaye and "pestle-with-the-potion" routine by trying to explain that public schools are really private, whereas grammar schools are public and so on; however, army recruits, by and large, tend to be grammar school and soccer products and hence the shortage.

I had had no intention of getting involved in that day's affair, feeling thoroughly fragile, but I was also light-headed enough to listen to some emissary of Costerbadie's frantically trying to round up enough people to make up two teams. I do not recall anything about the game except that I felt awful getting out of bed, felt just as awful tottering around the rugby field, and equally poorly when I got back to bed. Predictably I was fine the next day and back on parade when I was summoned to Costerbadie's presence, a man with the looks and temper of Montgomery, but clearly without his fortuna. He made it clear that had it not been for my display of team spirit yesterday and general asininity (not his assessment, mine), he would not have noticed me. As it was, however, he was recommending me for a commission, and, pending my appearance before a War Office Selection Board (WOSB), here I was once again a lance corporal, acting unpaid and temporary. Squash, in 1939, had made me a friendly alien; rugby, in 1943, might make me an officer.

WOSB was not to convene for another month, and meanwhile I was very much on probation. Drill sergeants and other Base personnel invariably viewed putative officer-cadets with dislike and as a blatant case of class discrimination, which of course it was. If they could catch such a body in any misdemeanor, they would report him to Costerbadie, who invariably would then withdraw his recommendation. This led to one of the very few instances of quick thinking that I have ever been guilty of. A small fire broke out one night in the neighboring hut, enough sparks, flames, smoke, and water to keep a lot of us amused. So much so that I promptly overslept roll call next morning and found myself on report. I thereupon fell into lamentations worthy of Olivier's *Oedipus Rex* and for kindred reason: I had lost the sight of one eye!

The medical officer was predictably incapable of finding any damage but, mindful of the fire the night before, indulged in some learned theories involving sparks, smoke, corneas, and retinas, with all of which I enthusiastically concurred. I left the medical station bandaged to Halloween pumpkin size and in this state of obvious and grave injury reported to Costerbadie, who, assuming this to be the reason for my roll-call absence, dismissed the case. If quick-witted lying is one of an officer's assets, he probably did right.

## 2

The War Office Selection Board, located on a large estate not far from Aldershot, saw about thirty candidates at a time, destined for every branch of the army, clearly on the assumption that leading a bayonet charge or a mule train required the same abilities, which may very well be true. Consequently, I knew no one and did not know whether anyone else present was hoping to be a tank officer. As I found out much later, rugby and Costerbadie literally may have saved my life. While all of us ultimately ended up on the Normandy beaches at about the same time, we did so in different locations, and the tank units to which most of my class at the training regiment had been allocated took particularly heavy losses.

After a cursory "where did you go to school?" routine (among a certain class of Englishmen an almost reflexive enquiry), the WOSB officers, about six of them, got down to business. We were split into groups of six, told to change into "fatigues," and each group, led by one officer, disappeared into the landscape at a fast trot. Every once in a while we would stop and be told a lurid tale. We were facing a crocodile-infested, unswimmable river, we had lost all our weapons, and we were being hotly pursued by cannibals, on whom we had eight minutes' headstart. We were carrying three heavy sacks with vital though unidentified contents and had found a rope. There were some trees here and some more thirty feet away, "across" the river. We had eight minutes to get ourselves, the sacks, and the rope across the river, since our pursuers were not merely voracious and non-swimmers but had no ropes of their own. Having left us in this awkward situation, our officer would then settle under a tree and doodle on his notepad.

No one had been designated to take charge, and the whole purpose of acting out this fantasy was to find out who would take the lead, what he would do and how the others would react.

Ten minutes later, we would be on our way, either having escaped or being prepared for the pot, but with our fairy-tale spinner having taken copious notes, and some minutes later we would again face some horrendous dilemma, this time on the North Pole or at the Khyber Pass. This went on all day long, and while I recall no details, I vividly remember that I had a simply wonderful time—like Peter Pan in khaki.

Late in the afternoon, we ended up at a particularly tortuous obstacle course, where I fell off a rope to land in a small lake about fifteen feet below. Since it turned out to be more of a swamp than a lake, I re-emerged looking and smelling like the monster of the Blue Lagoon and continued in that state for the remainder of the day, hopefully earning suitable brownie points for being determined, albeit disgusting. Come evening, we all ate together, joined by all the WOSB officers, doubtlessly intent on establishing whether we ate peas with a knife or used language that would scare a mess steward. We slept like logs and at dawn started all over again, extricating ourselves from a whole smorgasbord of Boys' Own adventures, interspersed with that ever-present obstacle course. Obstacle courses are to the army what tickets are to traffic cops; if you can think of nothing better to do, that is what you go for.

Three vastly enjoyable days of this pleasant outdoor nonsense were followed by a batch of elaborate and mystifying psychological tests, ranging from Rorschach to cheating at cards, and long personal interviews by psychiatrists asking senseless questions and pondering evasive answers. Why do I want to be an officer? Because I look cute in uniform and because someone else gets tea for me; what kind of a damn silly question is that?

At the end of it all, our WOSB masters went into conclave and an hour or so later informed us of our fates. Some were "returned to unit," and the remainder were told they would be sent on to an Officer Cadet Training Unit (OCTU); I was both delighted and amazed to be among the elect.

Most infantry OCTU schedules lasted only three months, but tanks required a six-month OCTU period, whether because the subject matters were held to be more complex or the cadet trainees to be less bright was unclear. In addition to OCTU, tanks required six weeks of pre-OCTU, during which a goodly number were supposed to stumble by the wayside and never make it to OCTU proper. OCTUs (the word seems as silly as the concept) are just about the ideal place to verify Gore Vidal's contention that it is not enough to succeed, others must be seen to fail. He is, of course, quite right.

In all, it would therefore take seven-and-a-half months to defy the laws of nature and turn all of us pig's ears into silk purses, and the venue for this unlikely attempt was to be Royal Military Academy Sandhurst, the most hallowed of British Army territories. Military academies do not approve of wars, they tend to interfere with the laws and customs of peacetime soldiering, which is the purpose for which places like Sandhurst are intended. Consequently, Sandhurst had closed down for the duration and had made its facilities and staff available to the War Office for whatever ruffians it could find to engage in vulgar and unseemly war activities not meant for gentlemen. The War Office, in turn, had allocated the premises to the Royal Armored Corps. I would never dare state that I have "gone to Sandhurst," but for six months I lived "as if," since the entire peacetime training personnel had been retained. One maniacally screaming sergeant is much like another, except that Sandhurst sergeants all were ex-Guardsmen, which made for ramrod-posture and even noisier imprecations.

However, first there was the pre-OCTU hurdle to negotiate, situated at Blackdown in Surrey, not far from Sandhurst and less than an hour from Piccadilly by truck as I was to find out.

Coming to Blackdown was coming to another world, and, to complete that metamorphosis, I started out with a different army number. No. 335662 Officer-Cadet Lynton had now severed all links with the nether military regions and had, in the uniformed sense, become a certified gentleman.

The first striking aspect about Blackdown was the body of officers who were to command and train us. Pioneer officers had been oddballs almost by definition, and Costerbadie and his minions had left no particular impression, but this lot were all fugitives from the pages of *Town & Country*, flawlessly tailored and exquisitely languid. In time-honored *Scarlet Pimpernel* tradition, they combined dandyism with rows of medals testifying to palpable heroics. Most

Blackdown and Sandhurst instructors tended to be highly decorated combat officers on temporary leave of absence, presumably to instill bravery in the likes of us. They almost invariably belonged to un-horsed cavalry regiments of legendary age and distinction, whose uniforms reflected the panache and color blindness accumulated in centuries of serving in outlandish places. Offenbach would have loved them.

They were complemented by an assortment of drill sergeants, Guardsmen all, straight as a church tower (and straighter than some), and with tailor-dummy perfection of creases, boots, and buttons. Since a Guardsman's visor is in exact line with his nose, he should theoretically be blind. Don't you believe it; just like the bumblebee, a Guards sergeant defies the laws of physics.

There were about two hundred cadets at any one time at Black-down pre-OCTU, as against about six hundred at Sandhurst OCTU subsequently. Being officer-cadets led to the traditional farce where everyone calls everyone else "Sir," though with a difference, as the Blackdown regimental sergeant major clarified in his opening ad-dress: "You will call me 'Sir' at all times," he bellowed, "and I shall call you 'Sir' at all times, but when you say it to me, by Christ, you'd better mean it—Sir!"

We also now qualified for pretty fancy uniforms, complete with ties (last worn in Cambridge well over three years ago) and flashy lapels, shoulder tags, and cap badges, all proclaiming us to be poten-tial officers and gentlemen by inference.

The other members of my troop were predominantly Eighth Army veterans, battle-hardened corporals and sergeants who had either fought in every Western Desert battle or claimed to have. I have been a walking encyclopedia of Eighth Army folklore ever since my Blackdown days. There were also a surprising number of Cana-dians, all of them basketball fanatics, none of whom managed to convert me.

Discipline was ironclad, continuous, and imparted at extreme vocal registers; you constantly moved in a welter of bellows and screams that boiled down to: "If it moves, salute it; if it does not move, paint it," which is tantamount to the army's First Commandment. Godliness is a negotiable principle in military circles; cleanliness is not. We cleaned, polished, and burnished everything; weapons, boots, stoves, finger nails, belts, stray stones, interspersed with constant inspections by a variety of our betters looking for that forgotten speck. On one such endless scrutiny, the officer of the day, having poured over every item of mine from rifle barrel to blanket edges, summarized his endeavors in his own mind then turned to the sergeant and said, "Take that cadet's name. Dirty ears!" There went my weekend leave.

Most weekends, however, I either had cleaner ears or more lenient officers and so spent a great number of them in London. I still marvel how, on wages of some five dollars a week, I managed to have so much fun and not be in debt. Of course my journalist friends at Le Club were as rich as Croesus by comparison and as generous as they were affluent; through them, I had access to American PX and USO canteens, a profusion of affordable pleasures wholly beyond the dreams of the average wartime Briton and hence continually and cordially detested by him. Even so, it seems in retrospect to have been an economic sleight-of-hand worthy of Schacht or even Ronald Reagan.

Not all London excursions were pure pleasure; maneuvering a three-ton truck around the Inner City was not one. I had never driven a truck before, and the three-ton species is particularly intractable. Convoy techniques in large towns were part of our training, and London was understandably listed as a large town. If you have never stalled a truck on Piccadilly Circus in peak traffic, you have never known real panic. I have, both. Aside from truck driving, Blackdown's mechanical instruction was surprisingly immobile. We learned how to mount and dismount from tanks (I was almost expecting to be taught how to saddle them), what to do in them, how to command them (still today a hazy topic to me), but all of it in stationary tanks. Of course, we also learned how to clean tanks.

Otherwise, the training was far from static; everything you did, you did "at the double": you ran to the parade ground and on it, you ran to the canteen or to the washrooms. The daily route march consisted of assembling loaded like a mule and setting off on a ten-mile march. The first mile you marched, the second you ran, then march a mile, run a mile, and so on, while being sick at intervals in between. By the third week, you ran all of it and sometimes were not sick once! Finally there was the obstacle course, the army's version of occupational therapy, which was run once before breakfast and once before dinner, every day, and over a specimen designed by a syndicate of orangutans and beavers. You were constantly either swinging from branch to branch thirty feet above the ground or squirming through leaking pipes four feet below it. All this to the accompaniment of bloodcurdling screams: "Christ, pick up those flat, bloody feet—Sir!" and similar encouragements by a horde of physical instructors swinging effortlessly from tree to tree alongside you and, in all respects, seeming very close to their orangutan forebears. After six weeks of Blackdown, we had reached a stage of physical fitness that made it doubtful whether we would need tanks to cope with the Germans. Unarmed combat seemed a much more promising alternative.

Having brought us to a state of barely leashed violence welded to a pathological preoccupation with cleanliness and saluting, Blackdown, in the autumn of 1943, forwarded about two-thirds of our original number to nearby Sandhurst for further processing.

## 3

Sandhurst is both impressive and attractive; set in a fenced park of several hundred acres and surrounded by miles of woods, it is a vast, harmonious neo-Georgian complex of buildings, grouped in an open rectangle around an immense parade ground. The day I arrived was the only one on which I ever had time to admire the architecture or the scenery. Compared to Sandhurst, Blackdown had been positively somnolent!

We were progressively becoming more gentlemanly and officer-like. Now we were allocated just two to a real room, with a door and real beds, and with a batman who polished buttons to snow-blindness level. He and others of his calling at Sandhurst were all peacetime holdovers, a martial variant of McDougall and similarly addicted to meandering reminiscences. According to ours, Harold lost at Hastings because he was no Sandhurst graduate; it is as good an explanation as any. Set against these novel luxuries was the fact that here you were not just moving at the double, you were forever out of breath! Ten minutes from wake-up call to standing on the parade ground, dressed fit to be inspected by the King (or the drill sergeant, which was worse); five minutes to get off the parade ground and reappear dressed for whatever the next activity called for; two minutes for some natural needs; no time at all for others. Walking became a wholly forgotten skill; you either ran or stood like a statue. The daily ten-mile march was no such thing; we ran the entire distance in full equipment and in just under an hour. Halfway through our Sandhurst time we could do all these things without either thought or sweat, and none of us have ever been as fit as we were then. The entire panoply of peacetime Sandhurst surrounded us; screaming drill sergeants, even taller, straighter, and noisier than at Blackdown, wireless specialists, driving instructors, gunnery experts, cryptographers, mechanics. There must have been about five such people for every one of us cadets, and the "personnel to guest" ratio claimed by the Ritz or other hotels has never impressed me since.

Major Ronnie Aird, MC (that is, recipient of the Military Cross, a hero's decoration), commanded our squadron (Sandhurst cadets were divided into four squadrons of about one hundred fifty men), an infinitely elegant, infinitely weary cavalry officer—a sleepy version of Basil Rathbone. He was charming and urbanely effective and after the war, for many years, the much-admired secretary of the MCC, the Marylebone Cricket Club, which is the governing body for world cricket.

His Number 2, Captain Reginald Gordon-Lennox, Coldstream Guards, equally competent, was the complete antithesis—highly strung, sardonic, poisonously witty, and cynical about everything except classical music. He was, in due course, heir to the Dukedom of Richmond, a prospect that he considered just as ridiculous as the world he lived in.

I remember the chief physical instructor, a delightful teddybear of a man, extraordinarily sweet-tempered, particularly when contrasted with the muscle-bound sadists who made up his staff. He later became Sir Matt Busby, the best-loved and most successful manager in British soccer in the postwar years.

However, they all pale against Regimental Sergeant-Major Brittan, Grenadier Guards! Brittan stood somewhat over six feet ordinarily and close to seven feet when on parade, chest thrown out to look almost spherical and chin tucked in to a point that convinced many people that Brittan's face ended at his lower lip. Some said he could be heard in the next county; others that he could carry to the next country. There was little doubt that his voice could smash glasses half a mile away without undue exertion. To be the object of his undivided attention was the nearest thing to standing beneath an Apollo missile at blast-off. The astonishing point about Brittan was that he was really a kindly man, without a way or place to show it. A regimental sergeant-majors were concerned, a species that could browbeat Lenin into believing in class distinction; provided they deigned to talk to such a civilian at all.

According to Kipling and similarly hyperbolic experts, a hush falls over the jungle when the tiger appears, and at Sandhurst, too, you always knew. One moment cadets were crashing about, screamed at by their drill sergeants, and the next moment all was utterly still. Brittan had appeared at the edge of the parade ground, immense, ramrod-like, totally immobile, the silver knobbed RSM cane held precisely parallel to the ground. Then a scream like tearing metal, "Carry on, instructors," and all would be noise and confusion. He was a terrific guy. I never once talked to him.

Each squadron was divided into five troops of about thirty cadets each. Every second week a new intake of thirty men would arrive, and the most senior troop then training would "pass out," first by the formal ceremony of a passing-out parade at Sandhurst, thereby becoming second lieutenants, and subsequently in assorted pubs in the Camberley area.

Passing-out parade, invariably attended by royals, domestic or foreign, or at the very least by a stray field-marshall, was a wonderfully arcane affair. Except for the troop passing out, all cadet troops would be drawn up, in hollow square and parade formation, in front of the main administration building, where a set of wide and shallow steps led to a colonnaded arch, which, in turn, gave access to a vaguely Pantheon-like hall within.

All officers would be standing on one side of the steps, all in full dress uniform, a sight that should have brought both Gilbert and Sullivan out of their graves, and all surrounding whichever visiting personage was gracing the proceedings.

In the middle of the square, immobile, alone, and resplendent, was the passing-out troop, trying to breathe without being noticed, since Brittan was watching from six feet away. The visiting dignitary would then embark on a brief address (we hoped), occasionally delivered in intelligible English, but invariably dealing with honor, bravery, loyalty, God, and other military accessories. He would then inspect the troop, accompanied by the Sandhurst commandant (in my time, Colonel Hutton of the Fifth Royal Tanks, DSO† and two bars, MC and two bars, a desert tank commander of legend, who visibly loathed these occasions), Brittan, and the officer in charge of the troop (Gordon-Lennox, when our eventual turn came).

Assuming no one dropped his rifle, invoked God in Hindustani, dropped dead, or otherwise interrupted the proceedings, the king, field marshall, or whoever, would then instruct the commandant to "pass out" the troop, and Hutton in turn would so instruct the troop officer, who would relay the order to Brittan. The fact that all of them stood within four feet of each other inhibited no one from shouting as if he had been shipwrecked. Brittan, seemingly without drawing breath, would then literally blast the troop off their feet. The troop, in rigid formation, would stalk up the steps (we must have practiced that half-a-million times), into that hall, and in so doing, presto! would change from caterpillars into butterflies. Once in that hall, you were an officer!

The high point of the proceedings, however, was not the troop trotting to its just desserts, but the Sandhurst adjutant on a white

---

† The Distinguished Service Order, or DSO, is the second highest British military decoration, after the Victoria Cross, which is mostly awarded posthumously. The Military Cross, or MC, is the third highest. A bar signifies that a second (or third) DSO or MC had been awarded.

horse, following them up the steps, step by step, and thereby ending the parade. This equestrian absurdity had been instituted in the 1850s and had become a Sandhurst tradition, to the chagrin of the incumbent adjutant who evidently was allergic to horses or vice versa. To keep both tradition and the adjutant alive, they had found a horse literally yellow with age which, it was rumored, was being white-washed occasionally to keep up appearances. It barely managed to negotiate the steps and was certainly much too preoccupied with its own ailments to inconvenience the adjutant. One of its ailments clearly affected its digestion; it was the most flatulent horse in the south of England! The only humor in the whole passing-out caper was to stand in utter, stony silence, the passing-out troop having already gone, and watch horse and rider gingerly looking for the next step to negotiate to the constant accompaniment of thunderous equine farts. This may not strike you as all that funny, but then you were not at Sandhurst.

All that was still six months ahead for me, and those coming months were to consist of, successively, weeks of wireless training, then weeks of tank driving, then map reading, followed by gunnery training, and finally, commanding tanks, first singly, then in troops and finally in squadrons.

Wireless training was fun despite my pathological aversion to technical matters. At the end of the course I did manage to dissect and reassemble an entire wireless set, which worked perfectly well despite the fact that I had several screws and dials left over, for which I had not been able to find a location. Morse code messages I loathed and do to this day; it is just not natural to communicate in squeaky dots and dashes, and people who do should be avoided.

We were taught to drive tanks by trying to steer some very old Sherman tanks over very undulating terrain, with all hatches closed and the instructor sitting on top of the turret telling you what to do on the "intercom." The "intercom" was one of three frequencies always used in tank wireless sets; the other two were the "A" frequency, used to talk to tanks within sight, and the "B" frequency, which would carry twenty miles in speech, and well beyond that in Morse, if someone could be troubled to send and someone else could be inconvenienced to read it at the other end. The fourth frequency, which was constantly "on net," was the BBC, though the army did not encourage that. I had some problems with driving a tank; a tank is quite heavy and, going downhill is a real bitch to control, and I happened to be a remarkably poor tank driver. Going downhill at ever-gathering speed, being constantly late in shifting down, and, hence, being out of gear most of the time did not greatly concern me, since I had about twenty tons of steel all around me, but it visibly aged some of my instructors sitting on top of the turret. They passed me through the driving course very quickly; it seemed the safest thing to do.

A tank does not turn but pivots from the center; if the front turns left, the rear turns right correspondingly. During a night exercise in nearby Guildford, I wiped out two storefronts before that penny dropped. Sandhurst took a remarkably casual view of such vandalism; aside from some comment from Gordon-Lennox that there was no call to assist the Germans more than necessary, I heard nothing further about it.

Map reading exercises were distinctly more enjoyable; Sandhurst had attracted some passably pretty ATS girls to drive little utility trucks, and you sat next to them fiddling with maps, wireless, and high strategy.

The general concept was that you and your tanks (represented by half-a-dozen similar trucks) were to reach a specified lateral line on the map, about one hundred miles away from your starting line, and you had a finite number of hours to get there. You were held to "come on the air" every fifteen minutes and give an accurate map reference of where you were; aside from that, you could adopt any itinerary or speed you chose. The "enemy," again a bunch of trucks, was supposed to intercept you; he, too, had to give an accurate map reference every quarter of an hour and for the rest could do whatever he wanted. The idea was for both sides to know and plot out where the other one was; it may sound a bit puerile, and it was, but it made for nice drives through the countryside.

Gunnery training, on the other hand, was sweaty, noisy, smelly, and inhibiting; the latter because every newspaper constantly harped on the disparity between German and Allied tank guns. This happened to be quite true and remained so throughout the war; German tanks were far superior to any British or American tank as far as armor or guns were concerned, two rather key elements in tank warfare. In terms of crews and engines, they were probably a match for each other, and there was no question that Allied wireless was superior; so at least you could talk about the Germans before they hit you. Back in Sandhurst, we kept firing at derelict German tank hulls, only to see the shells just bounce off. The answer of course was to close in, but whether that was going to be such fun later on was no certainty. In the event, it was no joy at all. To run the gauntlet trying to get a German tank within effective range while for the past half-mile or more you have been solidly within his range is character-building, to put it mildly.

The best time of all those six months at Sandhurst was the week spent in "battle camp" near Mount Snowden in north Wales in late November, to give us some exposure to infantry operations and teach us some handy skills, such as house-to-house fighting, night patrols, massacring sentries, and similar skulduggery. It brought to mind my Ringway outings, and I thought it very useful. Given my instant and total panic when faced with any mechanical breakdown, I never quite believed that tanks could be relied upon to last through a day, so always anticipated situations where, like it or not, we would have to fend for ourselves on our feet. It never came to that; but I remained unconvinced right to the end. However, that was not the main reason for my remembering Wales so well, nor the fact that "battle camp" conditions meant live ammunition being used, which added a *je ne sais quoi* to the proceedings. I know *quoi*, as it happens: it added being scared, that is all. Of course only instructors used live ammunition, never cadets; Sandhurst might condone accidents, but not homicide. The way "live" ammunition was used in such circumstances was for instructors, acting as "enemy," to fire tracer bullets on fixed trajectories, a foot or so above the ground; if you crawled to your target, like it said in the manual, and if the instructor had stayed away from the pub the night before, you had nothing to worry about . . .

While in Wales we were also introduced to the mysteries of mine detection and removal, a particularly nasty way to spend one's time. Tank mines only explode under tanks, and while that does the tank no good, it is not going to cause you more than a headache, if that. There are any number of anti-personnel mines however, each one more unpleasant than the last, all tricky to spot, terribly scary to lift, and devastating when detonated. Until the Viet Cong honed their skills, the Germans were the undisputed masters in devising truly horrible mines.

What sticks most in my memory is how quite unbelievably fit we were. Every single day we jogged to the top of Mount Snowden, well over three thousand feet up, and in full equipment, which included disassembled machine guns, ammunition cases, and other paraphernalia. On one climb, we did it bottom to top in forty-three minutes flat, which remained a Sandhurst record till well into the 1960s. Every night we slept wherever we stopped, rolled in just one, usually damp, blanket, and that in mid-November in light snow and not a sniffle among the lot of us! There is an enormous sense of well-being, a real "high" in being in fabulous shape; they say that is why people jog or pump iron. Maybe so; battle camp near Mount Snowden in mid-November, that is where it was for me.

There was another, much more debatable, circumstance that got the adrenalin pumping; just about all of us found house-to-house fighting exhilarating. There were a number of empty house shells in the area, and the concept was to go slamming into them, submachine gun blazing, lobbing grenades around blind corners, and generally being destructive. At the time I thought I enjoyed it because no one was shooting back. I found this not to be so later on, and that, lamentably enough, there is some kind of bloodlust in just about all of us, particularly in "close quarter" situations. The combination of fear, excitement, noise, confusion, and momentum makes the destruction of lives as well as of property, an almost orgiastic experience. You do not have to be a Kali worshipper to experience it. You do not have to be proud of it, either.

Aside from all else, there was the memorable scenery of that part of Wales: bleak, slate-gray mountains, usually glistening in the rain, often shrouded in fog, a beautiful and strange country. The locals tell you that Owen Glendower never died and has lived in those mountains for the past four centuries; once you are in that part of the world, you at least consider it a possibility. It is so wild and remote that, by 1943, some of the realities of war had not penetrated to those valleys; we had omelettes made of real eggs!

It may have been due to that diet that, throughout that week, I displayed a Napoleonic mastery of terrain, awing fellow-cadets, instructors, and not least myself; whatever the angle or exercise, I invariably seemed to spot the ideal "dead ground," or ambush, or crevasse, or whatever—a Jewish Clausewitz, no less. It was an aptitude I never displayed before or since, but it greatly improved my Sandhurst standing.

In our final weeks in Sandhurst, we were not merely fit as wolves, but also, thanks to our batmen, the hourglass of military fashion. Despite their name, British Army batmen are neither scientific nor fictional; in depots or on bases such as Sandhurst, they are aged, cynical, herniated, and grumbling old soldiers, obsessed with creases, boots, buttons, and general cleanliness. In the field, batmen are generally juvenile delinquents, not much given to neatness but with a well-developed thieving instinct for eggs, extra socks, and hot water, and an unfailing ear for gossip.

Strutting through London on a weekend, gleaming, polished, and creased, we could have given Georgie Patton a run for his money, and my additional *bonbon* of sporting parachute wings did no harm either.

# 4

As time went by, and it became increasingly clear that we would actually stay the course, the prime question became which regiment would we join, or which would have us. Wartime temporarily blunts some prejudices, but does not eradicate them, so Groucho Marx's observation that he would not join a club which would have him as a member was as valid as ever.

To some few of us, the choice was predestined; if your great-grandfather had battled with the Zulus at the head of the Nineteenth Lancers, that is where you went—Zulus or no Zulus. To most of us however, the basic choice was between the donkey-wallopers and one of the original tank regiments. Joining the cavalry meant stunning uniforms, impeccable social standing, and hobnobbing with both your peers and real peers; joining a tank regiment meant lower mess bills and a higher survival rate. In peacetime, a Horse Guard officer might spend in a month what a Royal Tank Regiment (RTR) officer could not earn in his entire career; wartime had curtailed truly Homeric mess bills, but Veuve Clicquot was still more expensive than a pint of bitter. As to the survival rate, there was a third and more lunatic alternative reserved for heroes and headcases. You could join a Reconnaissance Regiment, which meant patrolling ahead and on the flanks of advancing troops in very light tanks or armored cars and taking quite appalling losses. Still, while alive, you were a member of legendary regiments and some evidently believed that being a dead Eleventh Hussar was socially more acceptable than being a live Tank Regiment member. In some circles, that was quite true.

I obviously opted for a Tank Regiment and hoped to be accepted there; there was no particular reason to try for Third Royal Tanks, except that regimental folklore had it that Third and Fifth Tanks were *primi inter pares* and why not the best?

About three weeks before the passing-out date, final RTR notices were handed out, and some twenty of us knew that we had somehow slipped through. Not only that but we were also told which regiment had accepted us, so as to allow time for uniforms to be tailored (to be donned within about thirty seconds after having duly passed out). Among all the military tailors available in Camberley and London, I picked Gieves at One Savile Row. In retrospect I assume that the address impressed me; Gieves was famed for naval uniforms and for its steep prices, neither of which should have been a selling point with me. RTR uniforms did not present much of a challenge to a military tailor; one tank regiment distinguished itself from another merely by differently colored shoulder tabs. Third RTR had green tabs, which led to a lot of Irishmen being in the regiment, or maybe it was the other way around. Cavalry uniforms were a far more demanding undertaking; some came only in twill, some only in light beige, some had flaired jackets, others skintight trousers (and some of those in color or tartans), and some uniform jackets had black buttons or cloth buttons or six buttons or twelve buttons—none of the cavalry regiments ever quite left the nineteenth century—nor should they have.

Everyone in tanks, donkey-wallopers and RTR people, wore the black beret, but the beret badges of course differed widely, and only

RTR regiments wore black berets off duty as well, whereas excavalry types would then revert to all kinds of arcane headgear. The catch about this entire uniform aspect was that it only involved dress uniform, which you obviously never wore in the field. Once in a very long while, when things were really quiet (when peace had broken out, for instance), the rear echelon trucks, where all these belongings of yours were stowed, would move up and you could then assume officer-and-gentleman disguises. While in the field, just about everybody was dressed "Eighth Army style," either because they were used to it, or more likely, because they wanted others to think so. It consisted of an old battle jacket without markings of rank (supposedly to discourage snipers; except in Normandy, we never came across any, and those we did meet shot at anything that moved, never mind the markings), a colored foulard scarf in lieu of a tie, a pair of corduroy trousers, preferably as "sand colored" as possible, and a worn pair of Clark desert boots. That and the black beret made up the uniform; when it got cold or wet, you wore a "tank suit" over this potpourri. The tank suit, a bile-colored forerunner of an astronaut's outfit, had numberless zippered pockets, was alpaca lined, and wind- and waterproof; it tended to asphyxiate you, but you stayed dry. If you had an efficient batman, he would "find" some fur-lined flying boots, preferably RAF issue, which were warmer than their German or American counterparts; army boots in tanks were an invitation to frostbite.

You were supposed to wear a pistol, but hardly anyone did; by the time the Germans were that close, you should be elsewhere. Good binoculars were essential and were a problem until we went into action; once German binoculars became "available," we were in good shape. English glasses are very good for opera, provided you have good seats.

You were supposed to have your map case with you at all times; presumably so that, even if you did not know where you were heading, in case of your capture, the Germans would.

Together with some extra socks, underwear, and washing kit, that was really all you took along on a tank, all of it rolled into your bedroll, which also held blankets and whatever your own other particular basic needs were, anything from hunting horns to portable toilets. The bedroll was the critical difference between being in tanks and comfortable and being in the infantry and in trouble. The infantry just trotted around and everything they needed, aside from some ammunition and a little water, had to be brought to them by trucks. Trucks do not like to go where people shoot at each other, and that was where the infantry was supposed to be; so there was this dilemma. . . .

Not so with tanks; you piled, laid, or stuffed every conceivable item into your bedroll, a large, rectangular, waterproof expanse of stiff canvas, which you then rolled up like a huge jam roll, secured with two leather straps, and hooked onto the back of your tank, near the exhaust. This not only kept all your stuff warm and dry, but a pile of bedrolls (there were five people in the tank) even gave us some protection against snipers and shrapnel—or at least you thought it did. And anytime you stopped, it took not more than a couple of minutes to brew tea, make beds, write a letter, shoot a pheasant, change your socks. Whatever you needed, you have had it right there.

In addition, you owned (you purchased all these items and for cash) an immensely heavy metal suitcase, so designed primarily to withstand termites—which some might not view as a priority risk in western Europe—and which was the size of a large coffin. Yours, together with those of your fellow officers, was stored somewhere near divisional headquarters or it could have been somewhere in South America, for all you knew or cared. It contained your dress uniform and similar peacetime paraphernalia; I saw it once between June 1944 and May 1945, and opened it for the first time three months after that. It was totally indestructible; mine once fell off the top deck of a cross-channel steamer and has had a two-inch dent in one corner ever since. I still own it; I can neither sell it nor give it away and, so far, have been unable to lose it. It will undoubtedly outlive me.

The last weeks at Sandhurst were hectic, particularly in our troop where the competition for the "belt of honor" seemed very tight. Each officer of course owned a leather belt, the famed "Sam Brown," which he only wore with dress uniform and hence hardly ever. It was, however, a long-standing Sandhurst tradition, now adopted by Tank OCTU, that the officers and instructors of each troop would, on passing-out day, designate the best all-around cadet who would then be presented with a "belt of honor" (a "curate's egg" of satisfaction and irritation since, by that time, he had of course bought one of his own and supernumerary Sam Browns were about as easy to get rid of as metal suitcases).

Nonetheless, we all tried as hard as we could, and it was an open secret, in the final weeks, that there were three contenders, and amazingly, I was one of them. Presumably my impersonation of Hannibal in Wales was the cause, but in the end good sense prevailed, and I was voted second and could keep my own belt. The passing-out parade was a strangely quiet affair, after all those weeks of witnessing other such ceremonies, but that was doubtlessly due to our marching ahead of the adjutant's horse.

So there I was, sometime in April 1944, Second Lieutenant Mark Lynton, Third RTR, still an enemy alien of course but somewhat removed from POW Loewenstein digging in the streets of Quebec less than four years ago, and from Private Lynton, Pioneer Corps building Gloucestershire latrines just last year. Same war, though.

# 5

I spent a short and most enjoyable leave, much of it taken up marching up and down Piccadilly for the sheer thrill of being saluted and saluting back. Every newly commissioned officer succumbed to that, and, as a result, English soldiers mostly steered clear of the area. The Americans and French only saluted their own, and the Australians did not salute anybody, so they had no problem. All in all, it took time and luck to find victims.

I then joined Third RTR "somewhere in southern England."

Third Royal Tank Regiment had joined the Eleventh Armored Division in December 1943, and was its senior and most experienced tank regiment. The division had been constituted late in 1943 in preparation for the Normandy invasion, and its emblem—a charging black bull on a yellow background—was to become as well-known as the "desert rat" worn by the famed Seventh Armored Division in Africa. Third RTR, quite possibly the most battle-tested tank regiment in the entire British Army (I shall always believe that and you might as well too), had left Seventh Armored Division and the

Western Desert to form the nucleus of the new Eleventh Armored. They had been joined by three other veteran tank regiments, Second Fife and Forfar Yeomanry, Twenty-third Hussars, and Second Northampton Yeomanry, as well as by the Inns of Court Regiment as its reconnaissance element, all names redolent of Waterloo, or Agincourt, if you prefer.

The fact that Eleventh Armored Division thus had five tank regiments instead of the habitual four clearly marked it as being intended as a "breakthrough" division, an honorable but somewhat dubious distinction. Third RTR and Twenty-third Hussars were to work together in one armored brigade, commanded by Brigadier Harvey, a much-decorated desert veteran, and the entire division was led by Major-General "Pip" Roberts, aged thirty-seven, which was about as old as you can get in tank circles. Pip, so called both for his boyish enthusiasm and his bare ability to look over a table top, had actually commanded Third RTR in the desert, while amassing decorations, promotions, and renown. He was an absolutely charming man with an inexplicably sunny disposition and a continuing affection for Third RTR, which meant we were constantly lead regiment — a little less affection would have made me happier.

Third RTR was overwhelmingly made up of Western Desert veterans, who had served in all the Eighth Army campaigns and spoke a "desert rat" language of their own, like film technicians, investment bankers, and other "in" people do.

You took a shufti instead of a look; you were at the sharp end when being shot at; nubile women were bhints; of course you never drank tea but only chaw; when you broke through enemy lines and into open country, you went swanning. There was a whole *vade mecum* of similar gibberish, and to be accepted by Third RTR, you had to learn it before you even took your beret off.

Very much like the opposing Afrika Korps, for over three years Eighth Army had been quite isolated from the rest of the war and had coalesced into an elitist community, fiercely loyal to itself and its shared experiences, and much more in empathy with Rommel and his three Afrika Korps divisions than with any allied forces outside the Western Desert. The British had a weakness for Rommel throughout the war, but Eighth Army really knew and loved him; they would

have traded him against any two British generals at any time, and that
certainly included Montgomery—they would have given him away as
a bonus.

Eighth Army people kept very much to themselves, even after it
was dissolved, and since Third RTR was the only Eighth Army unit in
Eleventh Armored Division, they talked to no one else and were
considered both awesome and insufferable. In all the time I was with
Third RTR (actually not much over fifteen months), they only talked
to other ex-desert rats and to Commandos or Paratroops, who did not
speak their language but who at least displayed that mixture of
slovenliness and violence that reminded them of the good old days.
Newcomers, like myself, were viewed with disinterest and wary
mistrust by the ranks, and with friendly indifference by fellow officers;
obviously until you did your part, you would not be a member of the
club.

Chris Bourne, the regiment's second-in-command, was an exception. He had joined Third RTR a week before I did, having just
earned a DSO in Burma by extricating his tank unit from a Japanese
ambush in a three-day fire fight, and a captain with a DSO (Britain's
second-highest decoration) was good enough even for Third RTR.

It was accepted doctrine that any decoration earned by any rank
below major was likely to have been truly deserved, whereas those
awarded to colonels and above were viewed with, usually justifiable,
skepticism. Majors and lieutenant colonels, the "in-between" ranks,
were seen as borderline cases; sometimes they deserved their medals,
sometime they were just lucky. If anyone got a Victoria Cross, he
always deserved it, but then, since in many cases he was dead when he
got it, he might as well.

I got to know and like a great number of people while with Third
RTR—being shot at together creates a bond of sorts—but I do not
have close memories of many. Annual regimental dinners go on and
on, and doubtlessly will until the Second Coming, but I have never
attended any of them.

There were, of course, some Third RTR members whom I recall
vividly, starting with the three regimental commanders I served
under. David Silvertopp, another famed veteran of the desert, where
he had won both an MC and DSO, was a textbook commander:

decisive, competent, humorous, and humane. He led Third RTR brilliantly from Normandy to St. Anthonis, on the Dutch-Belgian border, where he was killed. We were all standing in the market square when some captured SS troops were brought in, whom obviously no one had thought to search. One of them threw a grenade, which killed David and a couple of other officers; shooting everyone in that SS group was no consolation.

This may seem a rather cavalier way of referring to what, under the Geneva Convention's rules for the humane treatment of prisoners of war, was clearly a war crime. It is not that the Geneva Convention articles were hardly bedside reading at the time, it is just that such incidents did, on occasion, happen.

War crimes, isolated and unreported, involving shooting, looting, or rape, are an inevitable part of an ongoing war. When committed on a large scale, such as at Malmédy or My Lai (not to mention the Russian advance through Germany), the media will report them, and, if the perpetrators also eventually happen to lose the war, they may be brought to trial. Revenge, such as for Silvertopp's death, however, did occasionally happen and was never reported or punished, any more than instances where, carried away by the "heat of battle," people did shoot men on the other side who no longer presented a real threat. It did not happen often, but it happened.

David Silvertopp was succeeded by David Brown, a scholarly and retiring person who never really established himself in the wake of the charismatic Silvertopp. He was with us for less then three months and never became part of the regiment; he did however lead it in outstanding fashion during the Ardennes battle, which earned him a DSO and a brigade command. His successor, Teddy Mitford, commanded the regiment till well after the war and was a splendid specimen. We had absolutely nothing in common, and consequently we became quite close. Teddy was a member of the notorious Redesdale clan and a brother of the famed Mitford sisters, who were prominent in every field from fashion to fascism. Teddy, while looking and acting like the classic British nobleman—elegant, weary, bored, and vapid—had a very keen mind and a wide range of interests. He was a totally imperturbable commander, and to hear Teddy directing a hectic and noisy tank battle as though bidding a rather unpromising bridge hand was enormously reassuring. He had been one of the founders of the Long Range Desert Group, a quite extraordinary outfit about which more books have been written, lies told, legends woven, and unbelievable feats left unrecorded than any other unit fighting in North Africa. Teddy had two rows of ribbons to show for it.

I recall Major John Watts, MC, who commanded A Squadron when I joined it. John was charming, handsome, dumb, and a superb leader; he got stupidly killed in April 1945, shot by his own tank machine gun in some mix-up in the night. His successor, Neil Kent, an Eighth Army veteran like all the others, was red-haired and as dramatic as his hair: he was funny, irreverent, and, much later and for a brief spell, a Hunter Douglas employee. Predictably, he was a better tank commander than a marketing man. Neil lost part of his hand in a fire fight in Germany and was succeeded by Captain Freddie Dingwall, MC, a tall, gaunt, mournful Don Quixote–type given to sudden outbursts of manic gaiety involving much destruction of glassware and sundry personal property. Freddie was wounded during the Elbe crossing, and Dickie Dixon then took over the squadron. Dickie was cherubic, serene, and unshakably competent; he owned a substantial appliance company, which, after the war, became riddled with ex-Third RTR personnel, but prospered nonetheless. Robin Lemon, whom I remember well, was only a lieutenant and a mere twenty years old, looking about twelve; this had not inhibited him from earning one MC in the desert and would not prevent him from gaining another, together with two Croix de Guerres, in Normandy and Germany, being relentlessly heroic while looking consistently like a wide-eyed choir boy. Major Jack Dunlop, MC, Walter Pidgeon's twin to look at, and as darkly handsome, had the extraordinary experience during the Ardennes campaign of having a sniper bullet go in one cheek and out the other. He lost his teeth but gained a dimple in both cheeks, which made him even better looking.

A tank regiment has about thirty officers, and I recall most of those with whom I started out. In the ten months between Normandy and the end of the war, well over half of them were gone, mostly wounded, rather than dead; but the attrition rate was still awesome. I remember Captain Paddy Hear, MC and Bar, a gigantic, brick-faced Irishman with a limitless capacity for drink and fights. Like all other

Irishmen I met in Third RTR, he just liked to do battle; preferably with Englishmen, but in between he was quite prepared to take on Germans, just to keep in practice. Paddy had a tin ear, a voice like a fire siren, and, either when drunk or happy (usually a co-mingled state with him), would launch into an interminable epic extolling Third RTR's exploits in the desert; it had about two hundred stanzas, each ending with " . . . and swanning off, and way ahead, forever there were seen, old Paddie and Third Royal Tanks, a-wearing of the green." Third RTR was a regiment of renown, and it undoubtedly deserved two hundred stanzas; it had fought on the retreat to Dunkirk and on the beaches there; it had fought on the retreat first in Greece and then in Crete, and on the beaches there; it had been involved in every armored action of Eighth Army in the Western Desert for three long years, shuttling up and down the coastal strip with the changing fortunes of the "Benghazi Handicap." It had led the breakthrough at El Alamein and the pursuit of Rommel all the way to Tunisia. It was the most experienced and bloodied tank regiment in the Allied armies.

As you would expect in so seasoned a regiment, it comprised a great number of highly experienced, battle-tested, and decorated men, and there were numberless occasions when freshly minted Second lieutenants, such as I, literally owed their lives to watching and listening to the people they theoretically commanded. Everyone knew that these old hands were spoon-feeding us greenhorns, and it would have been suicidal to ignore their views. For some weeks, I would have been an obituary item several times a day had it not been for Peter Elstob, my troop sergeant and an altogether extraordinary man. Starting life as a well-to-do playboy, he had studied at Oxford and the University of Michigan, then he had fought in Spain with the International Brigades, and when war broke out, he joined Third RTR and had fought with them everywhere. He refused a commission on principle, and did so till the end of the war; subsequently he became a successful author and co-owner of the Players' Club, one of the liveliest theater-cum-dining spots in London till well into the 1960s, and where all ex-Third RTR people were *ex officio* honorary members.

So much for background canvas; now to get back to the war.

# 6

The Third RTR landed east of Bayeux on June 13, 1944 (seven days after D-Day), and for weeks was involved in nasty and costly slogging matches in the bocage country around Caen, which included participation in the bloody mess of Operation Epsom and the battle for Hill 112, followed by the murderous futility of Operation Goodwood. When German resistance broke, Third RTR covered 350 miles in seven days, took Amiens in a night attack, and liberated Antwerp on September 4. We then pushed north, via Malines and Louvain, to Nijmegen, but were beaten back in the attempt to link up with the paratroopers in Arnhem. We fought for some weeks in the Dutch Roermond-Helmond-Overloon triangle, then withdrew to Poperinghe in Belgium to be outfitted with new tanks. We were interrupted in doing so and were rushed back to participate in the Ardennes battle, after which we completed our refitting and participated in the assault crossing of the Rhine at Wesel on March 27. Third RTR took Osnabrueck in another night attack, did successive assault-crossings of the Weser Canal and Aller River, passed through Bergen-Belsen and Uelzen, took Lueneburg, did another assault-crossing, this time of the Elbe near Lauenburg, then took Neustadt, Neumuenster, Bad Segeberg, and Flensburg on the Danish border (along with the Twenty-third Hussars who took Luebeck, further east, that same day), thereby effectively cutting Germany in half.

Except for that month in Poperinghe, the regiment was continually in action, frequently spearheading the division, and since Eleventh Armored, in turn, often led the entire Second British Army, it was not uncommon for the lead tank of the lead troop to be the very pinpoint of the entire Allied thrust; a melodramatic but unhealthy posture.

There is a widely held belief that once the Allies broke out of the Normandy beachheads, the remaining war was just a breeze, except for a few hiccups like Arnhem, Ardennes, or Huertgen Forest, and the mention of twenty-mile-a-day tank runs reinforces that view. But a few figures show a different picture. From the day Eleventh Armored landed in Normandy to the day of German surrender, the war lasted 330 days. The division started with 400 tanks, which meant 2,000 men, and of those, 602 were dead on May 8, 1945. Among them were

201 tank commanders and 78 officers. Allowing for the traditional ratio of three men wounded to one man killed, that means more than 2,400 people either wounded or killed, thus we turned over the entire division more than once; not exactly a walkover.

Oscar Wilde thought that to lose one parent was a tragedy, to lose both seemed like carelessness; the same observation might well apply to tanks, and most of us actually lost three or four during those eleven months! These were tanks you actually occupied, and I was in my fifth tank by the time it was all over. A joyride it may have been, but not always—Third RTR, despite leading the division more often than not, drew both on its experience and its *baraka*,† and was thus both savvy and lucky—after a fashion. We lost eighty-eight men killed between June 1944 and May 1945, which included twenty-three tank commanders, of whom thirteen were officers. It just depends on how you define luck; twenty-three out of sixty and thirteen out of thirty does not really sound all that fortunate.

I had expected that, when in action, people tended to be scared in varying degrees and I probably more than most. I had not anticipated that the longer they were in action, the more frightened they got. For one thing, the same people tended to be at risk over and over; while any army believes in rotating fighting troops, it also tends to call most often on those who have the most experience. So, as you get more experienced, you get into an ever more scary Catch-22 situation, since the one firm belief amidst this welter of noise, confusion, and potential injury was your faith in the law of averages. Every time you went in and came out unscathed, that was one chance you had used up; the more often it happened, the greater your belief that your luck could not hold. A good number of "battle-fatigue" cases or nervous breakdowns, or whatever the medically fashionable term might be, were caused by this gnawing and increasing fear that it would be your turn next time. One aspect of this crazy logic was that being lightly wounded made for inordinate cheerfulness; the wound ended the cycle, and you were back at square one.

---

†an Arab word co-opted by the French Foreign Legion meaning good fortune or destiny.

The result was that you never found experienced people volunteering for anything; new recruits did that, most likely would get hurt, and thereby be part of a pathetically self-fulfilling prophecy. All this held doubly true in a tank, where you had four other guys to think of, any one of whom might prefer living to being a legend.

Fire was the constant and specific nightmare of all tank people, particularly since a tank, hit and on fire, would as likely as not have a jammed hatch or damaged turret, which might make quick escape impossible. All tanks tend to burn. Only armor-piercing shells can really affect a tank, and they penetrate as a solid piece of metal rotating at immense speed through the tank wall and melting it to white heat in the process. That was the old-fashioned way; in the years since, they have come up with anything from hollow-charge to rockets to stop tanks, but in the end it is always the same white-heat effect causing a fire to break out, which is inevitable since the inside of a tank is full of flammable material, anything from spots of oil to discarded socks. In "our" war, there were two likely ways of getting caught in a burning tank. One was to be fighting in a Sherman tank, as most of us did until late in 1944, and which was widely known as a "Ronson." It was claimed that a Sherman could be set alight by a near-miss, and I would not necessarily doubt it. The other way was to join the Guards Armored Division, where for a while they had the idiotic habit of polishing the insides of their tanks with petrol and paraffin.

An equally unpleasant, though less frequent, incident was when a shell had sufficient velocity to penetrate one turret wall but not to exit on the other side. In addition to starting a fire, that shell would then ricochet around the turret and literally reduce the inmates to pulp. That did not happen very often, and besides, when it did, everything would be over very quickly and the fire part would not trouble you. On one side of the ledger was the fact that lots of things that could hurt infantry, anything from mines to blistered feet, could not touch you; on the other hand, if you did get hurt in a tank, chances were that you got hurt pretty badly, so the score tended to even out—except for those hot meals, of course. If, as in my case, you started out commanding a troop and, eleven months later, were temporarily looking after a whole squadron, it had nothing to do with merit or ability—it was just sheer luck of survival. To be less ghoulish, one of the intriguing aspects in operating out of tanks was that you began to see landscape quite differently. You constantly and, in the end, reflexively identified attacking positions or cover grounds for your own tanks, or spots from which some harm might come to you. Never mind the flowers and the bees—all you saw and memorized were ridges, woods, and bends in the road.

The reason why, sometimes even to us, the months after the Normandy breakthrough seemed comparatively uneventful was that for years we had all been fed on reports of vast battles and huge armies, the confrontations on the Russian front, El Alamein, the Normandy beachheads, and nothing that immense and dramatic had happened. After Normandy, death just came in penny packages—but it came regularly. Armies are supposed to advance in a coordinated fashion (as they supposedly do when they retreat, but only the Germans consistently managed to do that), with each division allocated to a certain sector and covering each other's flanks. Within each division, each brigade would take turns leading, at times for hours, sometimes for days, depending on how much fighting was involved; within each brigade, each regiment would rotate; and so on down the line, to the individual tank. It so happened that Eleventh Armored division consistently appeared to be the lead division, and so far ahead that it lacked flank support, or so anyone in the division would swear to. It also so happens that any tank crew you ask will swear that they were lead tank throughout the entire war.

The primary purpose of a lead tank was to find out where the enemy was, and the enemy's main idea was to spot that tank first. As a lead tank, you started moving with as much circumspection as the terrain allowed or your superiors would let you, and all the other tanks kept well under cover while watching what might happen to you. You never exposed more than one tank at a time, if you could help it; once the lead tank was round the corner or over the hill, the rest would follow. Unless you found trouble that is, which generally meant that someone shot at you. Dealing with Germans, that almost invariably meant that an 88-mm gun opened up, far and away the most lethal gun in World War II. The iron rule with 88-mm guns was never to wait for the second shot; the Germans would almost never fire till they had you well in their sights, and if they missed on the first shot, that second 88-mm round would almost certainly kill you. So you had to do something fast, and if you could think of something smart to do—hit it with your own gun or find good cover under which to think things over—so much the better.

If you could not think of anything smart, the other tanks would have heard that 88 mm or would see that thick black smoke from your tank and at least know where you had been, which did not necessarily mean that they knew where that gun was, unless you had dealt with it or at least had reported it. So the next tank up might find itself lead tank and go through the same procedure, aside from trying to collect whatever survivors you might have. And that is how you spent your day. Of course you were not unlucky all the time, but come the end of the average day, you might well have lost three or four tanks and five or ten people. In the process, you might have covered thirty miles, and all this would be reported by the army and certainly by the press as a speedy advance against very slight opposition—and so it was, but it did not come cheap.

Of course if things went well, it could be a blast, literally—like the day when Robin Lemon got his second MC. He was lead tank, and he edged round the bend of a wooded road, and we heard him say in childlike wonder, "Well, I'm darned; it's a Tiger." Tigers, of which the Germans had mercifully few in the west, were the most feared tanks of the war, so heavily armored that you had to be within a few hundred feet to do damage, whereas they had an 88-mm gun, which could blow you apart at a mile range. The best way to deal with Tigers was not to meet them, or else to get the RAF to attack them with rocket-firing Typhoon planes. That could work out reasonably well provided you made sure that your own tanks were well marked and that those pilots knew where you were. To Typhoons diving in at maximum speed, one tank looked pretty much like another.

Coming back to Robin, we heard him say, "Trying to get in close; driver, advance," followed by an enormous bang, then Robin saying with the utmost calm, "He missed me." Then there was another crash and Robin's comment, "Missed; gunner, traverse left two degrees; fire," followed by another crash, a lot of smoke and Robin reporting, "Got him this time; driver, advance."

That is how it was supposed to be, according to the manual. Talking about radio traffic, the thing to remember (or try to) was not to show or share your anxieties over the air; it did you no good and it upset others. It also helped if you said no more than necessary, and sometimes not even that. Keep on imagining that you were Gary Cooper; it was better to seem catatonic than panicky.

Tanks do not fight nor move at night, except under very unusual circumstances. The Sandhurst-approved procedure was to go into "leaguer," the armored version of the covered wagon-circle: all fifteen or so squadron tanks arranged in a big circle, guns facing outward, and just some gunners and wireless operators on watch, with the rest of the squadron sleeping inside the circle. The problem there was that you got wet if it rained and hurt if someone started shelling the place. A safer way was for each tank crew to dig a kind of mass grave, put tarpaulin sheets, bedding, and themselves in there, then before going to sleep, have the driver roll the tank right over you and your communal tomb. This kept you dry, safe from shells, and quite happy as long as claustrophobia was not one of your afflictions. The thing to do, however, was to test the ground carefully, before you built your underground Hilton; a tank weighs about forty tons and has a tendency to settle when immobile. We once woke up with about a foot between the edge of our hollow and the belly of the tank; we did not think it was as funny as the other guys did.

The best and safest way, though not necessarily the most comfortable, was to pick a house in the neighborhood, run the tank through it from the rear so as to have the house collapse on the tank, and then just make sure you could operate the gun turret in case of need. It gave you splendid camouflage and the added satisfaction of ruining German property. The problem with that approach was that you had to sleep inside your tank, like a large and very grubby embryo. Lack of sleep and terribly cramped posture were what everyone remembers most and longest about tank warfare. Chronic lack of sleep was, in some ways, a tougher thing to fight than the Germans; we never got enough sleep and at times were literally groggy, so that bad decisions were made and people got hurt in consequence. No one I know ever got used to being so short of sleep.

You did, after a fashion, get used to the fact that a tank is all edges and corners, and all of them are steel. A tank commander sits on a tiny piano stool and views the world through a sort of periscope with the turret hatch closed; that is the theory. In practice that is conducive to poor vision and ultimately to suicide; in RTR regiments no one ever closed a turret hatch or used a periscope. If the hatch was closed and you got hit, there was no telling whether you could open it in time, and that periscope had far too many dead angles to be of any use, except maybe for girl-watching.

So a tank commander just put his head and shoulders out of the turret and kept looking around. Admittedly that was not much recommended when there were snipers or shrapnel in the neighborhood, but we did it even then; anything was better than feeling cooped up inside that turret when an 88 mm might open up on you. In due course this collective sense of claustrophobia was shared by all tank regiments, and particularly by the donkey wallopers; going into action with head and shoulders well in sight probably reminded them of cavalry charges.

RTR regiments added a touch of idiosyncratic lunacy, since they were the first ones to wear the black beret—no one in RTR regiments ever wore anything else, regardless of shot and shell. The other folk wore helmets when in action, sensibly putting survival above tradition.

Travelling in a tank meant you balanced on a three-inch wide ledge in the turret ring and tried to wedge your feet somewhere (preferably on the gunner's shoulders if he would let you) so as to have your hands free for binoculars, map reading, microphone, or making empty gestures. Your feet and back were in bad shape after a week and in terrible shape after two, and you were in constant and crippling discomfort from then on. It is just fortunate that in those good old days, no one had invented "back trouble" yet; otherwise all of us tank people would be suffering from it to this day.

Though it was not described so alliteratively back in the 1940s, "peer pressure" played an enormous part in all this—not wanting to be perceived as the coward you were. It certainly influenced a great many of the things I did, except for the rare occasions when noise, confusion, and the general "*élan* of battle" produced that crazy sense of elation that just made you go for it. The rest of the time you feared loss of face more than loss of limb, which made literal but no other sense.

Did I ruminate much about all this while rattling round the countryside? Hardly ever, since trying to cope adequately with the situation at hand was a full-time occupation; not having time to be scared is a truism and there were some additional factors. Third RTR had been around the war for quite a while and had seen and dealt with a lot of situations; there was a professional air about a lot of my colleagues, that was both reassuring and challenging when it came to my own performance. In addition, there was a sense of curiosity that goes with being new boy on the block; eleven months of action is a long time in some respects, but not long enough to lose a certain sense of excitement and even anticipation. Most of all, there was an enormous and wholly unpredictable element of luck involved, so I just went on and coped as best I could with whatever I encountered.

My recollections of the Normandy beaches, the subsequent slog-ging match around Caen and in the wooded region around it, and the ultimate breakthrough are all no different from numberless reports about all of these events; there have been so many hostilities since, that telling about it seems like research into the Punic Wars. I do remember the constant and terrible contrast between a bucolic and sun-bathed countryside and the carnage littering it, and how I felt about the first dead body I saw, a feeling I never lost. Dead people look unreal; there is a waxen, puppet-like, "never having been alive" look about them that makes them seem like tailor's dummies; they may scare you, sometimes disgust you, but they will rarely elicit a sense of human rapport and grief. They are not only gone, they look as if they had never been. Sometimes, it seemed like proof of the reality of a soul or a spark of life. It seemed otherwise inexplicable that, within a fraction of a moment, someone who was palpably alive was now so remote and alien that there was no sense of human association at all.

Late that June 1944, there was another of those surreal incidents in which I seemed to be involved in those years. My tank took a hit in the wooded area near Caen, which killed the two people in the driver's compartment, but only resulted in very minor flashburns to the three men in the turret. As a result, we ended up in a brand-new U.S. field hospital, about three hundred beds under canvas, doctors by the score, nurses by battalions, and enough medical equipment to deal with the Black Death. We were the first three patients in it and, by the time we left two days later, no one else had shown up. Why such a M.A.S.H. outfit should have been in the British sector and for what catastrophic emergency was unclear both to the staff and to us. It may have been some elaborate hoax, rather like my Avonmouth oil tanks; more likely, somebody had just mislaid the entire outfit—the military have a tendency to lose things casually and a mere hospital might never be missed.

In any event, the food was memorable, and given the lightness of our injuries, the availability of comic books was much more important than the level of medical expertise.

Whole libraries have been filled with dissertations on the strategy of that period, how Montgomery and the British and Canadian component of the Allies were to immobilize the Germans by constant frontal attacks, so as to allow Patton and the U.S. troops to hook around the right flank and break through. Maybe that was the plan, perhaps these luminaries had even talked about it and, though less likely, knew what they were doing; none of it percolated down the line. We just slugged it out with assorted Panzer divisions, like a couple of punch drunk fighters, and after a while they literally ran out of gas, and we got lucky. When we did break through, we had beaten the Germans, but not because we were better at fighting. I have no doubt at all that, even more than in World War I, the Germans were the best fighting soldiers around, and by some considerable margin, both in the east and in the west. Special outfits like the Commandos, Marines, or Paratroops obviously do not enter into such a comparison, but on the "warriors for the working day" level, the Germans were unparalleled. It had, in my view, nothing to do with physique, courage, ideology, or even training; it had everything to do with creating and maintaining cadres of tough, determined, and intensely motivated corporals, sergeants, and junior officers who kept their bunch of people together and moving much better than we ever managed to do. Some people claim that the German tendency towards blind obedience makes for good soldiers. Maybe so, but I am convinced that the key is leadership at ground level, so to speak, and no one was as good at that as were the Germans. It was particularly noticeable anytime we managed to get them off balance; if you did not push your advantage immediately, and if you gave them any time at all to catch their breath, they would rally almost instantly and you would have to start all over again; which is exactly what happened in Normandy for weeks. To be an effective combat leader at that level requires just two attributes. The men must feel that you look after them and their welfare, and you must display personal physical courage. It is easier said than done.

We came up a good deal against SS Panzer divisions. Being certified Hitler enthusiasts meant they had the pick of weaponry— almost all Tiger and Panther tanks, Germany's best, went to SS divisions and that in turn meant it was generally rough going up against them. It did not, however, mean that you were dealing with murderers and war criminals. The Waffen SS was a large body of elite military troops; the SS as such, was a much smaller group of mur- derous individuals, disguised in fancy uniform, who never did any fighting at all but rather were fanatical Nazis personally sworn to Hitler and originally intended as his bodyguard. People seem con- fused about this to this day; somehow it was always very clear to us.

# 7

I am firmly convinced, as others have been, that we did not win the war; Hitler lost it.

Until the Normandy break-out, there was not a single instance in six years of war when the Allies seemed able to deal the Germans a decisive blow that would have decided the war.

Hitler, on the other hand, had at least five such opportunities.

The "miracle of Dunkirk" in June 1940 was not the escape of the British troops, but Hitler's inexplicable decision to halt his Panzer divisions short of the beachheads. He could most certainly have forced England's surrender, and to this day the German inaction remains a mystery.

In December 1941, German troops were within sight of Moscow when the Russian winter caught them in flat terrain and in need of warm clothing. Had Hitler halted the advance and consolidated the line, the Germans could have withstood the winter and the Russian counterattacks, and they could have forced the Russian surrender in spring 1942.

Even after the reversals of the 1941 winter campaign, the Germans could have overcome the Russians had they taken Stalingrad in October 1942. Or had Hitler listened to Manstein's and Guderian's advice and pulled the Sixth Army out of the closing Stalingrad trap in December of that year, he could have renewed the assault on the Volga in spring 1943 and achieved a decisive victory.

His fourth and last opportunity to beat Russia was "Operation Citadel" on the Kursk-Orel front in July 1943. Six thousand tanks met on one battlefield to fight the greatest and longest tank battle in history.

The Germans should have operated "according to the book" and that had been written by General-Oberst Heinz Guderian, the finest tank tactician so far known, and whom Hitler had dismissed after Stalingrad. Guderian's relentless credo was "Nicht kleckern sondern klotzen!" and his unvarying aim was to create a "Keil und Kessel" situation. Mass your tanks and hurl them at the enemy like a mailed fist (klotzen), rather than dissipating them (kleckern) in thin extended lines. The concentrated force of tanks will form a wedge (Keil) bursting through the enemy lines; the wedge would then fan out and turn back on itself to form a cauldron (Kessel), in which large numbers of enemy forces would be trapped to be mopped up by the infantry and artillery.

The German Kursk offensive was commanded by Hitler, not by Guderian, and it kleckert to a standstill—

The last and most decisive opportunity the Germans had to win the war outright was in Normandy, on June 6 and 7, 1944. Utah Beach was a near disaster and so were our parachute drops. The weather conditions (and hence supplies and reinforcements) were dubious, and Rommel, commanding the invasion front, was dedicated to meeting the Allied assault right on the beaches and to throwing us back into the sea. To do so, he would have had to commit his "strategic reserve," notably half a dozen crack tank divisions, within the first forty-eight hours of the invasion. Given his faith in his own tactical instincts, I am convinced that he would have done so, that he would have convinced his superiors, von Rundstedt and Hitler, and that he would have hurled us back into the water.

But on June 6, Rommel was in Stuttgart celebrating his wife's birthday, and there was no one on the spot to dispel Rundstedt's and Hitler's conviction that the landings were a feint and that the real assault was aimed at the Pas-de-Calais. The tank divisions were not committed in time, and when Rommel returned on June 8 to take charge, the beachheads were secure, and we could no longer be dislodged.

Those forty-eight hours saved us; had we been thrown back, it might have taken years to launch another such invasion.

## 8

Having got out of the Normandy bottleneck, Third RTR's night dash to Amiens has become part of British tank folklore. It supposedly started with Pip Roberts sending us a signal that "it's moonlight tonight." For one thing, we never received it, and for another, had it been code, we would not have known what it meant. If on the other hand Pip was giving us a weather forecast, he had the wrong crystal ball, because it poured all that night. Nothing was planned, it just happened. The ten days or so between the time we broke out of the woodlands and the day we reached Antwerp were the only time when any of us experienced a real blitzkrieg, an extraordinarily exhilarating sensation, which made you feel reckless and invincible and greatly encouraged unnecessary foolishness. Actually Third RTR had had a sampler of it in North Africa, first against the Italians in 1941 and later in the pursuit after El Alamein. But thrashing Italians did not really count and racing through the desert was not at all like liberating parts of France—unless you prefer couscous to Calvados.

So there we were about thirty miles outside Amiens, in the dark and the rain, when David Silvertopp had the notion to keep moving up the road, so we did. It did not trouble us that, as we were going along, the column was getting longer, and a lot of blacked-out vehicles were joining us from various side roads. No one shot at anything or spoke to anybody, and it was very wet and very dark, so we just nudged our way along until first light, when we hit the outskirts of Amiens and got fired on from both flanks. One side we found to be the German garrison, which seemed reasonable enough, and the other we assumed to be the French resistance fighters, a melodramatic, unpredictable, and generally ineffectual lot who liked to play with firearms. The light was poor, their aim was worse, and it took us a while to work out that both thought we were on their side. What in the dark we had assumed to be an unidentifiable and mobile version of the cabin scene in A Night at the Opera turned out, at dawn, to be a cross-national potpourri. During the night, a goodly number of German vehicles, mostly trucks, even some staff cars, had joined our column, all retreating towards Amiens and all assuming that that was what we were doing. Coffee tasters can do blindfold tests, and tank people can distinguish engine noises and tank silhouettes, but to a truck driver, one tank looks and sounds pretty much like another in the dark, and so there we were, a mixed bag indeed.

Silvertopp's decisiveness, the Germans' evident reluctance to make a stand (Amiens had no tactical significance and the garrison troops were elderly and poorly prepared), and the Resistance's rapid loss of interest in playing at soldiers in the rain all combined to sort matters out rapidly. We did indeed take Amiens, but there were too many Inspector Clouseau elements involved to make it the model of a coup de main.

It did however establish Third RTR's reputation throughout Twenty-First Army Group as being lucky, as being a "go for broke" bunch, and as experts in tank warfare at night; we assiduously cultivated all three myths, hoping that the first was true and that we would not be called upon to make good on the others.

The apotheosis of this headlong dash through the countryside came on September 4, when A Squadron, Third RTR, liberated Antwerp all by itself—a uniformed and emotional version of the "kid in the candy store."

Once again, there was no plan involved, just luck. We had been barrelling along as lead squadron of the division, some ten miles ahead of the rest of the regiment, and, for all we knew, half of Belgium ahead of the division. This kind of configuration, in ordinary circumstances, would be a shortcut to a bronze statue or a court martial, but those were heady days and no one had time to read Clausewitz, even in translation. Anyway, the whole concept of distances became very relative and variable depending on how often or how intensely you got involved in the shooting part of the war. Our own squadron headquarters, some hundred yards away, at times appeared as safe as an atomic shelter, and regimental HQ, a mile or so back, seemed like the Club Med. As for brigade headquarters, let alone division HQ, they might as well have been back in England for all the contact we ever had with them or their lifestyle: shiny boots, meals on plates, toilets with doors, whisky in glasses, clubland living, or so it appeared to us "at the sharp end." So, when it came to how far we seemed to be from anyone else, it just depended which end you were looking from.

That September morning we had reached Boom, about ten miles from the outskirts of Antwerp, where a bridge crossed over the Albert Canal and effectively bottlenecked the approach to Antwerp—and still does. We did not know that immediately—military maps are notoriously reluctant to indicate any manmade landmark; since they only seem to get revised every century or so, that seems reasonable enough—so we were just intent on having a "shufti" and hoping for the best.

Since Normandy, we had been carrying a few infantrymen on the back of each tank, who came in use when one had to deal with snipers or bazooka men. The infantrymen in question were generally somewhat less certain that this was a good way for them to travel, but by and large managed to console themselves with the prospect of constant hot tea and other home comforts of tank life. Since the back of the tank was almost consistently a Standing Room Only situation, we never paid much attention to just what all these human limpets were up to, particularly when many of them might also now be celebrating civilians.

In our rush through France and now Belgium, we had become rather blasé about the liberated and duly grateful populace, who would throw flowers (useless), pâté and sausages, (very welcome), bottles of various kinds (great; mind your head), or themselves (depended on who) at us; generally we would just wave languid thanks at the multitude.

As we went through Boom, it took a while for me to realize that one of these civilians was trying to tell me something, and given the general noise level (with a twelve-cylinder Rolls Royce tank engine, you hear a lot more than the clock ticking), it took me even longer to guess that it was something more specific than just what a miserable lot the *boches* had been and how much he loved us. What he was telling me was that there was a bridge, that he knew where the Germans had laid charges, and that they had not blown it up yet! To cut that part of the story short: we got there, we got over the bridge, and now we really started racing towards Antwerp.

At first there was the usual cascade of flowers, edibles, and bottles (the French and Belgians are very good at this, since the annual Tour de France cycling event keeps them in steady training for supplying moving targets). As we approached the outskirts of Antwerp, the place was literally black with people, all shouting, waving, weeping, a solid wall of ecstatic noise, an explosion of joy, and none of us who was there will ever forget it. The tanks were literally moving over a carpet of flowers, and each turret was covered with an ant heap of men and women embracing us and each other, waving British and Belgian flags. It was incredible, unforgettable, and indescribably moving.

Confusion was of course utter, since among this welter of emotion, there were also some Germans to take care of, and there were enough of them to maintain a semblance of warfare among this riot of sentiment. Every once in a while, mostly at street intersections, we found ourselves in a Keystone Kop situation, our tanks were moving on one boulevard and some German tanks or half-tracks were moving back on a parallel street, and each one was taking a couple of quick potshots at the other. There may have been some casualties in such mêlées, but I do not recall any. I do remember my co-driver suffering a slight concussion from a thrown wine bottle (which he drank, that concussed he was not).

We finally ended up in front of Antwerp City Hall, all fifteen tanks of A Squadron, maybe 250 men all told, including the infantry, all of us garlanded, smeared with lipstick, and surrounded by the unceasing screaming of a rapturous and hysterical population—it was absolutely incredible!

A suitable vignette to all this unreality came when John Watts, the squadron commander, attempted to let regimental HQ know where we were and, mindful of codes and procedures, referred to "being in the middle of the Big Place," only to get the reply "repeat; not understood." So he tried a couple of times to be suitably discreet, only to be faced by the other end being correspondingly obtuse, until finally he yelled into the microphone: "For Christ's sake; we're in the middle of Antwerp. That's where we are." And we all heard the reply over our own earphones, "Give map reference. You must be mistaken." That is the kind of day it was. On the same day and at just about the same time, Guards Armored Division took Brussels and they, too, were disbelieved by anyone they tried to tell it to. In any event, A Squadron had Antwerp to itself for a full twenty-four hours (the rest of the regiment got distracted by some mopping-up operations on the flank, much to their disgust), and Third RTR had the city as their own for another two days before division, Army Corps, Army Group, and Uncle Tom Cobley all turned up. In the light of subsequent events, particularly the Arnhem debacle, we should never have stopped, but—and particularly at that time—we were pharisees, not prophets.

Except for a very desultory guard detail (rapidly reduced to a state of alcoholic coma, where someone could not only have stolen our tanks, but the City Hall to go with them), we all set off, more or less individually, to share in the joys of a jubilant and celebrating city. Two tank crews of mine ended up in an imposing mansion that (greatly to their surprise, to hear them tell it) also happened to be a house of ill-repute and vastly expensive. The latter obstacle was waived for "*les libérateurs*," who disappeared from view for the entire three days and practically had to be hoisted back into their tanks, in the presence of a bevy of young ladies, who had turned out *en masse* and *en peignoir* to wave them on to greater deeds.

One or two incidents stick in my mind, which gets happily woozy even now at the thought of it all. There was Peter Elstob and his tank going astray, when we first moved into the city, and ending up at the Scheldt estuary, where a large German cargo ship was making for the open sea. It is very likely that Peter was the only tank commander in World War II who sank a ship. Somewhat later that day (or maybe the next day; who knows or cares—), there was the spectacle of Father Halloran. The British Army did not allocate clergymen to specific units nor seemed to distinguish between denominations; there just were a number of ambulant couriers to God who tended to turn up here and there. Father H., an ex-paratrooper and with a brogue so thick it would have baffled Sean O'Casey, had somehow strayed into Third RTR and into Antwerp that day. I came across him late in the afternoon, carried on the shoulders of a dozen or more Anversois, all drunk as owls and Halloran himself drunk as an Irish owl (which is really being smashed). There was a mob of celebrating citizens all around them, and every once in a while Halloran would rally from some sodden contemplation, trace wide and asymmetrical crosses into the air and shout, "Bless you all, you lovely bastards!"

None of us clearly recalls where we spent all of those seventy-two hours and how; it was just one huge party, and although Antwerp is a large city and there were very few of us, there was an elliptic quality to all those celebrations, and we kept on running into each other, being handed on from orgy to orgy. The Germans gave us no trouble, since they had all temporarily been locked into the cages of the Antwerp Zoo; not quite as Neronic a solution as it may sound, since the zoo had been emptied years earlier. The whole Antwerp fantasy had an equally bizarre sequel. Some time in 1946, the mayor of Antwerp asked for one of the tanks of A Squadron, to be installed as a permanent monument on a large granite block, facing towards the Boom road. I have no idea why I kept a record of the registration numbers of the tanks I had in 1944–45, but I did; that tank you now see standing on the road from Antwerp to Boom is mine! Wave to it as you drive by—I always do.

# 9

By the time we were on the move again, the Germans had caught their breath, and we started slugging it out all over again.

We just got a few miles north and over the Dutch border, and then they held us in the Helmon-Roermond-Overloon area, and when we got pulled out later in September to try and link up with the

Arnhem drop, they blasted us off the map just outside Nijmegen. I recall one morning just after dawn, when we were having yet another try on those dreadful dyke roads, which run like ridges across the Dutch landscape. Our tanks were silhouetted against the skyline—which is a tank man's nightmare—and we lost seven of them in less than ten minutes. For several weeks we froze, cursed, fought, and got nowhere, before suddenly being ordered to deposit our tanks in Antwerp Harbor and proceed by truck to "somewhere in Belgium" to start training preparatory to the arrival of brand-new models and the eventual Rhine crossing.

Coming out of Normandy, we had exchanged our Shermans for Cromwells, a new English tank, which was faster and lower, but still had to be maneuvered virtually within spitting distance of a Tiger to do any damage. Now we were to exchange Cromwells for Comets, of which we were told many good things, and which indeed turned out to be a pretty good tank. It still was no match for a Tiger or Panther, but you could at least have a sporting try.

Awaiting those Comets, we were driven to our unknown destination, which turned out to be Poperinghe, a tiny town close to Ypres, and of which it could well be said, as someone once said of Russia, that it had more history than it could cope with.

Ypres is a place of sinister memory, since some of the longest and bloodiest battles of World War I took place in that corner of Flanders. The Menin Gate in Ypres, a smaller and rather uninspired cousin of the Arc de Triomphe, carries the names of ninety thousand British soldiers who were killed in the immediate area and never found, and, just like Verdun, it is a countryside drenched in blood and sadness.

Ypres was very much part of the actual battleline then, and Poperinghe, then as now a tiny sleepy market town, was the nearest rest area for exhausted troops coming out of the line. It was the birthplace of "Toc H," the brainchild of "Tubby" Clayton, vicar of St. Martin's-in-the-Fields in London, who conceived of this forerunner to USO canteens in a large requisitioned house in Poperinghe, which became a haven and byword to literally millions of British soldiers. When we got to Poperinghe, the original "Toc H" still stood there, and so did Tubby Clayton, on one of his periodic visits to his creation, a frail, small, kindly, almost saintly cleric, and a terrible bore.

Poperinghe turned out to be a thoroughly Breughelian town, with robust Flemist zest for doing everything to boisterous excess. Just look at any Ostade or Jan Steen painting; there is something irresistible and irresistibly Flemish in that sanguine enjoyment of everything life has to offer. It was a town of perhaps twelve thousand inhabitants and, as is often the case in such places, totally dominated by one family clan. Albert Lahaye had been mayor in perpetuity, or at least from around 1905 until his death in the 1930s, and his widow, jolly, formidable, tightly-corseted, and always in black, was the unquestioned Queen Mother. There were five sons who, between them, ran everything: one of course was the mayor, another the assize judge of the area, and yet another was the town's notary and principal attorney. Son Number 4 ran the family brewery (an almost limitless cash cow, given the Belgian propensity for beer; but the family had also diversified into real estate and virtually owned the town by law, as well as in fact). The youngest son had been sent to Brussels to be active in national politics and, after 1946, was several times a cabinet minister and even prime minister once or twice. Just to make sure that control remained airtight, three of the brothers had married three sisters, whose family owned most of the remaining countryside in the area. The politician was unmarried when we knew him, and the brewer had broken away from the fold, had gone to Ostend to find and marry the ravishing blonde daughter of a struggling grocery store owner, and had imported her to Poperinghe. Arlette was stunning, wore Brussels clothes, and was tolerated by the family and deeply distrusted by Poperinghe's population. She simply could not have had the time to pursue all the Messalina-like activities that the local gossips attributed to her; but she was never idle, as a number of Third RTR people could testify. Her husband adored her regardless and was so classic a case of *cocu complaisant* that the entire scene could have been lifted right out of *La Femme du Boulanger*. The Lahaye clan lived all over town, each on very substantial property, with gardens, domestics, dogs, horses, and vast wine cellars, and once a week everyone would gather for dinner "chez Grand-Mère," which would include about twenty-five people and a multi-course meal lasting till well after midnight.

Clearly the clan had first pick as to who would be lodged where; Grand-Mère naturally got Colonel Brown, the judge got John Watts, and the brewer adopted John Dunlop of B Squadron, who soon after began showing signs of gathering exhaustion and, when seen with the gorgeous Arlette, seemed to be held up by her rather than walking arm-in-arm.

Although quite low on the totem pole—I had only just been promoted to full lieutenant—I was picked by Sylvain, the notary, and his wife Angélique, probably because, unlike the other Lahayes, their English was poor and they wanted a French-speaking lodger. Arlette could not speak English either, but there was no need to—she had other assets.

Angélique and Sylvain lived in a rambling, whitewashed ranch-type mansion, with wings going off in all directions, on the outskirts of town. They had two children in their early teens, innumerable dogs, almost as many maids, and a few horses. They were absolutely charming. Sylvain practiced law from his study, and it did not appear to take up much of his time; he spent some of his hours playing the oboe, which was unfortunate, and the remainder of his time being a delightful and erudite conversationalist. He was cultured, diffident, quiet, gentle, and very kind; Angélique shared his kindness and education, but was a constant tornado of activities. She could handle six different chores simultaneously with effortless ease. In Poperinghe, that involved kids, dogs, servants, driving, riding, shopping, and entertaining; had she been in New York, she could have run the archdiocese as well as the public transportation system simultaneously. They were wonderful people to talk to; bright, educated, and yet genuinely uninterested in the outside world day-to-day. You could engage them in endless discourses involving Voltaire, Plato, or Proust, all the meaningfully meaningless subjects which I had not heard about since leaving Cambridge. Sylvain once drove me around some nearby land owned by Angélique which included Wytschaete Ridge, another infamous name of World War I. I did not confuse him by telling him that my father had won his Iron Cross just here in 1916, and that my father's commanding officer at the time had been Hauptmann Erwin Rommel.

Naturally all Lahaye house guests were included in the weekly dinners "chez Grand-Mère" and altogether there was a great deal of entertaining among the Lahaye clan. Those Lahaye meals, with a

Rubens-like ambiance—opulent silver, crystal, and china, endless, delicious courses, and limitless, wonderful wines are with me to this day—as they were then for days on end, since none of us had heard yet of Alka-Seltzer. All of us were distinctly idle, awaiting the arrival of those new Comets and meanwhile just keeping soldiering to a minimum; one roll call in the morning and that was it.

Although no one else could aspire to the feudal comforts which Lahaye lodgers enjoyed (my bathroom had a black sunken marble tub; Angélique had seen a movie with such a tub and Claudette Colbert in it, and had half a dozen installed all over the house; sans Claudette, unfortunately), all of Third RTR, about three hundred men in all, were well taken care of by the people of Poperinghe.

The oddest setup, giving rise to endless and never-resolved speculation, involved Barry Peerless and the Twins. Barry was another of those nursery fugitives, who looked about sixteen but was twenty-three, a captain who had won his MC fighting all over the Western Desert with Third RTR. Still, he looked, acted, and was simply cherubic; strangers patronized him, women mothered him, his men adored him, and he smiled at one and all with curly-headed innocence. He had been lodged with a small, elderly, friendly, and stone-deaf widow who had identical twins, tall, blonde, buxom, and inseparable, a couple of juvenile Valkyries. They immediately adopted Barry, and Poperinghe being a tiny town, you could see that trio arm-in-arm half a dozen times a day. Barry, as always, was happy, vague, and silent; the twins looked happy, triumphant, and silent—no one will ever know.

This idyllic existence was heightened by a thick layer of snow that had fallen by late November. To leave after one of those Homeric Lahaye evenings and walk a mile or so to Sylvain's place through crisp snow on a still, star-lit night made it seem a very bearable war.

## 10

On December 16, the Germans launched their Ardennes offensive, slicing through the American positions in that area. There was a lack of both interest and respect for U.S. troops among the British soldiery at the time, based very largely on ignorance. The Americans had not been impressive on their first outing in North Africa, the only time when they and the British had directly fought together. Third RTR had been there and was dismissive about their efforts. Nothing during their stay in England had endeared them to their British colleagues; they were too rich, too noisy, too successful with girls, and there were too many of them. About the only interesting thing about Americans was that there were also black troops, then still an intriguing novelty in England; that these were in fact segregated, was an aspect we were unaware of.

All we knew about Americans since the Normandy invasion was what we had read in the papers, which mostly featured Patton, who sounded as much of a son of a bitch as Montgomery, and was an "expensive" general, to boot. Montgomery was not likely to win any popularity contest with Third RTR or any other British troops, but he did have two things going for him. He would tell you what he intended to do and then do it—other British generals told you nothing, and then it usually became painfully clear that whatever they were not telling you was not working anyway. More importantly, Montgomery was an "economical" general; he may have missed opportunities and wasted material (he certainly had done so time and again since Normandy), but he did not waste lives if he could avoid it. Troops like generals who keep them alive and that was the beginning and end of Monty's popularity.

Patton, on the other hand, seemed a "blood-and-guts" clown, forever taking unnecessary risks at his soldiers' expense, and old hands like Third RTR despised and feared such grandstanding glory hounds and disdained troops who seemed to admire such antics. Omar Bradley, on the other hand, seemed cautious and competent, but then you never read much about him. No one ever viewed Eisenhower as a fighting general; he seemed a kind of administrative coordinator and spokesman, and anyway was operating so far in the rear as to be on another planet. In short, the news of American setbacks did not particularly concern us.

That changed, however, on the evening of December 18, when trucks raced us back towards Brussels, some seventy miles away and clearly in the wrong direction as far as the Ardennes affair was concerned. Halfway there, on a truly dark and snowy night, we found our old Cromwells, which tank transporters had deposited, and spent the remainder of that night doing the best "refitting" job I ever saw, outside of the movies. The tanks were lined up on one side of the road, moving up at a walking pace (going towards the Ardennes, this time) and an endless stream of trucks was coming up alongside bringing machine guns, ammunition, petrol, rations, wireless sets, and all the bits and pieces that had been stripped out of our tanks, and which had been awaiting shipment back to England. Over the next three hours, in the pitch darkness and constantly moving slowly forward, we completely refitted some sixty-five tanks, and just before dawn, the regiment was battle-ready. For once, all the pegs and all the holes had been round.

With our wireless in place, we also got news: the Germans were pushing hard, the Americans were in trouble, 101st Airborne was cut off in Bastogne, bad weather was making flying impossible, and Montgomery was taking command of part of the front and intended to throw in British troops to "plug the gap."

We had no idea where that gap was, but we did know that the only British troops anywhere near the area were Twenty-third Hussars, our sister regiment, also being refitted not far from Poperinghe, and Third RTR; everyone else was still up in Holland somewhere. Twenty-third Hussars had similarly spent the night doing mechanical acrobatics, and all that day, December 19, both regiments raced east on frozen roads to reach Namur by nightfall. From there we started out to cover the several bridges crossing the Meuse, and by midnight we were in position, hull down, guns traversed, waiting for the Germans to come for the bridges. Which they did, at dawn on December 20, some six hours later, and we beat them back.

It would be absurd to claim that we and Twenty-third Hussars won the battle of the Bulge, (although we do so claim, of course), but it is a fact that the Germans' key objective was crossing the Meuse to go for Antwerp and the petrol depots there. To do that, they had to cross those bridges, and except for us, no one would have prevented them. It is of course also true that by the time they reached those bridges, they were already running out of fuel and were too spread out and disorganized to follow their original battle plan. Even had they crossed the Meuse, it might not have made much difference: that offensive had lost its impetus and was spent. To say that we met and threw back the furthest German spearheads of the German Ardennes offensive is perfectly accurate, though. It was not much of a fight, as it happened, and by midmorning on December 20, we were ourselves across the Meuse, pushing east, and for the next three weeks, until January 9, the rest was mostly a mopping-up operation.

The most memorable aspect of that whole Ardennes outing was how cold it was; I have never been so cold in my life. We kept the engines running round the clock, as they would have seized up on us otherwise, and cases of frostbite considerably outnumbered any other kind of injury. I tend to feel chilly on a summer night on the Riviera, but this would have awed an Eskimo; it was bitter. It had its moments, though; there was the incident of Jack Dunlop losing his teeth, and another when I came close to losing other parts of my anatomy. Tanks are reasonably well-contained, but plumbing is not included, so I was squatting in the snow in a shallow ditch a few yards away when I suddenly heard a snuffling cough and something dark and seemingly immense leapt right over me and into my gunner's sights, who promptly shot it.

It is somewhat unusual to come across a live wild boar with your pants down; it was huge and was kept refrigerated on the back of the tank and brought back to Poperinghe; it proved absolutely delicious.

By far my bloodiest recollection of the Ardennes interlude involved my assisting Barry Whitehouse, our regimental medical officer. His father, Sir Beckwith Whitehouse, a gynecologist of vast renown, had insisted on Barry becoming a doctor, a prospect that Barry viewed with distaste, to the extent that he ever showed any strong feelings at all. He had been an invariably amiable, silent, and impeccably courteous member of the crowd I used to run around with in Cambridge, where I had last seen him in May 1940. Midway through Normandy, our medical officer got killed, and Barry replaced him, having evidently obtained a medical degree meanwhile. He was a superb regimental doctor, whose role is not necessarily to be an outstanding physician but to get to wounded people quickly and deal with them calmly and reassuringly. Looking as remote and as sheep-like as ever, piloting his jeep to places that would scare off a tank,

Barry was imperturbable to the point of seeming comatose and imparted calm and confidence which, aside from morphine, is about all a good battle MO is supposed to dispense.

It was a mid-afternoon, bitterly cold as usual, snowing a little, and Barry had just come by to check about generally and to pick up a drink or two, when one of my forward tanks reported a couple of civilians who wanted "to say something in French." So I joined Barry in his jeep and we discovered these two men to be a local farmer and his brother, both living a couple of miles up the road. The brother's wife was in labor with her first baby, and they pleaded for medical assistance. The Germans being at least another two miles beyond the farm, and Barry barely ever saying a word in English, let alone in French, I decided to join the three of them to see what could be done.

Barry looked at the prospective mother, clearly in considerable distress, told father and brother to stay out of the way and told me to start boiling vats of water, look for clean towels (yes, sir, Dr. Kildare!), and start scrubbing down the kitchen table (not in any movie I could recall). Twenty minutes later, the wife was under morphine and on the table, I was ducking about with hot water and towels, and Barry was doing a cesarean section, a much bloodier enterprise than I had imagined. Half an hour later, mother and baby were back in bed, father and brother were crying almost as loudly as the baby, and Barry and I were imbibing a bottle of *eau de vie* and surveying this domestic idyll. Just before nightfall, the proud father turned up once more among my tanks with two baskets full of eggs; it seemed a shame that Barry did not have a few more maternity cases in the neighborhood.

On January 9, we pulled out of the Ardennes area, still cold and covered with snow but with no more Germans in sight, and my first and lasting impression of it all was how beautiful a part of the world it was; the woods are lovely, dark and deep—yes, indeed they were! Having handed back our tanks for final disposal, we returned "home" to Poperinghe for a series of Rabelaisian celebrations commemorating Christmas and New Year, which we had missed, and of course the fact that we had "sauvée la Belgique" (saved Belgium)—more or less.

Our new Comet tanks arrived in due course that month, and with them, the reminder that the war was not quite over yet. The Comet seemed a quite acceptable piece of machinery, but a good deal more complicated than Shermans or Cromwells to handle and fire, and we spent most of our days in workshops and on nearby gunnery ranges trying to figure out which lever did what. Having done that daily stint, we were ready for more sociable and varied action in the evening which, in those last weeks of respite, increasingly meant heading for Brussels. We certainly had not tired of the pleasures Poperinghe had to offer, but the Brigade Club in Brussels was just too alluring to resist. Paddy Hehar, its organizer and ad hoc manager—who came from a line of con men and smugglers reaching way back to the Spanish Armada—had parleyed someone out of a most sumptuous *petit palais* on the Avenue Louise—Brussels' Fifth Avenue and then some—and declared it out of bounds to all except officers of Twenty-ninth Armored Brigade and their guests.

The bar never closed, the food was exquisite, served by elderly Belgian waiters with white gloves (who doubtlessly had done just that for German officers six months earlier; Belgians tended to be a bit pliable during that war), and there were always a number of strikingly pretty women around, whose nationalities were indeterminate, occupations vague, and intentions obvious. There were also some sumptuous bedrooms upstairs, for rest or recreation, as the case may be. It was probably the most elegant *maison de passe* since Louis XV's Parc des Cerfs, and Paddy richly deserved the Croix de Guerre which he got just about then—though possibly for some other distinguished deed. In retrospect it amazed me that we would, night after night, set out in an open jeep and drive well over two hours in the dark and on terrible and crowded roads to get from Poperinghe to Brussels and do the same trip back, starting out at 4 A.M. to be in time for morning roll call. At the time it seemed a perfectly natural thing to do and skidding four hours through the snow never deterred any of us.

It was at that time, starting in mid-February, that the Germans began launching their V1 and V2 missiles on London, and, occasionally, on Antwerp and Brussels. V1, known as doodle bugs, were unnerving little bastards; you knew that once the engine cut out, the thing was coming down, and the engine always seemed to stop right on top of you. On one particular occasion, I recall diving into some passageway, only to have another horizontal body literally passing underneath me. I landed right on top of Brigadier General Harvey—

superior officers presumably have superior reflexes. The bomb landed
miles away. V2 rockets were something else; if you heard them, you
were all right. Not everyone heard them, however; one of those
supersonic monsters hit a movie house in Antwerp and Third RTR
lost quite a few men.

There were happier visitations. Marlene Dietrich suddenly turned
up one night in our Poperinghe mess, on her way to American troops
nearby. There she was, a living legend, leaning against the bar in
black jodhpurs, riding boots, and a man's white shirt, looking about
thirty and absolutely stunning. While we were falling over each other
acting hospitable, she and Teddy Mitford discussed arcane recipes,
both being ardent amateur cooks. In the middle of all this, Barry
Peerless, duty officer for the night, came in to warm up and for a quick
drink, and was duly introduced by Teddy Mitford. La Dietrich really
did her thing; leaning against the bar rail, she must have looked at
Barry for a full ten seconds in total silence and then said in that
million-dollar voice of hers, "Ah, (pause) and how are you (long pause)
young man?" Barry—who anyway was the blushingest man I ever
saw—was crimson and catatonic. I saw him later, standing in the
snow. "She spoke to me," is all he was able to say. Dietrich, in her day,
had that effect, and not just on Barry. . . .

# 11

Our lotus days in "Pop" were clearly coming to an end; in mid-March
we moved to Aerschot to rejoin the remainder of Twenty-first Army
Group, a huge assembly of men and weapons that Montgomery had
gathered to force the Rhine.

Shortly after our arrival, Monty himself addressed us and a
number of other tank regiments and, in his cocky, self-assured, and
nasal way, outlined just how he was going to knock the Germans for
six. Even to a cricket enthusiast, war is not cricket, and Monty was
just being his irritating self. To be fair, he could not have found favor
with RTR people even if he had promised instant peace followed by
three years of paid leave. While in the desert, Montgomery got into
the habit of wearing a black beret, with an RTR badge alongside his

general's insignia, which RTR people found as laughable as if he had worn a tutu.

We did cross the Rhine on March 27, Monty having made sure that the RAF and artillery had pounded everything to dust—a scene, as Gibbon would have said, easier to deplore than to describe.

The crossing over pontoon bridges was wholly without incident, except for Churchill appearing (just as Twenty-third Hussars were putting over the tanks) and supposedly insisting on peeing into their Rhine. We did see him stand there, but we only saw him from the waist up.

The Germans kept fighting right up to the last days in April, and there was no real collapse of resistance until we crossed the Elbe. All along the pattern went "tank coming round corner—88 mm opening up—tank burning—next tank forward—infantry mopping up woods where 88 was," none of it headline news stuff, but all of it nasty and costing lives. The reason I am writing more about this penny-ante war in Germany than about that "big picture" war in Normandy the previous year is precisely because so much has already been said about the one and so little about the other. You can get just as hurt by one man as by an entire division.

Our advance line ran roughly straight north, and in that part of Germany, most waterways run from east to west, so the Germans had a series of natural defense lines and tried to make full use of them. It was a one-sided contest since the Allies had overwhelming air superiority; but wherever there were no planes to help out, we still had to go toe-to-toe. The first time it got lively, appropriately on April Fool's Day, was in forcing the Weser-Ems Canal. The Germans had dug up a few surviving dive bombers, which made first laying and then crossing pontoon bridges both noisy and uncomfortable. Except for a direct hit, high explosive shells cannot do much damage to a tank or its crew, but they are a nuisance. Once over the canal and while crossing a rather marshy meadow to head for a nearby wood and thick shelter, I misread the ground directly ahead and, ordering a tight turn, got one side of the tank bogged and threw a track. That is not fatal, just wearisome. You picked some extra track links off the back of your tank and, at the cost of a lot of heaving, swearing, incipient hernias, sweat, lost tempers, and broken fingernails, you spliced the whole thing together again. That is what it says in the manual and that is what we were about to do when a couple of German fighter planes came out of nowhere and opened up on us with machine guns. The five of us skipped smartly to the rear of the tank to find cover, and the planes went into a tight turn and came at us from the rear. So we hopped round the front, and they seemingly entered into the spirit of things, turned around, and came from the front. Meanwhile half of A Squadron, all safely tucked away in the woods, had come out of their tanks and were standing at the woods' edge, having hysterics. This must have gone on for five minutes or so till the Germans lost interest; not before we had lost both breath and temper, though.

After everyone calmed down or stopped laughing, we got the track fixed.

A couple of days after that, once again in drenching rain and depth of night, Third RTR took Osnabrueck by a combination of luck and poor map reading. We had managed to get lost in the woods and were trying to navigate ourselves back to the main road, which ultimately was supposed to get us to Osnabrueck. At a crossroad, in the middle of nowhere, I hit a mine, which took out my tank but fortunately none of my crew. In such a case, a tank crew is supposed to go back to rear echelon and try to find another tank, whereas any officer so involved is supposed to commandeer the nearest tank and take command.

This I proceeded to do, only to find that the nearest tank rattling through the night was the squadron commander's. Since, unlike the subways, a tank column running nose-to-tail is not really conducive to transfer travel, I had no option but to hang on. Literally, as it happened; the tank was of course full, and its back was crawling with infantry, so the only place left was to stick to the turret like a piece of gum. It was not only very damp, but bloody dangerous; you had to be a human yo-yo to avoid being decapitated by the odd tree branch. To add insult to injury, running into that mine had caused a truly cretinous display of "conditioned reflex." Ever since Sandhurst, we knew that it was an iron rule that an officer goes nowhere, not even to his Maker, without his map case; never mind why, you just didn't! A couple of hours earlier, we had had a short altercation with a small SS unit, which had resulted in no casualties on our side and my "finding" a latest model Leica camera. I had been the proud, if not lawful, owner for about an hour when we hit that stupid mine. The stupid tank started burning, and I, even more stupidly, bailed out plus map case but minus the Leica.

By the time I remembered the camera, the whole turret was glowing like a traffic light. No good deed goes unpunished; I never "found" quite as good a Leica again.

The road that supposedly led to somewhere near Osnabrueck, actually ended in front of Osnabrueck Central Station and so did we, to our total surprise and Pip Robert's congratulations. I recall Osnabrueck as a semi-deserted and burning shambles and as the place where Peter Elstob proved that eccentricity is a gift!

We certainly felt and were grubby, but I do not recall why Peter convinced me that this was the time and place to have a bath. The hindrance to our getting one was the reported "werewolf" movement, a wholly absurd myth invented in Eisenhower's entourage, whereby German grandmothers were hiding grenades in their camisoles and even toddlers might carry plastic explosive in their diapers. None of us had ever seen or heard of a werewolf, not even a cub, but we were still suspicious. Peter solved our dilemma in sovereign fashion. While the rest of our two crews were brewing tea (a tank crew invariably brews tea when not in immediate and mortal peril, but sometimes even then), he and I marched into the nearest house, routed the inhabitants from the cellar, ordered them up to the bathroom, and filled the tub. There was a father, mother, and two kids, and it might have been more sensible to lock them into a room, but it did not occur to us at the time. Instead, we both undressed, and while I scrubbed Peter's back, he kept the family at pistol point, and then he scrubbed me down while I pointed the pistol. Imagination boggles at what those four must have thought of us. By the time we came out of the house, tea was ready. Peter, ever inventive, left Osnabrueck with a wire cage fastened to the rear platform of his tank and six chickens in it. We cut Teddy Mitford in on the egg supply, so he did not mind, and within a few days most Third RTR tanks looked like miniature farmsteads, with chicken, hams, and sausages festooned all around the turrets and spare tracks. It never seemed to interfere with the fighting ability of the tank. Peter's tank got caught by a bazooka a week or so later, but being Peter, he grabbed the chicken and left the map case; that is why he did not want to be an officer, I guess.

You are very much mistaken if you believe that the British never looted. It is true that, somewhat like the Russians, they never looted very intelligently, whereas the Americans and French, with eventual retirement in mind, tended to be impressive thieves, but items like food, drink, and the odd trinkets for girlfriends were invariably taken, and there was also a good deal of wanton destruction, just for the sheer hell of it. In that respect the British and Americans resembled each other, smashing things in a spirit of good-natured mindlessness, whereas the Russians and French were openly retributive in doing so. Whatever the motives or reasons, all four nationalities burned, smashed, and looted their way through Germany; the only difference was that only the Russians ever molested civilians. Once they were disarmed, we just ignored men in uniform; there were too many of them and anyway we had no disposal instructions of any kind. Quite a few just went home, but being used to discipline and good order, most of them marched themselves to whichever POW camp they could find in the neighborhood. That was the strange part about them; once the Germans stopped fighting, they mostly appeared aimless, disoriented, and submissive. But a mile up the road you would hit another bunch who still had weapons and someone to command them, and you would again have a real fight on your hands.

Moving up to the Aller, the next river line, we lost John Watts, and being a captain by that time, I temporarily took over command of A Squadron and did the best I could for the next month or so. At the Aller that was not particularly good, though not unfunny. A Squadron was lead squadron—for the 500th time, or so it seemed—and we got two troops across the river before the Germans blew the only bridge. The Aller was about one hundred and fifty feet wide at that stretch, there were thick woods on both river banks, and it was getting dark. I happened to be among the eight tanks gathered on the far side and was ordered by Teddy Mitford to stay put, and he would

arrange for something in the morning; whether that would be reinforcements or a burial party was not clear. So we went into "hedgehog
formation," all hatches closed, and spent a rather noisy night under
mortar and machine gun fire and, occasionally, some light shelling;
there were evidently no German tanks around, so it was all more of a
nuisance than a peril. It ended at first light with someone banging on
one of the tank turrets and yelling, "Come out; it's safe," which did
not exactly make us feel like John Wayne, particularly since we
should have shot whoever it was while they were approaching
us–and would have if we had not been so sleepy!

As it turned out, the situation had a Hollywood touch to it after
all; shortly before dawn, Brigade had put a company of Commandos
across the river upstream in rubber dinghies, who had circled round
the German positions from the rear and had attacked, using knives
and strangling wires only. There now seemed to be a strangled or
knifed German behind every second tree; it is a wonder they did not
scalp them.

The sequel to the Aller episode came some two weeks later
when one of my crew members reported a case of gonorrhea. Men
were supposed to inform their officers when they had been infected
and where, though I never found out what the officer was supposed
to do beyond commiserating. In this case the locus of the occurrence was both clear and improbable. Trooper Armstrong had left
the tank during that night across the Aller, while all hell was
breaking loose, to find a convenient bush. An understandable,
though foolhardy urge. Somewhere in the dark he had met a "female
person" (his deposition) whom he took to be a Displaced Person,
which seemed an apt assumption under the circumstances. Trooper
Armstrong and this female person, notwithstanding shot and shell,
got to know each other in a biblical sense, and here he was,
reporting sick. No cross examination would shake this unlikely tale,
and it was agreed by all that this was a quite extraordinary display of
determination under fire. From there, it took just a few drinks to
convince ourselves that Armstrong should be recommended for a
medal, and that same night the recommendation went up to Brigade
and Division, countersigned by Teddy Mitford. Harvey at Brigade
and Roberts at Division, being the people they were, thought it

absolutely hilarious, once they knew the facts, and lent their support, so that by the time the document moved on to Army, we had convinced ourselves and everyone in sight that Armstrong was a thoroughly deserving case and the award a foregone conclusion. When a call came from Army Group for some supplementary details, I drove back the thirty miles or so (Army Group was getting quite venturesome; the war was almost over) and unfolded the entire and clearly splendid tale to some marvelously elegant and stupefyingly stuffy staff major.

He did not think it funny at all, no indeed; he listened to it all stony-faced and then tore up the recommendation. Poor Armstrong got VD and nothing else; there is no justice.

The morning after the Aller brouhaha, on April 12, we heard of Roosevelt's death, a shattering piece of news. During a war, and particularly while in combat, your horizon tends to narrow considerably, and politics was, in any case, not among Third RTR's preferred topics of discussion, but Roosevelt was very special. He had been around almost forever, he was idolized in England; he was part of one's family. In all these years, time and time again, we all had heard that patrician, Harvard-accented voice over the radio—"they have asked for arms and we shall give them arms, they have asked for ships and we shall give them ships"—we just knew that he was behind us and that, in the end, things would be all right. His had been one of the two clarion calls that had kept everyone hoping and moving forward; his and of course Winston's. No one who heard Churchill will ever forget that lisping, slurred, menacing growl and the raging challenges of that voice. When Cicero ended his orations, people said, "How well he spoke," but when Demosthenes finished speaking, people shouted: "Let us march!" Who ever heard "we shall fight on the beaches, we shall fight in the fields, we shall fight in the streets, we shall never surrender" had heard Demosthenes. Churchill sustained and saved England, there is not a doubt about it. But he could not have done it and we would not have been here without FDR. All these thoughts went through my mind that morning. "There is no armor against fate; death lays his icy hand on kings. . . ." There are moments when time stands still and every detail remains etched in your mind.

It was early morning, we had lined up the tanks and were sitting by the roadside ditch, brewing tea as usual. One or two tanks were keeping a wireless watch by staying in contact with regimental HQ, but most of the others had run out an extension cable from the turret and were listening to the BBC, a habit that the army deplored, but tolerated. I remember the sudden and total silence at the announcement and then several men sobbing; it seemed wholly natural that they would. Most of all I remember that I was sitting not ten feet away from a dead German lying in the ditch, and here I was mourning a man I had never seen, and I had no emotional response at all to a dead fellow human being right in front of me. The bell tolls differently for different people.

It always surprised me that even disguised civilians such as we were (Teddy Mitford and a few others were the only professional soldiers among us) rapidly became very unemotional about the Germans. Except in rare instances, such as when Davis Silvertopp got bushwhacked, no one ever displayed active anger or hostility, let alone hatred towards them. They frequently irritated you and often scared you, but all you were doing was your job, which was trying to take territory and kill them, and they were doing theirs, which was to hold territory and kill you. There was no sense of chivalry as there was in the desert, or at least as it appeared in Third RTR's memories of it, but there was a total absence of hatred or even dislike. As a German Jew, I should have felt differently, but I did not and still do not. I fought and killed Germans, and they often frightened me, but I did not dislike them; I often respected them. Fighting soldiers are not far removed from the mentality of professional mercenaries. Flag-waving patriots are few and far between where there is shooting, and they usually do not live long; real haters stay home or at base camps.

It is true that I have an altogether maverick reaction to Germans; come the Day of Judgment I will probably still think that Germany and Germans is where somehow I "belong" and that everywhere else was an *ubi bene, ibi patria* alternative. I have been enthusiastically and happily *bene* in many places, Cheltenham, Cambridge, England, Holland, and, more than anywhere else, the United States, and so, in the end, might claim truly to be *civis mundi* which is what I would like to be.

April 16, my twenty-fifth birthday, started as low comedy and ended in stark horror, though, strictly speaking, that came the next day. We started the morning with tea, laced with Steinhaeger (a local variant of Schnapps; it tasted like mouthwash and left you with a head like cracked cement, but it was plentiful), and feeling suitably benign, I led my lot up a little slope, and the whole squadron settled "hull down" to look around. Tanks should be "hull down" whenever possible; it just means that they only show their gun and upper turret and have found cover for the remainder of the vehicle. There you are, now you are an expert.

Looking over the ridge, we spotted a wide meadow leading down to a small stream, which was perhaps thirty feet across, and a blown bridge. Across the stream were some twenty houses, hardly a village, and nothing except fields and wood beyond; not a soul, not a sound, very idyllic. Even so, you do not just run a bunch of tanks across open meadows without making sure that really no one is going to bother you; any such interference would come from the village, and someone had better find out. The Steinhaeger must have made me do it: first I volunteered to have a look, then I decided to do so on foot, and lastly, since there was water but no bridge, to do so *au naturel*. Wearing nothing but a silly grin and a haltered pistol round my neck, I trotted down the meadow, waded a waist-high stream and ran briskly round the village, dripping wet and naked as a baby.

It was not so much fear that made me rush, but the fact that April 16 is not yet summer. Having sprinted once round the place, to the accompaniment of vulgar hilarity up on the ridge, I waded back across and up the meadow, declared the place untenanted, put on some clothes, and we were ready to move. While I was capering around bare-assed, however, orders had been received to swing off to a flank, so we saw no more of that silent and somnolent village. An infantry unit moving to it later that morning saw plenty. There were apparently several scores of Germans, well camouflaged in cellars and on rooftops, and there was a small pitched battle with quite a few casualties before the village was as quiet as I had thought it to be. Like good soldiers, the Germans had clearly opted to ignore one naked nut, in favor of waiting for someone more substantial to pick a fight with. The "Reiter ueber den Bodensee"†—sensation is now old hat to me . . .

Our new orders tied in with some puzzling rumors we had picked up over the divisional wireless net (when not listening to the BBC, we used to eavesdrop on our lords and masters way back in the rear, which was not encouraged either); Army Corps appeared to be talking to some high-ranking SS people and even Monty was supposedly involved. We had no idea what was being talked about, but we were now moving east instead of north as we should have been. The answer came that afternoon. Twenty-third Hussars, just next to us, had been contacted by some SS officers under a flag of truce, who explained that about ten miles further north, stretching right across their and our advance line, lay a large German detention camp riddled with typhus. Fighting over the area would result in typhus spreading to both sides, and they therefore proposed a twenty-four-hour truce during which the German troops would withdraw to a predetermined line well north of the camp, we would move through the area, and fighting would resume at noon the following day. Shades of Fontenoy. As Faulkner said, the past is not dead, it is not even past. The proposal was so outlandish that it was clearly beyond divisional competence, hence the rumors about Montgomery, who may well have been involved, not least because he was an incurably nosy general. Looking back, it puzzles me why that truce was agreed to since no one believed the story about a typhus-ridden camp, and speculation about what it really was ranged from underground poison-gas factories to rocket sites, in any event, something unpleasant, and why would the Germans give up territory for any reason? However they clearly did persuade some august authority, so we were

---

†"The Rider over the Bodensee" is a famous German ballad wherein a medieval knight rides in deep winter through a blinding snowstorm in search of the Bodensee (Lake Constance, on the German/Swiss border) and at last sees a farmhouse. He knocks and an old crone opens the door. He asks her how to get to the Bodensee, and she says "You have just ridden over it." He stares at her in disbelief and then drops dead off his horse, in the shock of realization. So one refers to the "Rider over the Bodensee" syndrome when by sheer blind luck and ignorance catastrophe has been avoided.

ordered to leaguer on a predetermined line, move right through the putative camp at first light, and be ready and in position to fight again at noon.

The camp, however, was not putative, it was Bergen-Belsen. I doubt that anyone knew that it was there, except people in the immediate vicinity. The whole question of camps and the average German's knowledge of them is too complex to deal with here. Among German refugees in pre-war England, I had heard occasional references to Oranienburg, Buchenwald or Dachau as concentration camps in Germany, where Jews were being detained, maltreated and sometimes killed. I had never heard of Auschwitz, Maidaneck, Treblinka or any of the "death camps" in former Poland, where genocide was taking place. None of my English friends ever mentioned anything about camps; no one I ever met in the Army ever did; I do not know whether it was lack of knowledge or lack of interest.

I am therefore not qualified to guess, let alone judge, when or whether the average German citizen could or should have known, and, more importantly, could or should have reacted. Bergen-Belsen—which none of us had ever heard of—was, as we heard much later, never meant to be the terrible place it became. Grotesque as it now sounds, it was originally intended as a "rehabilitation center" for detainees of other camps, who had by some providential means, obtained their release but whom the German authorities did not want to re-appear in public in the shape they were in. They were to be held in Belsen while being fed back into some semblance of health. After the outbreak of war, there were no more releases anywhere, and Belsen became a concentration camp similar to Dachau, Buchenwald and other camps located in Germany, where people died from disease, starvation and the malignant cruelty of guards, but not as automatically doomed victims of a vast system of genocide, as was the case in the extermination camps in the east.

In the final weeks of the war, lack of food and unchecked typhus and other epidemics did turn Bergen-Belsen into the place we saw.

We drove up and into Belsen at dawn; my tanks were the first through the gates, and we were under orders to keep moving as fast as possible and not to dismount for any reason; troops behind us were supposed to take care of whatever required attention. We certainly did not leave our tanks, but it was impossible to move fast through one huge charnel house, with hundreds of skeletal figures lying and crawling everywhere; we went through Belsen at a snail's pace, a vision of unimaginable horror. So much so that to this day I cannot describe it. To see the "heart of darkness" does not mean you absorb what you see; some of it I still shut out.

We must have been in Belsen for no more than an hour; an eternity . . .

Promptly at noon, the war started again and with us well in time for it. Within the hour I lost my tank and two men of my crew to a bazooka and, by the way of a belated birthday present, spent two days in a hospital being treated for some fairly spectacular but quite innocuous burns. It was a nunnery, temporarily converted into a field hospital, and virtually my entire treatment consisted of learning how to knit. The other choice of occupational therapy was to read the Bible, but knitting seemed less taxing. It actually is not very complicated and immensely restful. I started out on socks, but since I only spent a couple of days with those kindly nuns, I never learned how to knit a heel; I remained a "straight line" knitter and by now am no longer even that.

Third RTR was racing through the Lueneburger Heath, when I rejoined it, and we were going as fast as we could, surrounded by fleeing deer, crashing trees, and ear-splitting explosions. The Germans had turned Lueneburger Heath into one vast ammunition depot, and dry weather, and some careless shooting on our part, had set a good part of the countryside on fire; it was not a place for loitering. We spent half a day dodging or charging through flames and saw more deer than we ever believed existed, including some real Monarch of the Glen specimens. The region had always been full of wildlife and no one had pursued it for years; after the war ended, we did a good deal of untidy hunting in the area. That day it looked like a scene out of *Fantasia*.

We were approaching the Elbe, the last great water obstacle separating us from Hamburg, Luebeck, the Danish border, and effectively the end of the fighting war. "We" meant Eleventh Armored Division and Sixth Airborne Division, the two spearhead formations that had led the British forces ever since the Rhine crossing, and who were constantly competing for being "firstest." It was a perfectly absurd ambition, but war is a perfectly absurd undertaking. Talleyrand said about the shooting of the Duke d'Enghien, "C'est pire qu'un crime, c'est une erreur,"† and that sentiment should be chiselled in granite over every military barracks.

We had expected sustained fighting in trying to cross the Elbe but encountered no resistance to speak of, so we kept on rushing helterskelter northwards, never in any "headline" situation, but consistently losing a tank here, two or three men there. It sounds insignificant, and doubtless was to all those global strategists, but it made us both unhappy and nervous. Not all the time though. There was a rousing little interlude in Pinneberg, a township close to Hamburg, where we tangled with some German paratroopers and, one thing leading to another, ended up joining our infantry on foot in an old-fashioned house-to-house hoedown. It was just like battle camp in Wales, only noisier; I recall it as hugely enjoyable, which just shows you how weird we had all become. On this particular occasion about half a dozen of us ended up in the vault of the local bank, literally knee-deep in bundled bank notes, enough money to buy Las Vegas (then, not now). As senior officer on the spot, I was asked by my fellow warriors whether it would be worthwhile to take some bundles along. Morality did not unduly burden any of us, but I advised against taking the trouble, since the deutschmark would without a doubt be totally devalued; and so it was—more than six months later! A couple of my guys, clearly skeptical of what any officer said at any time, grabbed an armful of bundles nonetheless and probably think of Germany as a land of opportunity to this day.

## 12

The war was beginning to unravel quite quickly, to wit Jock Sterling and the paper delivery. By now the usual procedure was no longer to leaguer in the open, but to requisition some nearby houses, round up the inhabitants, and lock them into the cellars with enough food, drink, fear of God and of us, to last them until we moved on next day. We had done so in some village north of Hamburg (Hamburg itself

---

†"It's worse than a crime, it's a mistake."

was a Sixth Airborne objective and not on our attack axis) when we were visited by the storied "Jock" Stirling, commanding First SAS. Special Air Services were even then the most secretive of all those "off the record" outfits; no one knew what they were doing, how, or where—or why, for that matter. They had an almost mythical reputation of being a bunch of cutthroats with public school educations (a very plausible combination), and their commander, Jock Stirling, was credited with deeds that made later James Bond movies wholly redundant. Here he was, in full Western Desert regalia (people in outfits like SAS live in a constant time warp; he could have turned up as Richard the LionHeart), accompanied by his driver and one of the equally legendary SAS jeeps. These were reputedly nothing more than an aircraft engine mounted on four wheels, with a heavy machine gun bolted to each side. Looking at Jock's there certainly seemed nothing else, no doors, no windscreen, no seats to speak of. Colonel Stirling (three DSO's, three MC's and on and on), a gigantic Scot with an awesome capacity for liquor and an uncertain temper—a very volatile mixture if you add the weaponry—insisted that he could drive all the way to Luebeck and back, a one-hundred-and-fifty-mile round trip, unimpeded by the entire German army still milling about in the area. You do not argue with an SAS colonel, even when he is sober, nor when he insists that we all bet fifty pounds that he could not do it. So we bet fifty pounds and he did it; he was gone for about four hours and in return for those fifty pounds told us the way to travel—SAS fashion. You come up to any locality as quietly as possible, preferably in poor light, then go tearing through the village, town, or whatever, all guns blazing, horn blaring, and out at the other end with the gas pedal to the floor, before any of the locals have gotten their act together. Next place, same procedure; but pick a different route for your return trip, along the lines of the old Bulgarian proverb, "Never steal twice from the same hen coop." The concept had an air of Bulgarian unreliability to it in our view, but it worked for Stirling that time—he brought us that day's Luebeck paper to prove it. It subsequently took us ten days to cover the same distance.

During that period also, I found the bedroom with the black satin sheets. We had ended up at a very large park and villa, ample enough to house the whole squadron, and having locked the castellan of this spread and sundry servants into the cellar, we had drawn lots for the master bedroom, and I got it. Cecil B. de Mille would have approved of it: black satin sheets, canopy over the bed, bed standing on raised pedestal. He might have been more critical of the fact that, dog-tired as I was, I fell into this cradle of sin with my overalls and boots on. Next thing I knew, the lady of the house, a buxom Gretchen type, shook me awake; she probably had a spare key to the cellar. I kept on dozing off while she embarked on some complicated story involving the approaching Russians, the nameless horrors they committed (she named some), and her desire to avoid such inconveniences. After a while—it had been a long day—it dawned on me that she was indicating her readiness to suffer now the indignities she wished to deny to the Mongolian hordes, so—it really had been a very long day—I told her that the person to talk to was next door and fell asleep again. The person next door, it turned out, was my wireless operator, a dour and taciturn Scot. When I saw him next morning he inquired after the reason for this nocturnal visitation (since he spoke no German and barely any English, Gretchen's message may not have been quite clear to him), listened to my story, and then said solemnly (the Scots tend to be solemn when it comes to drink, women, or fighting), "Verra thoughtful of you, Sor; much obliged." The Russians never came that way, and virtue is its own reward.

While nearing Neustadt, a small town north of Hamburg, the "telephone caper" occurred to Teddy Mitford. He had come across some engineering unit restringing telephone wires who had told him that they had, quite by accident, tapped into the Neustadt Exchange a few miles up the road. He summoned me to join him, since I was the only German speaker in Third RTR, and suggested I try to phone the Neustadt garrison and talk them into surrendering, rather than put everyone to the trouble of fighting for it. I do not believe, incidentally, that anyone in Third RTR ever knew exactly where I came from; no one asked, I did not tell, and the Tank Corps was more likely to read *Beowulf* in the original than look at Pioneer Corps records.

I got hooked into the line, asked for the Neustadt commandant, and promptly got put through to him. After that it became pure farce.

Pitching my voice somewhere between Erich von Stroheim and Dr. Anthony, I outlined a scenario of hundreds of tanks, clouds of planes, and swarms of paratroopers, all bunched down the road for the declared purpose of obliterating Neustadt. The party at the opposite end, hearing of this imaginary Armageddon, clearly felt that Neustadt hardly warranted so much attention, and politely inquired what we wished him to do. On being told to fly white flags, sheets or whatever, from every building, assemble all his troops on the main square, men on one side, arms on the other, and do it all within ten minutes, he appeared to view that as an eminently sensible suggestion, provided he be allowed to phone his superiors to advise them that he was retiring from this war. Since Teddy and I imagined the entire conversation to be just a slightly inane interlude between fights, I in turn agreed, and our regiment then proceeded to move on to Neustadt in the usual cautious fashion, lead tank round the corner, have a look, move up the rest, lead tank forward again, and so on, until the lead tank reported Neustadt in sight and a sea of white flags everywhere! Weapons and men had been disposed of as instructed, and recovering from first being surprised and then hysterical, we decided that this was clearly a more fun way to fight the war, and I set off for the Rathaus to find another phone and another city. In the Rathaus I found the mayor in his office, and not only him, but his wife and two teenage children as well, all lying stiff, still, and dead, having taken potassium cyanide. It was the first time I had come across such a sight—though not the last. He was not, as we later found, a particularly active Nazi and certainly no war criminal. The suicide puzzled us, but those were not times when even such ghoulish sights left much impression. I recall, many months later, talking to a German politician in Kiel about the incident and our reaction to it, and I remember him commenting, "Manchmal ist es schwer, ein Mensch zu sein."† I do not know whether he meant the mayor or me.

The next place to phone into submission was obviously Neumuenster, thirty miles away, the main county seat of the area and a town of about fifty thousand people. I got an immediate connection, was put through to the adjutant of General von Wesselink, Officer Commanding Neumuenster District, and was about to describe the

---

†"There are times when it is hard to be a Mensch"—now it is up to you to translate Mensch!

immensity of the threat overhanging Neumuenster and everyone in it when the adjutant briskly told me they had already been informed. General von W. wished to avoid unnecessary bloodshed and wished to hand over Neumuenster and his command to an "authorized negotiator," whom he and the adjutant would meet under a flag of truce on the main road halfway between Neustadt and Neumuenster. It was not clear to Teddy or me whether the Germans were having us on, or whether, efficient as always, they had already turned telephone surrender into a systematized military procedure. No way to know except by finding out, so I climbed into my "dhingo" scout car (there was one allocated to every squadron; arguably the ugliest and least comfortable vehicle ever devised, but could it move!) and set off as the "authorized negotiator." Sure enough, at a crossroads some fifteen miles further stood a large, open, black Mercedes, flying the pennant of a German lieutenant-general on one side and a white flag on the other, with two ramrod-stiff drivers in front and a gaunt, tall, haggard-looking general in the back, with a major by his side. The two of them got out, I got out, and there was a whole minuet of salutes, stiff handshakes, eye contact, more salutes—just as you have seen in the movies! Wesselink wore the mandatory Knight's Cross and monocle, but also long pants and he carried a stick (he had lost a leg commanding an infantry division in Russia, as I found out). His adjutant, however, was straight out of central casting, complete with duelling scars, Knight's Cross and Oak Leaves, and jack-boots which required sunglasses for close inspection.

My outfit, though equally striking, was somewhat more arcane: oil-stained, greenish overalls, a very threadbare black beret (earphones are hard on the ears, but ruinous on berets), fleece-lined brown RAF boots, and a red silk scarf.

It was agreed that they would follow me back to Neustadt to discuss formal arrangements; when we arrived, we found not only Teddy, but also Pip Roberts, the divisional commander, whom Teddy had alerted to witness Third RTR's latest toy. Wesselink clearly was unsure of what to make of this trio, all of whom wore similarly dirty overalls, none of whom wore any insignia of rank, and who, in the case of Pip, looked about age sixteen and small for his age. What probably put him at ease was Teddy Mitford, who wore a Sulka scarf, offered cigarettes from a gold case, and could display aristocratic detachment that would cow a grand duke. We agreed that Wesselink would return to Neumuenster to arrange for an "orderly surrender" of some ten thousand men under this command, and that Third RTR, followed by the rest of the division, would move to Neumuenster the following day. Wesselink suggested that one of us should accompany him back, and when it came to language skills and expendability, guess who? So, shortly after lunch, we set off again, this time in Wesselink's Mercedes, and I was in a real uniform for the first time since Poperinghe. On the way to Neumuenster, making some stilted though not unfriendly conversation, Wesselink seemed eminently correct, very Prussian, a bit stuffy, not unlikable; his adjutant was never asked to speak, so he never did. Suddenly the car came to a screeching halt and the drivers shouted: "Achtung! Flieger!" Wesselink, adjutant, and both drivers went scrambling for the nearest ditch, bad leg, stick, gleaming boots, scars, and all. Secure in the knowledge that any plane in the neighborhood would be ours, I remained seated—till it occurred to me that I was sitting in a black Mercedes. I just made it to the ditch before the first rocket-firing Typhoon came howling down the road.

There were two of them; they both missed and, having set the adjoining wood on fire, did not bother to try a second pass. So back we clambered into the car andthe beginning of a memorable afternoon.

One of the minor chances Hitler overlooked to win the war was the use of the Heinkel 262 jet fighter, the first operational jet plane developed anywhere, which flew at least twice as fast as any conventional plane the Allies had in the air. Hitler had never authorized full production of this extraordinary plane, which he could have done at any time after 1943, and only in the very last weeks of the war were some spotted in the air at all. We had seen them once or twice, with squat, small, stubby wings, rather fat-bellied, and so blindingly fast and making such a whooshing noise that we had taken them for some variant of a VI, particularly since they never came by twice, probably due to a very limited action radius. I was due to find out a little more about HE 262 that afternoon.

Just before reaching the outskirts of Neumuenster, Wesselink pointed to an airfield a mile or so away and indicated that the Luftwaffe did not fall under his jurisdiction and any arrangements made by him would not be binding on the Luftwaffe commander. The

Neustadt euphoria had not yet worn off, and I promptly suggested to Wesselink that he drop me off at the airfield; I would settle matters, and Wesselink's driver could pick me up again in half an hour to take me to "downtown" Neumuenster. The moment I walked into that Luftwaffe HQ, I wished I had not. The place was crawling with young pilots, all looking alike: blond, in their early twenties, almost every one wearing his Knight's Cross, all fighter pilots and looking cocky as hell and about as likely to surrender as to wear a yarmulke. Upon asking to be taken to their leader (what other formula would you have suggested?), first nothing at all happened, and then, after a long silence, someone asked "Warum?" a reasonable enough query since it was quite evident they had heard of no surrender, nor seemed likely to listen to such a suggestion. I was about to embark on my increasingly unconvincing *Muenchhausen* story when a door opened and everyone froze to attention. Out came a strikingly good-looking, dark-complexioned man in his mid-thirties, in an immaculate uniform, and for the first and last time I saw someone wearing almost the ultimate thing: Knight's Cross with Oakleaves and Crossed Swords! This certified hero looked at me and said in accent-free English, "My name is Oberst von Bomgard. Come with me."

A moment later I stood in Bomgard's office, with several of his officers crowding around, whether as honor guard or potential prison escort depended on how you gauged the situation. Bomgard listened in silence to my brief review of our negotiations with Wesselink and their outcome, thought it over for a moment, and said, again in perfect English, "General Wesselink must take his responsibilities. I must take mine. I do not wish to negotiate." Then, totally ignoring me, he turned to one of his officers and said, "Alle Geschwader startklar. Abflug in zehn Minuten,"† and the man disappeared as through a trap door. Just then Bomgard's phone rang and listening to Bomgard's end of the conversation, this is how it went (everything connected with the Neumuenster episode was so extraordinary that I made verbatim notes right afterwards so can really recall everything that was said): "Ja, Herr General, habe es gerade selbst

---

† "All formations ready to start. Take-off in ten minutes."

gehoert. . . . Einer von ihnen ist hier bei mir. . . . Nein, habe nicht die Absicht. . . . Nein, nein, ich fliege aus. . . . Ja, in 5 Minuten. . . . Ja, Stavanger, war auch mein Idee. . . . Nein, glaube nicht dass der was tut. . . . Danke, Herr General."†

He then turned to me and said in his BBC English, "You understood what I said, of course. We leave for Norway. I shall leave you now." As he was walking to the door, one of his minions said, "Eigentlich sollte man den mitnehmen‡ (it had occurred to me that that thought might occur to them), whereupon Bomgard said icily, "Seien Sie nicht so bloed; Krieg ist kein Indianerspiel"* On reaching the door, he turned and formally saluted me; shades of Conrad Veidt! The entire blond horde followed him, and since Bomgard was clearly the lodestar of their young lives, each one of them stopped at the door, turned, and gave me a rigid salute as well. Moments later I was standing alone in Bomgard's office and, looking through the window, saw the whole airfield crowded with planes, all warming up and beginning to turn onto the runway. Every last one was an HE 262, perhaps thirty altogether, and quite possibly all the jets the Luftwaffe still had. Very shortly afterwards, the whole lot was airborne. I heard later that they duly surrendered in Stavanger the following week. They must have refuelled in various places, since Stavanger is a long way from Neumuenster, but that was Bomgard's problem, not mine.

Meanwhile, back on the ground, a very senior Luftwaffe NCO came to a crashing salute in Bomgard's office and reported that, on instructions of Oberst von Bomgard, he and all other ground personnel were to place themselves under General von Wesselink's orders and surrender to us.

It seemed a good deal longer than half an hour since I last saw that black Mercedes, but there it was, at the door—

---

†"Yes, General, I just heard it myself. . . . One of them is with me now. . . . No, I don't intend to. . . . No, no, I've ordered take-off. . . . Yes, in five minutes. . . . Yes, Stavanger was my thought as well. . . . No, I don't think he'll do anything. . . . Thank you, General."

‡"We really should take him along with us."

*"Don't be stupid. War is not a game of cops-and-robbers."

I was driven to Wesselink's headquarters, surrounded by a constant flurry of salutes and clicking heels on the way. The car was flying Wesselink's pennant and any army will tell you to salute a bag of potatoes or a potted plant if it should happen to come by and if it carries a general's pennant. Incidentally, except for the Waffen SS and an occasional Luftwaffe member, I never saw anyone in the German forces give the Hitler salute; it is a ridiculous and tiring gesture and it had been a long war.

It became a totally unforgettable evening, capping a wholly unforgettable day. Wesselink's quarters were above his officer's mess, in a very handsome old villa just next to the main barracks, and I was shown to a simply, but impeccably furnished bedroom, complete with hovering batman and well-appointed bathroom, and informed that the general and his staff expected me downstairs for drinks at 6 P.M.; civilized wars are better than others! It was my first bath since Osnabrueck, and while I wallowed in the last remnants of Germany's wholesale loot of Europe (French bath salts, Norwegian pineneedle soap, Greek sponges), my stone-faced batman pressed my uniform and did things to my boots that had not been done to them since Sandhurst.

Coming down the stairs on the stroke of six (the military are the only people who are as manic about being on time as I am; not enough to create a real bond, though), I was met by Wesselink in full evening regalia, a profusion of red stripes, gold braid, ribbons, decorations, and stars, and he and I then marched down a line of about thirty officers, lined up strictly by seniority of rank. Wesselink would call out the officer's rank and name, who would then come to heel-clicking attention while I would raise a casual hand to my beret and try and look like a junior version of Louis XIV.

The drinks offered were an alcoholic map of Europe: French champagne, Dutch genever, Danish aquavit, Russian vodka; the dinner to follow was not exactly austere either. It made you wonder whether the Germans had engaged in military invasions or merely in culinary raids. The dining room was huge and undistinguished, except for the familiar faded rectangles on the walls. Since life-size pictures of Hitler and his henchmen were unlikely to thrill us, the Germans generally had plenty of time to take them off the walls. However, the only substitutes of similar "regulation" size were either pictures of Hindenburg or Kaiser Wilhelm, if they could still find them in the attic. Since there was some legitimate question as to whether that would make us happier, they generally just left the spaces blank; it sometimes made for a rather pretty geometric pattern.

Wesselink sat at the head of the table, and I on his right; the atmosphere started out cool and correct and became more animated with every succeeding glass; nothing like combat soldiers to indulge in hairy and hyperbolic tales, usually dealing with grotesque mismanagement rather than heroic deeds. I heard about awesome blunders everywhere from Murmansk to Monte Cassino and did my best to hold up the British Army's well-deserved reputation for studied incompetence. Wesselink, aside from being an attentive host and a surprisingly wide-ranging and articulate conversationalist, never once allowed the conversation to touch upon politics or any occurrence after the Normandy landings. Just before the end of the meal, he rapped his glass, looked around the totally silent table and said, "Meine Herren, kein Trinkspruch, nur ein Gedanke. Ich denke an alle Toten, in den Armeen, in den Zivilbevoelkerungen, bei den Kriegsgefangenen, in den Laegern, ueberall, in jedem Land. Wofuer sind sie gestorben? Meistens wissen wir es nicht. Und wo wir den Grund wissen, da war es kein guter Grund. In Deutschland nicht und nirgends. Meine Herren, wir muessen uns alle schaemen."†

Silence continued to be absolute; whether it indicated courtesy, contrition, disapproval, or bibulous coma was hard to tell. Wesselink then briefly outlined how he wanted matters handled the next day (disarmed troops assembled here, transport there, weapons in a third spot—it was all carried out to the letter and without a hitch), and then he dismissed everyone, but asked me to stay for some more coffee and brandy. We talked a little more about the surrender dispositions, and then he suddenly said, wholly out of context, "Das mit den

---

†"Gentlemen, no toast, just a thought. I am thinking of all the dead, in the armies, among civilians, among prisoners, in the camps, everywhere, in every country. Why did they die? Mostly we don't know the reason. Where we do know the reason, it was not a good reason. Not in Germany and not anywhere. Gentlemen, we must all be ashamed."

Laegern; man hat es gewusst und nichts getan."† I remember thinking that I was not at all sure what he was talking about; aside from
Belsen, we had neither seen nor heard of any camps. We talked a little
more about next day's technicalities, and then Wesselink asked my
views about the events of July 20, 1944, when Stauffenberg had
attempted to kill Hitler, but before I could make any comment,
(which would have been pretty trite, anyway), he came out with a
wonderful quotation from Schiller's *Wallenstein,* which I have never
forgotten: " 'Entworfen bloss ist's ein gemeiner Frevel, vollfuehrt ist's
ein unsterblich Unternehmen, und wenn es glueckt, so ist es auch
verziehen, denn aller Ausgang ist ein Gottesurteil.' "‡

He then got up, put out his hand and said cryptically, "Sie werden
es alles ja selbst bald sehen; Gute Nacht,"* and left.

At no time had Wesselink or any of the others commented on my
German, which clearly was as good as theirs. At the time it puzzled
me, but I was also never asked about it in all the subsequent time I
spent in Germany. Possibly people may have suspected the reason
and thought it indelicate or impossible to broach the subject. It is,
however, just as likely that it fitted right in with the Germans' truly
mythical concept of the capabilities and subtleties of the British
Secret Service. The suggestion that Hitler might in reality have been
a British agent might have met with some disbelief, but the concept
that a British agent might have lived in the middle of Berlin disguised
as a forty-foot German oak was well within the realm of possibility.

It has never been clear to me just what caused this dazzling
reputation of the British. Subsequently I had some exposure to one or
two Smileys, and to a lot of people who worked for assorted George
Smileys, and I am still not a converted believer. I can think of a
number of differences in the "tradecraft" (dreadful word; Le Carré
should have kept it to himself) of the various practitioners, but they

---

†"About those camps; one knew about them, but did nothing about it."

‡" 'In its mere conception, it is a base and blasphemous crime, but when ac-
complished, turns into immortal enterprise; and if successful is thereby forgiven,
for all things' outcome are God's judgment.' " It sounds much different when Schiller
says it.

*"You'll see it all for yourself soon; good night."

do not provide a real explanation. The Germans were organized and painstaking, the Americans had limitless equipment, funds, and enthusiasm but were poor analysts, the Russians had manpower, perserverance, and no analytic skills at all, and the French were subtle and intuitive but could not be bothered to gather facts. It is conceivable that the British mélange of humor, craftiness, self-deprecation, perfidy, luck, inspired guessing, amateurism, indolence, and almost four centuries of "having been at it" (ever since Walsingham and Queen Elizabeth) made them particularly suitable. Secrecy and deviousness tend to appeal to the British, the ability constantly to hide behind a bluff John Bull image being just one example, so maybe they are better at this game than others. Whatever the explanation, my ability to speak German the way I did was never once inquired about.

I slept as behooves a conquering hero, to be woken by that impassive batman, who informed me that both breakfast and car were waiting for me downstairs. When asked where I would meet Wesselink, that human robot looked as inanimate as before and said; "General von Wesselink hat sich gestern nacht erschossen."†

After I had gone to bed, Wesselink had evidently driven around to the various headquarters under his command to make sure that his orders were understood, then had gone upstairs, laid down on his bed, and shot himself with a silencer-fitted pistol. His batman had found him in the morning.

The surrender of Neumuenster would have delighted either Gilbert and Sullivan or the Three Stooges. The military part of it was no problem. All of Third RTR's tanks came rumbling into the market square, and all the German troops duly marched off to a "prisoners' cage," an inaccurate designation since most cages were merely open fields and some barbed wire; just a Bury St. Edmunds reprise. The problem was the Bürgermeister of Neumuenster, who, instead of swallowing something or at least staying home, insisted on handing over the keys of the city and some accompanying parchment, and could find no one to accept them. Complete with frock coat, chain of office, and

---

† "General von Wesselink shot himself last night."

blue sash, he kept on trotting from tank to tank, undeterred by shouts of, "Go away, Emil," and more succinctly put suggestions, trying to hawk those keys, and getting underfoot.

This *Fledermaus* interlude ended with Teddy yelling, "For God's sake, Mark, take his goddamn keys and let's get on with it."

So I took the keys—large, heavy, gilded, and fake—and dropped them in the bottom of my tank, where they probably still are; and we got on with it—with a little looting, that is. That same Gilbertian Bürgermeister had had the extraordinary but felicitous idea to have all inhabitants deliver all their guns, cameras, and binoculars to the town hall; being good and scared Germans (an irresistible combination when it comes to disciplined compliance), they had done just that. We were now requested by this same sashed simpleton to take all these neatly labelled goodies "into safe keeping," which we did with such visible enthusiasm, that it must have given pause to at least some of the former owners. We were however quite prepared to issue "receipts," very much an ad hoc document devised by Teddy Mitford and myself, holding out the remote possibility of an eventual indemnity at an unspecified time by authorities unknown. It would not have mattered if we had given them a chit with "Received with Thanks" stamped on it; as long as there was a receipt. You did not have to be Oscar Wilde to be unable to resist temptation; I got another Leica, nowhere near as good as my first, a couple of fair twelve-bore guns, with which I impersonated a hunting squire for the next two years, and a fine pair of Zeiss binoculars, which I own to this day. Neumuenster is of course still around, and I still think of it as my personal property; if I could find that parchment, I could prove it!

# 13

We moved from Neumuenster to Bad Segeberg that same day—an idyllic little resort town by a lake and surrounded by immense pine forests. The houses we requisitioned had diligently stocked larders and cellars, which we now proceeded to reduce just as diligently. That entire part of Germany had not been bombed or otherwise much affected by the war, which clearly was going to be over in a matter of days, if not hours. The day we moved into Segeberg, some of our divisional patrols had reached both Luebeck and Flensburg without encountering any resistance, and Eleventh Armored had effectively cut Germany in two. West of that dividing line, on the British side, the German forces were dissolving in a relatively orderly fashion; neither side made any attempt to fight, and the Germans, sometimes in large formations, at times just in small groups, all of them frequently still armed, were trudging off in various directions, most of them presumably heading for home. We made no real attempt to collect any of them, let alone direct them to POW camps; as long as no one was shooting at us, if they had some place to go, that was all right with us.

The situation was very different east of the Luebeck-Flensburg line; literally millions of soldiers and civilians were racing westward to avoid falling into Russian hands. There was some isolated fighting still going on, but overall it was just a tidal wave of panicked civilians and desperate soldiers, a torrent of trucks, cars, tanks, carts, bicycles, and pedestrians just pouring into the British sector, to get away from "der Iwan." What little action we saw in the last two or three days of the war and in the week following was as riot police, trying to channel this unceasing stream of dirty, desperate, and hysterically scared civilians and equally filthy, exhausted, and grimly despondent soldiers into some semblance of order, so that someone else could cope with the delousing, emergency childbirth, sudden death, and all the other Goya-like phenomena. Caught up in this maelstrom of disorganized and wholly disoriented humanity, just about the last thing we expected was the "black searchlight caper," and if that sounds like a live comic strip, that is just about what it was.

On our second night in Segeberg, the first in a while on which we all had had baths, a change of socks and underwear, and a concomitant change in attitude, one of the tank sentries reported a German officer outside, who was insisting on seeing someone who spoke German. That was how it began.

Hauptmann Geiger was a short, swarthy, twinkle-eyed man, about my age, massively self-assured and no wonder. A Knight's Cross was not unusual on a Panzer captain, but the "hand-to-hand combat clasp" in gold was. (Hitler invented the weirdest nomenclature for decorations.) This particular bauble meant that Geiger had fought hand-to-hand at least twenty-five times, which, for a tank person, is either heroic or careless. He was wearing full German tank uniform, a rather stunning ensemble based, I always suspected, on some road company performance of Lehar (a composer who could fairly be called a Hungarian Gilbert & Sullivan), which Hitler may have seen as a young man. Jet-black all over (tankmen were frequently confused with Waffen SS, which upset both parties) with a profusion of scarlet and silver pipings, black calf-high boots ending in some nifty black plus fours (rather like a golfer in mourning), and a liberal sprinkling of death head insignias (another SS-related gimmick that made for misunderstandings), the overall impression was faintly ludicrous, but German tank crews were nothing to laugh at.

Geiger informed me that his unit had had us under surveillance for the past few days and gave me a totally accurate report of our itinerary to prove it. Having thus watched us approvingly in operation (presumably barring a few hiccups, such as our bathing habits in Osnabrueck or our despoiling the citizenry of Neumuenster), his commanding officer had come to the conclusion that we would be the people he would surrender to, provided we observed his conditions. These simply were, that the unit—with all the men and equipment—should be handed over directly to a British team of technicians and scientists, and go with them to England, rather than be detained in any local prisoners' cage.

Geiger went on to explain that his was one of two tank units that had been in operation on the Russian front using equipment so secret and so effective that it represented another era in tank warfare. Their sister unit had been wiped out, but not before destroying whatever the gadget was (which clearly had limits to its effectiveness; otherwise how come?). Geiger and his crowd had fought their way out and had been shipped right across Germany to hold us, but had come too late to do any good. Instead, they had elected to retreat slowly in front of us and watch us, and were now proposing to surrender on their terms. If we did not accept them, they might fight, but more likely, they would first blow up whatever it was and then give themselves up. His reasoning was identical to what we had been hearing for some weeks past, and what I was to hear endlessly for the next two years. Just about all Germans then and for years afterwards believed war between the West and Russia to be inevitable and wanted us to be as well-equipped for that showdown as possible. After the bomb was dropped on Hiroshima, I hardly met a German who did not urge the use of it against Russia and the sooner, the better, as long as we had the advantage. The German fear and hatred of the Russians was not merely an amalgam of historical mistrust and antagonism but was based on the overriding memory of the merciless fighting in Russia, the scope and bitterness of which was wholly inconceivable to us, and the utter savagery with which the Russians retaliated, both in battle and subsequently in occupation. The Russian front was one huge killing ground; nothing, in any war, can compare with it. These feelings were of course wholly reciprocated by the Russians.

Geiger assured me that our scientists would be simply ecstatic at the sight of whatever it was they had. I relayed all this to Teddy, who believed it no more than I did, but since Geiger did not act suicidal (despite that hand-to-hand thing), and it seemed a bit late for the Germans to win the war, why not give it a shot? Besides, it was always fun to stir up some trouble and confusion back among the brass—

So I joined Geiger in his Kuebelwagen (the military forerunner of the Volkswagen and almost as good as a jeep), and we drove for about twenty minutes out of Segeberg and along various forest paths till challenged by first one sentry, and fifty yards beyond, another, and then yet another; the kind of security you associate with guarding the Coca Cola formula! We ended up in the depths of the forest, in the middle of a tank leaguer, all of them Tigers, Panthers, and Jagdtigers (a Jagdtiger, like a Jagdpanther, did not have a rotating turret, but carried an extra-heavy gun mounted on a fixed platform and was principally used to destroy other tanks)—about as scary a sight as I had seen since Normandy. Everything and everybody looked alarmingly competent, tough, and neat, and if anyone was playing at soldiering around here, I was the only one. The officer commanding the whole lot, a Count Dohna-Strelitz, littered with decorations just like Geiger, was impeccably courteous but managed to convey that the evident disparity in our ranks, experience, and social backgrounds did not warrant idle conversation. It took five minutes to establish the "ground rules," and another five for the entire unit to be on its way, and out we came again from the woods, Geiger and I leading the convoy in his Kuebelwagen, and the 88-mm gun of the first Tiger literally ten feet behind us, the closest I had ever been to a moving Tiger. Do not let them tell you any different—it was scary.

There must have been about twenty of these monsters and perhaps thirty half-tracks and trucks, and the whole lot came thundering into Segeberg to the bafflement and apprehension of the locals, who had very much an "enough already" attitude as far as the war was concerned. To their evident relief, this did not turn out to be some last-ditch counteroffensive; instead all the Tigers, Panthers, and trucks formed up in a leaguer on the local football field, tightly guarded by their own crews, and we, in turn, had a guard ring around them—real Chinese box fashion.

Inevitably and within a matter of minutes, this *quis custodiet ipsos custodies* situation (or "who's on first?" to make it simpler) led to both sides exchanging cigarettes and photos of babies and girlfriends. Combat soldiers take a very lenient view of fellow sufferers, regardless of which side they are on; lynching is for rear-echelon personnel. However, Teddy's orders in respect to "peeking" had been stringent, and, in any event, no one knew what to look for. Our report to higher authority had met with expected scepticism and the advice to switch from whatever we had been drinking. Unless we could come up with some kind of appetizer, we were clearly deadlocked on both sides. There is the old army maxim that if you play for time long enough, they will pick on someone else. Given time and a Micawber-like belief that things tend to turn up, Teddy and I hoped that they might. Consequently we informed Geiger that our masters had shown lively interest and would send experts the following day, all of which he duly reported to his commanding count who had, Achilles-like, retired to his tank. And something did turn up: Geiger and Count Dohna, evidently convinced both of our zeal and our discretion, promised us a tiny preview that night, just a glimpse, rather like throwing a single fish to a seal.

It was a moonless night, and I was once again heading out into the countryside. Geiger was at the wheel and Teddy and I were in the back of that Kuebelwagen. First he drove at a speed which dimmed-out headlights allowed, then he switched them off and really hit the accelerator. It was so dark a night that we could barely see him in the front seat, and while he had not given the impression of being nuts, I guess you do not have to be Japanese to go kamikaze. Before we could think of some way of saving ourselves, Geiger just as abruptly slowed down, stopped, and suggested that Teddy take the wheel and watch the road through a particular portion of the windscreen. Teddy did, said, "Well, I'll be damned" and proceeded to go even faster than Geiger.

Then it was my turn, and there it was: if you looked through a rectangular area in the windscreen, maybe six-inches-by-four, the entire road ahead was clearly visible in a pale greenish light for perhaps fifty yards or more. That was it—the "black searchlight," as some garbled press reports called it many years later. Geiger told us that every tank and vehicle in his unit was fitted with it, that the tank beam was considerably longer and had enabled them to mount numerous successful night attacks against Russian armor. I have no idea how it worked, and I doubt whether they knew; the fact was that, if you threw a switch, you got that beam, which was totally invisible unless you looked through the screen.

So we drove right back to the mess and called our masters then and there, told them all about it and expressed the conviction that if they showed no interest the Yanks would, which was one sure way to get some action out of them. Needless to add, the Americans got it in the end, but at least we tried.

By next morning the place was swarming with eggheads and security wallahs, one peering and poking about and the other making us swear all kinds of blood oaths that we had not seen what we had seen, and by mid-day everybody was gone and there was just the football field, looking a mess. Count Dohna, correct as Jeeves and aloof as a statue, had formally thanked me and made me feel like a deserving serf, and Geiger, with whom I had spent the best part of the past thirty-six hours, gave me his lighter as memento. I never saw any of them again nor heard anything about the gadget, until sometime in the 1960s, when there were press reports about night-sight equipment of extraordinary efficacy, which British and American tanks had been using in Korea, and of which the prototype was a German World War II development.

After the Neumuenster and Segeberg interludes, Teddy Mitford was insistent on recommending me for an OBE (Order of the British

Empire). He may have done, in which case the citation suffered the same fate as Trooper Armstrong's, and doubtless for the same reason. I had no medical problem though.

## 14

The day which began by disposing of our guests and their secret ended with Germany's unconditional surrender, an anticlimatic event in one respect and unforgettable in another. The fighting had been over for several days so the official announcement really meant very little. On the other hand, it meant that the war was really over, and there was a sensation of unspeakable relief, that we had managed to survive, that we were safe, that we had gotten away with it! We suddenly became very aware that we had never really quite expected to make it, and it left many of us with a peculiar and rather flippant approach to life. Quite a lot of us felt that we were living on borrowed time from that day on, a sort of huge and unexpected bonus, a real "gift of life," if you will pardon such a platitude.

Most people I knew got over that feeling and came back to normalcy; it never quite left me, nor has the belief in the arbitrariness of things. I would like to believe that one can be the master of one's fate, and sometimes, briefly, I do; most times I know better. Undeserved luck and random occurrence, that is what my life has mostly been about, and it has tended to make me a spectator rather than a participant. Being a spectator does not mean being passive, nor does it imply lack of ambition or lack of responsibility towards others or not caring for the affection and respect of those around you. In those respects, I am very much a participant, but I also have the conviction that the causal relationship between effort and outcome, or merit and reward, is very tenuous, and the overriding factor is random luck, *baraka*, happenstance, call it what you will.

That night one of my troop sergeants, having survived almost six years of fighting without a scratch, had a couple of beers too many and drowned in Segeberg lake. See what I mean?

Less than a day after the surrender, the rumor started that Third RTR was headed for Berlin as part of the British Occupation Forces, and it became official a few days later. We were to do so in late May, so for the next couple of weeks we were back in the peacetime army, with its manic obsession for cleaning inanimate objects. We scrubbed, brushed, painted, and polished our tanks; we did everything but flay them. They were not allowed to be moved or even breathed on; we assumed they would eventually be transported from Segeberg to Berlin by the Heavenly Choir. We suffered incessant visitations by lofty military personages, all exhorting us to ever greater exertions in polishing and painting everything in sight, to thereby extol to all and sundry, but particularly to the expectant population of Berlin, the virtues of the British Way of Life. We were even honored by an appearance of Monty himself, who indulged in his usual potpourri of sporting allusions and was his usual insufferable self. We polished, we drank, we painted, we drank, we scrubbed, and we drank; our efforts would have awed pharaonic slaves, and our intake dazed a Liverpool dockworker.

By way of light relief, some of us participated in the "capture" of Admiral Doenitz and his cabinet in Flensburg, just a few miles up the road. One of our infantry units was sent up to collect that crowd, and we went along just for the ride; not in our tarted-up tanks, needless to say. We all got our pictures in the London papers, which made it out to be the most dashing exploit since Prince Rupert last rode. It was about as exciting as watching grass grow: a bunch of elderly and very subdued characters, coming along meekly and without the slightest protest—all except Admiral Friedenburg, who swallowed cyanide in the lavatory. That he did so did not seem to upset Doenitz, but where he did it earned his disapproval.

## 15

The Berlin outing required some preliminary reconnaissance on the ground, which Teddy wanted me to undertake, and that outing was to be preceded by a briefing at army headquarters, then in Lueneburg. That, in turn, led, wholly accidentally, to the most "stop the presses" occurrence of my entire war.

In Lueneburg I was ushered into the presence of some noncombatant body of lofty rank, substantial girth, and rather more limited mental spread, who supposedly was to tell me all about Berlin. Although I had left that city twelve years earlier, I had the advantage over him since he had never been there, so it ended up, very amiably, with my telling him. Until the moment when someone came bursting into the room, yelling, "We've got Himmler! They're bringing him in." Evidently my portly friend was the senior person in the immediate neighborhood, and since this bit of news created predictable and instant pandemonium, neither he nor anyone else told me to leave. So I stayed, of course.

It got better. Our breathless Paul Revere turned out to be the security officer of some camp about thirty miles away, which had been set up as a catchment area for SS personnel. (Just as concentration camp inmates had numbers tattooed on their forearms, so all SS personnel had their blood groups tattooed in their armpits; spotting them was smelly but simple.) Two SS men had asked to see the commandant of the camp that morning, indicating that they were speaking on behalf of the Reichsfuehrer der SS, Heinrich Himmler, who was in Hut 7! After everyone had recovered from near cardiac arrest, it was learned that Himmler had decided that the best way to avoid detection until such time as he was ready to be found was to hole up in one of our detention camps. He had provided himself with Waffen SS papers and, together with his two bodyguards, had been sitting quietly in that camp for the past couple of weeks while Germany was being scoured for the "most wanted" Nazi left (with Hitler and Goebbels dead and Goering in custody). Screening techniques employed by the various ad hoc security officers, casually elevated to that occupation, were clearly on a par with Alien Tribunal practices, and the fact that this one spoke not a word of German was not helpful.

Himmler was duly led in a short while later, and, though it was never clear why he thought this a good time to reveal himself, we very soon discovered what he had in mind. I became a major player in this extraordinary event by the mere fact that I happened to be there when Himmler, standing in the doorway with various guards hanging onto him like leeches, addressed the room, "Sprechen Sie Deutsch?"

When you had been in Third Tanks long enough, you did not volunteer for anything, so first there was silence, then the man I had been talking with said to me, "You had better stick around," and so I stuck. Himmler looked even more colorless than his photos; he had shaved off his moustache and exchanged his pince-nez for horn-rimmed glasses, but otherwise had not attempted to disguise himself. He had papers indicating that he was a Waffen SS corporal by the name of Hitzinger, but he was also carrying various documents that left no doubt as to his true identity. They must have been in need of a Seeing Eye dog up in that camp.

The first thing we did was to clear the room, since half of Lueneburg appeared to have heard the news. The Army Intelligence authorities predictably belonged to the other half; no one turned up till hours later. The second thing—being British—was to order tea, which settled us nicely, if not necessarily Himmler. His problem (and clearly ours) was that he was only going to talk to Eisenhower personally! Staff officers can be wily, this one walked into the next room ostensibly to call up Ike, only to return with the news that Eisenhower was in Washington but Mongtomery would be prepared to talk to Himmler the next morning. It turned out to be a splendid piece of improvised misinformation, since, suitably embellished in translation, Himmler bought it.

All this took place in the late afternoon, and for the next couple of hours or so, we had a peculiar "treading water" situation, with neither Himmler nor us having any clear idea of what was going on—in other words a classic army situation.

We were obviously waiting for some more expert help to take Himmler off our hands, and he was waiting for Monty. Meanwhile I was translating whatever anyone in the room cared to say, and Himmler felt called upon to impress us with his own importance by hinting at the information he had for Ike and comparable deities. It did not require too much intelligence to puzzle out his clues and oblique references. Everyone knew that Himmler had also been in charge of German Intelligence operations, and he was clearly expect-ing to barter his life against information, specifically about spy networks that the Germans had created in occupied territories. Since Himmler evidently shared the general German belief that war between Russia and the Western Allies was inevitable, he was particularly coy and allusive about German spying operations in Russia, which he clearly believed to be of pivotal interest to Ike and Monty. I have no doubt that Himmler really believed that a deal could be struck.

As it happened, I became very involved in various Intelligence activities just a few months later and subsequently learned that the networks in Russia which Himmler had hinted at had in fact been set up and controlled by General Gehlen and had nothing to do with Himmler. Gehlen later became the first shadowy and successful head of Intelligence operations in the West German Republic, and it would be surprising if his networks did not have survival value as well.

That afternoon in Lueneburg we knew nothing about all that, and Himmler with his "nudge, nudge" hints, interspersed with wild mood swings ranging from morose suspicion to distressing bonhomie, was not all that enlightening. Obviously there were any number of questions one would have wanted to ask, but we were hardly the people to do it and were much relieved when an Intelligence colonel finally showed up to take charge. We briefed him on what had gone on so far and introduced him to Himmler as Monty's emissary (another inspiration by my cunning companion), which greatly reassured him.

It was decided to convert the office into sleeping quarters for Himmler by moving in a cot and posting double sentries at the door. The colonel, the staff officer, and I (still the sole linguistic conduit in sight) were to sleep down the hall, and we would all get together with Monty in the morning. By morning we hoped someone would have thought of the next smart move, or better still, would take Himmler off our hands.

Himmler was fed, went under heavy escort to wash and clean up, and settled in for the night. And so did we, but not for long. . . .

Shaken awake by a sentry, we raced down the hall only to find Himmler on the floor, bluish in the face, making gargling noises; there was a distinct smell of bitter almonds, just as there had been way back in the Rathaus in Neustadt.

Standing in the room were several high-ranking bodies, brigadiers and up, looking foolish, and so they should have. Someone produced a doctor who pronounced Himmler dead, despite the gargling—death by cyanide comes within seconds and subsequent motor reflexes are just misleading. He also established that Himmler had carried a cyanide capsule in a back-tooth cavity and only needed to grind his teeth once to ensure departure. It struck me at the time not merely as ingenious but also as gutsy—one false bite. . . .

What had happened was that these senior officers, a good deal less sober than they were now, had ordered the sentries to open the door and "let them have a look at the blighter." The news had been all over town, and they had of course heard it. Our orders to the sentries had been explicit, but privates do not tangle with brigadiers. Himmler evidently mistook them for additional Monty emissaries and had sufficient rudimentary English to convey that he was ready to make some deal. As soon as that penny dropped with the brigadiers, they evidently assured him that he would be lucky to live long enough to make a good hanging. They must have been convincing enough for him to grind his teeth.

Everyone was to blame: the brigadiers for being idiots, the sentries for being intimidated, we for being careless. In the event, no fuss was made at all, and everyone seemed just as happy to be rid of Himmler. I still think that he would have had fascinating things to tell (and would have told them!), but no one seemed to share my curiosity at the time. The Russians had made a considerable point of burying Hitler without a trace, to prevent any future "pilgrimage," and it was decided to do likewise with Himmler. I would have thought his potential as future martyr and hero to be very limited, but no one asked my opinion. Instead, I was ordered to round up four of the sentries, sling Himmler's body in the back of a truck, drive out to Lueneburg Heath, and dispose of him. We did just that, without a coffin, nor even a tree or bush in the vicinity; an hour later I could not have told anyone where we put him. No one ever looked for him, no one ever found him. He had been wearing a small metal swastika insignia on his tunic, and I still have that. I guess that is all that is left of him. To bring some slight focus to the entire anonymous, faceless event, the date was May 23, 1945.

The sequel to the Himmler episode was that everyone in the whole zone became acutely cyanide conscious. A number of people arrested lost teeth by having flashlights rammed into their mouths, to prevent their closing them. No one ever found another hollow tooth, but an amazing number of Germans did carry cyanide on their person. It was a good deal easier to come by than bubble gum in those days.

In the last days of May, I was off in my dingho, accompanied by batman and driver, to go to Berlin and find out just where we would be located. It was the first time that I saw the Helmstadt checkpoint, with exactly 196 kilometers of dead-straight autobahn running from there all the way to the Berlin outskirts. In the next two years, I was to drive over that stretch scores of times, almost always in "liberated" German cars, all of them flashy, and some of them furiously fast. In late 1946, two of us drove a 1936 Mercedes SSK (one of the greatest and most useless automobiles ever built) and covered those 196 km in exactly fifty-eight minutes; a record that is likely to stand forever. Needless to say, I was not the driver; I was not even looking—

There were no speed records to be broken in May 1945; the autobahn and everywhere you looked was littered with the detritus of the last weeks of savage fighting: burnt-out tanks and trucks, stretches of burnt and smashed trees, even crashed planes, and abandoned helmets, weapons, and equipment everywhere; the bodies had been moved, but nothing else. The autobahn itself was potholed and torn apart by shellfire, and driving along it was like a tackling the most treacherous kind of obstacle course.

At Helmstadt checkpoint I met my first Russians. The most unexpected feature about them, then as later, was the extraordinary diversity of origin: Mongols, Tartars, Kalmucks, Chinese—a human kaleidoscope. There was a noticeable scarcity of "European" faces since, as I heard in Berlin, the final Russian assaults had been spearheaded by Siberian troops and other formations coming from beyond the Urals. These were supposedly crack troops, especially rested and equipped for the final push, and that seemed plausible; that this torrent of Mongols and Tartars—Ghengis Kahan and his hordes come alive—would panic the German population had surely not escaped the Russians either.

Among the Russians I met there was a ferocious sense of hierarchy and discipline; all men may well be free and equal under Communist doctrine, but obedience in the Russian army was instant and total. They all seemed devouringly curious and, most of all, had an air of serenity and massive self-sufficiency about them. I had a great deal of contact with Russians for almost two years and found it hard to dislike them and impossible to understand them.

These are not the conclusions I drew at Helmstadt that day. I was surrounded by a couple of cheerful and curious guards, handling their weapons with hair-raising nonchalance (accidental shootings among Berlin Russians were at least as common as fender-benders in today's Manhattan) and studying my travel documents with absorbed interest. I doubt whether they could read, and they certainly could not read English, but they got a kick out of it, anyway. There was a great deal of back-slapping, vodka, the hand-rolled Russian cigarettes called *papyrossi* (which may reflect the Russian soul, but smoked like damp felt), and references to "Hitler Kaput"—you have all seen the movies.

This is as good a spot as any to refer briefly to the Russian invasion of Germany, some aspects of which were misunderstood even then, and certainly are no longer recalled now. The Russian dead numbered twenty million between 1941 and 1945, a number so enormous as to leave an impact on even so callous a murderer as Stalin, and which certainly justified the feelings of revenge and retribution with which the Russians tore into Germany. What was not known at the time was that the orgy of rape, pillage, and destruction that ensued, and which no German living then has ever forgotten, was official Russian policy. The Germans were supposed to suffer every imaginable horror, and they were supposed to remember.

The fact that Russian troops went about this with unflagging enthusiasm and relentless thoroughness is not that relevant. What is, is that in June 1945, about six weeks after the surrender, the Russian High Command ordered the immediate cessation of all these atrocities and had any subsequent offenders summarily shot; from that time on, raping and looting ceased for good. There was of course not much left to rape or loot by that time, and dismantling and removing factories and capital goods naturally continued. However, contrary to what many believe, particularly in Germany, the atrocities began and ended as a deliberate and organized action of terror and retribution. The savagery was both encouraged and controlled, and at no time were the Russian troops out of hand, in terms of their own discipline and chain of command. It was merely a vast replay of the Sack of Magdeburg and for the same primary reason—*pour encourager les autres*—so to speak.

While in Segeberg, we had driven over to Hamburg and had our first glimpse of a large city that had been almost wholly destroyed. In three successive nights during the summer of 1944, Hamburg had been exposed to raids of "1,000 bombers a night" and was virtually wiped out. Suburban areas still stood, and there were some buildings left in the town center, but literally square miles of the city had been smashed to the ground and then ploughed over and broken up again during successive raids. The city had suffered the dreaded "fire storms" caused by drafts set up by the combined use of incendiary and high explosive bombs, which raised hurricane-like winds sucking people, trees, and even buildings into the flames. For miles, Hamburg was one vast pile of rubble, twenty feet high or more, with just small footpaths dug out in between by survivors. In those three nights, possibly more than 50,000 people died, and most of them were never found. The summer of 1945 was unusually warm, and these countless unburied dead were expected to create severe health problems. It never happened; just lucky for everybody—

Nothing that I had seen in Hamburg prepared me for my first sight of Berlin. The city had not merely been bombed, it had been shelled and fought over, and it had literally ceased to exist. There was an occasional ruined, burnt-out shell sticking out from under mountains of rubble, and two huge concrete anti-aircraft bunkers still stood in the center of town, which could have withstood an atomic blast. For the rest, there was nothing, no houses, no trees, no streets and—at first sight—no people—the abomination of desolation.

The place was of course teeming with Russians and their equipment, everything from tanks to horse-drawn carts, and no one took the slightest notice of us. I spent the first few hours touring around that quite unimaginable heap of ruins, littered with broken vehicles, empty shells, burnt-out tanks, and all the aftermath of battle, all of which had been a city I had known intimately twelve years earlier. I went to look at the collapsed, burnt-out ruin of 10 Reichskanzlerplatz, which had been the five-story house in which I had grown up, and at the charred heap of rubble that had been the Franzoesisches Gymnasium, where I had gone to school. Since the building was less than two-hundred feet from the Reichstag, and hence at the epicenter of the last and most ferocious fighting, there was literally not one stone left upon the other. Having completed my personal pilgrimage, I joined hordes of Russians all wanting to see Hitler's chancellery and the bunker where he had died. He had not been dead three weeks but every trace of him and his entourage was hidden under a mound of graffiti, feces, and other mementos left by his Russian conquerors. The place did not just stink of death, it stank.

Talking about smells, there was a pervading smell of brick dust, excrement, burnt flesh, cordite, and smoldering debris that hung over Berlin, impossible to define, but instantly recognizable; you get into any city that has been bombed, shelled, and has unburied dead and you will notice it.

There were also some other odors: wherever you had Germans in any number, there was likely to be a smell of boiled cabbage; if there were a lot of Russians, you smelt wood smoke and papyrossi. I never associated Americans or Brits with any particular aura, and the only time I met Frenchmen was much later in Berlin, and they were all de Lattre's young men and wore white gloves and perfume. To leave it like that is not quite fair to de Lattre. Of the four top commanders I subsequently saw and listened to, Jean de Lattre de Tassigny, Marshall of France, was by far the most dramatic. Georgy Zhukov had a bear-like, granite quality about him, which made him more redoubtable than inspiring; Ike was "Old Home Week"—relaxed, folksy, likable, and appearing much simpler than he obviously was; and Montgomery was a waspish, highly strung, bad-tempered ferret. De Lattre had everything—imperial looks, style, panache, an impeccable tailor, and a matchless sense of drama. His actual record was impressive and his news value unrivalled; even Patton and MacArthur were bush-league compared to de Lattre in full panoply. He never removed his white gloves when shaking hands (which he did rarely and reluctantly), he changed uniforms twice a day and gloves every three hours, he rode into battle by jeep, looking like a fugitive from *Lohengrin*; si non e vero—it has been all written up endlessly and with ever more embellishments. There was de Lattre's night party on

Schwanenwerder in late summer 1945, forever to be remembered by those who attended, and I was one of them. The castles, terraces and gardens of Schwanenwerder, a small island on Berlin's outskirts, cover about fifty acres and the only illumination anywhere was provided by de Lattre's spahi troops, in red kepis and ankle-length white woolen cloaks, standing rigidly to attention, each holding a lit four-foot torch clasped in both hands. There must have been a thousand of them, and there had been nothing like it since Nero lit up his place with burning Christians. De Lattre would probably have preferred that, but presumably could not round up enough Germans that evening—there was more to de Lattre than just perfume.

Back in Berlin in May, you were immediately struck by the ant-like activity of civilians scurrying everywhere and that they were all children, cripples, or quite elderly. There were of course no able-bodied German men about, but the apparent absence of young and middle-aged women was peculiar to Berlin and the Russian Zone of Germany. The women who were there looked like a cross between a Kaethe Kollwitz drawing and the witch from "Hansel and Gretel," and that was not only due to the ravages of war and, more partic-ularly, those inflicted by the Russians. It had, I soon heard, become standard practice among women of all ages in the Russian sector to make themselves appear old, diseased, or crippled to the marauding Russians.

Russians were mostly just drifting about, with rape, loot, and drink in mind, generally in that order; Berliners, on the other hand, were feverishly busy surviving. Everywhere you looked people were frantically active: moving rubble, carrying water, trading food, goods, information, starting life all over. Within a matter of days, *Truem-merfrauen* (debris women) had formed up in huge and largely volun-tary gangs, moving bricks and rubble with their bare hands and a few surviving buckets and shovels. They literally moved hundreds of thousands of tons of debris over the next few months, and the *Truemmerfrauen* monument standing in Berlin today is one of the most justly honored and honorable memorials.

Already in the very first days after the surrender, specific areas had become "trading centers," particularly in close vicinity to the Reichstag ruins; these rapidly turned into vast, highly organized black market operations, where, by mid-summer 1945, you could buy any-thing and anybody. The trading currency until well into 1946 was cigarettes; nothing else. The cigarette rate varied throughout Ger-many, depending on supply; it was lowest in the U.S. zone and highest in the Russian zone, but always at a premium in Berlin. In July 1945, a single cigarette was valued at four dollars in Berlin, as against two dollars and fifty cents in Hamburg; a year later it was still worth two dollars in Berlin! By that time I was fully involved in Intelligence matters and had an official weekly allocation of twenty thousand cigarettes to take care of "payments for services rendered." It should not surprise anyone that maintaining an establishment of four motor cars with drivers and a permanent domestic staff of seven was well within my petty-cash budget. Had I been less self-indulgent and more alert, I might have acquired a good Van Gogh for a week's supply of cigarettes.

The first day in Berlin I started noticing the countless, pathetic bits of paper and cardboard on just about every wall, tree, or other prominent spot where they might be seen. I had seen them before in Hamburg, but they had not registered; after that first Berlin visit, I became aware that all of Germany was inundated with them. They were almost always handwritten, seemingly in a hurry, often misspelt, and in many cases, the weather had made them partly illegible. They were always short and indescribably poignant. "Hanna-mir geht's gut-bin bei Oma. Fritz and Kurt sind tot. Hans" "Trude. Habe Franz gefunden. Marie und Kinder sind tot." "Bitte Auskunft ueber Feld-webel Klaus Schmidt, 27st Panzer Regiment. Else Schmidt. Frie-drichsstrasse 19."†

Or just, "Egon, wo bist Du? Ich lebe. Klaere"

No one knows how many of these sad messages ever reached their destinations; perhaps they often were just a cry of anguish meant for all who read them. After a few weeks they were all gone.

I found the encounter with Russians in Berlin both intriguing and staggering. The sight of Russians with both forearms covered

---

†"Hanna—I am well—am with Grandma—Fritz and Kurt are dead.Hans" "Trude. Have found Franz.Marie and the children are dead." "Please need news of Sergeant Klaus Schmidt, 27th Tank Regiment. Else Schmidt, Friedrichsstrasse 19" "Egon, where are you? I'm alive.Klaere."

with wristwatches worn like an assembly of native bracelets was common (sixteen up to the elbow was as far as I once counted, but he had long arms and was in a hurry), as was hearing the triumphant yell, "Urrah, urrah," whenever they spotted a hapless civilian still owning one. The most memorable incident of horological heist I witnessed was later that summer, when I came upon an emptied watchmaker's shop and its terrified owner was being threatened by three clearly unfriendly Russians. This being in the British sector, I offered counsel to whichever side might listen to it and found that the object of contention was a large three-legged kitchen alarm clock, which the Russians had "acquired." Despite its size and function, they viewed the watchmaker's frantic protestations that he was unable to convert it into three or four wrist-watches as a display of Nazi obstruction, and were correspondingly displeased. Watches were not the only objects of Russian affections; they were enthralled by toilets or any other plumbing fixture that "made water come out of a wall," though their enthusiasm was not matched by any functional response. For months Berlin was just one vast outhouse.

Staircases did not hold particular interest for the Russians, but banisters delighted them. Again later that summer, I was due to meet with a Russian of lofty rank to coordinate some Intelligence matter of great immediacy and trifling importance. The general in question resided in a sumptuous, though battered, villa in the Russian sector. The most noticeable feature about the place was its marble entrance hall with a sweeping grand staircase leading upwards; noticeable since the general, his staff, and assorted friends were all noisily engaged in sliding down the banister, then running back up the stairs for another *Schuss* down. The only way to capture both his goodwill and attention was to join in. On the third slide down, I got him to take "time out" to talk to me.

Russians drank anything that was liquid or nearly so. Their capacity is of course legendary, and none of us could ever come close to matching it. There were, however, some carousal precautions that we learned and which proved useful. If you could manage to down a small glass of olive oil, or a similarly sealing and gagging substance, before you started serious drinking, it would line your stomach and keep you on your feet—for a while. If you can not face olive oil, try buttermilk—better than nothing.

More importantly, you had to eat constantly between drinks; not much, but the fattier, the better; pork cold cuts or heaps of butter held together by a little bread would do fine. None of this would do more than delay execution if you got involved in serious drinking with Russians, and the Russians knew no other kind.

Any get-together would inevitably lead to a first round of toasts honoring Stalin, Truman, and Attlee in separate and generous shots of vodka, followed almost immediately by another round, taking care of Eisenhower, Zhukov, and Montgomery. Having got those preliminaries out of the way, you started toasting people you really cared about, beginning with the mayor of your village (which naturally required the other participants to commemorate their respective dignitaries) and then tottering along various branches of your respective family trees, toasting as you went. In the wholly unlikely event that you were still conscious enough to cheer on the niece of your neighbor's wife or some such distant level of common bond, you might wonder in passing why the French were either never invited or never attended. They were not or did not; by the fifth round of vodka, who cared?

Perhaps the most memorable aspect about the Russians I met then was their stoicism and indifference to pain and to loss of life. You came across soldiers with seemingly unattended or neglected wounds that would have felled an ox, or with scars so huge and disfiguring that it was hard to imagine anyone surviving the wounds that must have caused them. I have seen Russians suffer accidents resulting in wounds and pain that would have you and me screaming on the ground; they would hobble away without a sound. They appeared totally unconcerned by death, their own or others: they seemed stoic to the point of being callous. The sanctity of life is an elastic concept, and where death in large numbers—by famine, floods, disease, or other apocalyptic events—is a constantly recurring part of the environment, the Western view of it may seem unduly squeamish. To illustrate the point and the contention that truly to understand Russians is beyond our scope, I recall a seminar I attended in Berlin later that year. The main speakers were Eisenhower, Zhukov, Montgomery, and de Lattre, who were to address several scores of Allied officers on how to win wars and comparable social skills. I cannot recall why I was invited to attend; I was about the only person present whom I had not heard of. During the ensuing "question and answer" period, Zhukov queried the delay in breaking out of the Normandy bridgehead. Monty replied, via his interpreter, that the number and density of the minefields we encountered had made it impossible to move faster. Zhukov's comment was brutally simple and equally scary. He too had run into minefields on his advance; his tactics in such case had been to hold back his tanks and ram a couple of infantry divisions through the minefields. They would get blown up and so would the mines, and he could then push his tanks right through the gap without loss of momentum. Thus, he asked again, what had held us up? End of my story.

Back in Berlin, the key issue was of course to discover where Third RTR was to be housed. Berlin had not yet been officially partitioned into the four sectors, nor was there any authority who seemed to know or care who was supposed to be where. For three days we drifted around the ruined city, eating and sleeping in various parts of Berlin as casual guests of friendly but generally wholly unintelligible Russians. I made progress on the third day by running into the resident British Military Mission, or rather, my driver did, by backing our dingho into the staff car.

Military Missions—British or otherwise—tend to be indefinable and self-perpetuating organisms, leading lavish and interminable lives based on jealously guarded anonymity, which makes it impossible to determine what they are doing, let alone to tell them to cease doing it. It can be a lifetime occupation if you keep a low profile and leave no forwarding address. This lot had a clear understanding of the criteria of success: discreet obscurity, sybaritic living, fast repartee, and lack of purpose. Predictably, their quarters were opulent, bursting with servants and Mercedes, and they had liquor stocks from five continents and enough caviar with which to build sand castles. It was equally foreseeable that they had no notion of who or what I was, but were wholly unfazed by such detail. Third RTR? Of course. Where were we going to be? In the Olympic Stadium, naturally; they had not had time yet to inspect it, but were sure that it would be eminently suitable; have another one, old boy. So I drove out to the stadium, which had been vast when I last saw it in 1933, and which Hitler had hugely enlarged for the 1936 Olympics. By now the infield was the size of several football fields, surrounded by concrete stands, seating well over one hundred thousand people. The place was wholly deserted and intact, except for a few burnt-out tanks and trucks near the approaches. It was as bare as, though less appealing than, a baby's bottom.

Unless we were content to hang out in the changing rooms and toilets of that concrete rabbit warren, we were going to spend that summer under canvas. Okay for us, but what about our "show room" tanks, and who was going to be suitably impressed by them? Clearly the thing to do was to drive back to Segeberg and report, which I did—only to be told that the Berlin move was off! We never heard why the move was canceled. Actually no British troops moved to Berlin at all until late that summer, by which time the four separate sectors and a quadripartite administration were in place and things proceeded in a relatively organized manner. The recurrent and obvious rumor about the cancellation was that we were being shipped out to win the war in the Far East. It seemed plausible that Third RTR would be needed to get things moving (these were pre–A-bomb days), but the thought held limited appeal.

## 16

Meanwhile we had received orders to move to Friedrichstadt, a place none of us had ever heard of, and chances were, would never see again. A pity, since Friedrichstadt is charming, quaint, and stuck in a late eighteenth-century time-warp—or was. It is way out at the edge of Schleswig-Holstein, a sleepy, delightful market town of around five thousand people. Meticulously laid out some two hundred years ago in a very attractive baroque grid system, it had small rectangular areas bordered by huge old trees, cobble-stoned streets, and small canals bisecting and surrounding the entire place. It had a distinct Dutch air about it, though I am not aware of any Dutch ever setting foot there; no one is likely to be drawn to that part of the world, and how this really delightful place came about still puzzles me. This was the Diethmarschen region on the western edge of Schleswig-Holstein, in a rich agricultural area dominated by a few large and reclusive farming clans, all intermarried and residing there since before the Vikings. They are the people of the *Schwarze Fahne* (black banners) peasant uprisings, immortalized in Gerhart Hauptmann's great play *Die Weber*—a taciturn, brooding, suspicious, and violent lot, forever rebelling, protesting, and acting unpleasant. Just as, according to Carlo Levi, Christ stopped at Eboli, so central authority appeared to have pulled up well short of the Diethmarschen and left them to their own dark devices.

True to their past and inclinations, the Diethmarschers could boast of more pre-1930 Nazi members than any other German region, and Hitler's frantic mouthings about soil, blood, honor, purity of race, tribal ties, and sundry other *Nibelungen* hang-ups were all issues that Diethmarschers passionately believed in. There was nothing west of Friedrichstadt except a huge dune area, several hundred square miles of it, housing several small fishing villages, numberless birds, and scores of seal colonies. There were a number of minor roads crisscrossing that dune region, all leading to one main ring road, which in turn, ran back to Friedrichstadt.

To reach town, the road crossed a wide canal, so that the bridge spanning it effectively provided the only access to the entire dune peninsula, unless you had a very shallow-bottomed boat. Someone in authority had had the smart idea of evacuating the few inhabitants still around and funnelling any number of stray German soldiers into this vast catchment area. By the time we arrived in Friedrichstadt, several hundred thousand soldiers, sailors, and airmen were "camping out" there, living in what housing they could find, in make-shift tents, or just in the dunes; the weather was good, no one was shooting at them, and the Red Cross (one of the few impeccably organized outfits I came across during the war) kept them fed. No one was guarding them, since none of them seemed keen to go anywhere. On the contrary, by the time we arrived, an SRO situation had arisen and a good deal of our time was spent preventing late-coming POW's from trying to crowd the island even more. Our duties, such as they were, consisted of posting a couple of tanks at the access bridge and keeping a casual eye on arriving stragglers and occasional Red Cross trucks. For the first week or so, we had no contact at all with that huge makeshift outdoor camp, except for Teddy Mitford's "daily folly." We had found—of all things—an ancient but, naturally, intact Rolls-Royce in Segeberg (Rolls are intact by definition), and Teddy had had it resprayed, chromed, and fitted with pennants and Union Jacks, doubtless in anticipation of "épater les bourgeois de Berlin."

Having been prevented from doing that, the next best thing seemed to be to awe that bedraggled multitude out in the dunes, and so, every morning, Teddy would set out in his Rolls, pennants flying, two motorcycle dispatch riders in front and two behind; to his regret, he had not found a siren to go with all this. He would whiz once around the entire island, which would keep him busy and happy, and left the Germans utterly indifferent and unimpressed.

After the first week, the island inmates began stirring from their catatonic confusion and things got a bit livelier. One fine morning I was called to the bridge (in all my time with Third RTR, no one else could translate as much as "Guten Morgen") to deal with two POW's who wanted to report the presence of "a war criminal." War criminals and nonfraternization were two buzz words of that year; mention of the first galvanized you into action and circumvention of the second occupied the remainder of your time ("What's your nationality?"—"Ich bin deutsch"—"Ah, Dutch; that's okay" was the standard Third RTR solution).

So off we went, two jeeps full of trigger-happy war-criminal hunters, being directed by our two informants to a house in the dunes some miles off. Once we got there, they disappeared into the dunes; I had not asked them why they had reported whoever it was in the first place, and, more to the point, I had forgotten to inquire who he was supposed to be. In those first heady days, the very word "war criminal" elicited a Pavlovian reaction, and you just rushed off madly in all directions. We surrounded the house and altogether managed to combine Elliot Ness with a Mohawk war party in approaching the place. The door was unlocked, which was a bit of an anticlimax, as was the fact that, tiptoeing around, armed to the eyebrows, we could find no one except a middle-aged, paunchy German, in his underwear and fast asleep. So, *faute de mieux*, we grabbed him; it took us a little time to get him to the jeep, because we had to help him find his glasses, since, without them, he could not find his pants.

He seemed a more likely prospect for traffic violations than for war crimes, but appearances did tend to be deceptive. He quite casually informed us that he was SS Gruppenfuehrer Bovensieben, a rank equivalent to lieutenant general, and, in that capacity, had been in charge of all SS and Gestapo activities in Denmark for the past three years. Presumably he had seen enough of Denmark and had just walked home over the border into the Diethmarschen. He seemed perfectly content to come back with us to Friedrichstadt and, duly locked in, promptly fell asleep again, like Alice's doormouse. Theologians and philosophers do not deal with wartime realities; conscience and sleep have no correlation.

We then called the nearest Field Security Section. We had been briefed about the "Intelligence situation"; in that the British Zone had been divided into five Intelligence areas, Berlin, Hamburg, Rhineland/Westphalia, Hannover, and Schleswig-Holstein. HQ for Rhineland/Westphalia was in Duesseldorf and for Schleswig-Holstein in Kiel. Each area had as many as twenty Field Security sections operating within it, each section being made up of one lieutenant or captain and half a dozen NCO's, all supposedly Intelligence personnel, as well as some drivers and clerical staff. Each such section was responsible for all "intelligence activity" in its allotted area, which did not prevent any number of shadowy "special outfits" from spooking around, seemingly answerable to no one. The entire structure was vague and chaotic, and if you knew your way around, as I came to do later that year, you could run your own fiefdom just about any way you wanted.

The local Field Security officer duly collected Bovensieben later that day and in due course a commendation for doing so. Bovensieben subsequently figured in various Danish war crimes trials and was then passed on to the Poles who wanted him for something; I do not know whether they tried him, but they hanged him.

The Bovensieben outing was my first contact with the Field Security world, which lived on an unimaginably lavish scale, even by our newly acquired Roman orgy standards. I began visiting the various FS sections in the area quite regularly, having nothing else to do and always being sure of there being wine and women in plenty and song in moderation. On one such visit, sometime in late May, I got entangled in the "Hitler's Last Will Shoot-out," one of the most widely reported and asinine exhibitions of gunplay since the episode in the O.K. Corrall. One of the hottest items sought by Intelligence in those days was Hitler's Last Will, of which there were supposedly three copies, and which had been carried out of a surrounded Berlin and to the West by three different couriers. By now just about everyone knows the content of that document, which is of marginal and purely historical interest, but at the time, it was assumed that it contained all kinds of revelations.

One evening, while having drinks with the FS officer in Schleswig (a half-hour drive from Friedrichstadt) and his latest "displaced" friend (a Chilean who had come to Germany as a child, he maintained; the dirndl she wore doubtlessly came from her Chilean grandmother), word came that one of those fabled couriers was in hiding on a farm a few miles away, complete with documents, and a greeting card from Hitler, for all we knew. This intelligence immediately assumed the aspect of a major, and hence fouled-up, military operation. The fact that Intelligence personnel were only peripherally acquainted with firearms and how to use them was not helpful either. Other security sections were alerted. I of course went along for the ride, and by the time we got near that farm, fifty people must have joined the posse. Someone suggested we wait till nightfall, someone else suggested surrounding the place, and someone else again had the wholly demented idea of throwing a double cordon round the house, to avoid both escape and any possibility of this scheme working out in any semblance of order. Add to that an elaborate system of whistles, bird calls, and other signals, as well as an arsenal that would have stopped a tank assault, and we were poised for disaster. Someone whistled, someone else bird-called, and off everyone went, firing everything they could lay their hands on. It may have been the extra Scotch or plain Third RTR caution; I just stayed well back and watched; it was not my party, anyway.

They managed to blow half the farmhouse down, hit five of their own people, two of them rather badly, and made headlines in the British press. When the smoke cleared, and they had looked after their wounded, they did find a man in the cellar, quite unarmed, with a tin of soup in his hand and, yes indeed, Hitler's will sewn into his tunic. By that time, I had joined those jubilant warriors and made a vital contribution to this major Intelligence coup (which it was truly held to be at the time) by producing a pair of nail scissors, thereby recovering the document elegantly and in mint condition. In turn, I was allowed to read it—it may have been the thirty-third copy for all I know, but it was not very inspirational.

The Bovensieben incident had broken some kind of logjam; hardly a day went by without someone reporting another "war criminal," and I spent a good deal of time "interrogating" them. None of them turned out to be more than very small fry, hardly worth harassing, certainly not worth hanging, but I had a good time acting as a cross between Torquemada and Ivan the Terrible and scaring the hell out of them. It was childish and childishly easy and does me no credit. It did not harm them much, either.

Military government as an institution did not yet exist, but we preceded them by blundering into the same inevitable trap that later caught all British and U.S. regional military governments.

Having started out by jailing all the Nazis we could find, we turned to the day-to-day business of running the place. Who knew about the waterworks, electricity supply, and sewage disposal? Well, the guys who knew were among the guys whom we had locked up. So we let them out again on a purely temporary basis, except that, like all temporary arrangements, the transition phase never ended. It seemed just so much more convenient to let them do the work needed, and by the time Military government took over in midsummer, these people had become indispensable and permanent fixtures. The whole de-nazification program in the British and U.S. zones was selective, shall we say, at best. The only people who remained in custody were either so prominent that the Archangel Gabriel would not have dared free them, or else so ineffectual that no one was missing them now. The real backbone of the Nazi machine, the middle managers and administrators, were back at their jobs within weeks of the end of war, and stayed there until they retired in the 1960s. Almost all war criminals uncovered in the past twenty years had almost certainly been in custody once before, in 1945, but just for a few days. The Russians and French dealt with the matter differently, since they had different objectives. They jailed their Nazis, and they stayed jailed, though the

French would overlook people for suitable inducements. Both the Russians and the French intended to dismantle their respective zones, partly by way of restitution and partly out of revenge. Whether anything worked in their areas (aside from their own accommodations) or how the Germans fared was of no concern to them, whereas it was critically important to the British and Americans. So we kept on shovelling people into and out of jail, like the famous Marx Brothers' breakfast scene. It was a dubious operation morally and an inept one in practical terms. Since French-German relations today are better than the German ties to England, our attitudes did not even pay off on a personal or political level.

There were less weighty matters to preoccupy us at the time. We had "liberated" a sumptuous motor yacht, complete with a crew of four, and had taken to cruising up and down the main canal in the late afternoon, having drinks on deck, and generally feeling like passengers on Cleopatra's barge, while the crew (expressly released for that purpose) kept the boat pointed in the right direction. One memorable occasion, Teddy, moved by some alcoholic and Nelsonian fantasy, ordered the anchor to be "dropped to port." Over went the anchor and as it happened not to be attached to any anchor chain, they just had to do without it. Since next morning Teddy could not even recall being on the boat, we never learned what he had in mind.

We all drank a good deal more than was necessary or useful, but none of us was as affected as Emil. Emil was a full-grown gander, which we had found one day sniffing up the remains of a glass left in the garden of the mess hall. Emil came waddling in every afternoon thereafter and drank whatever we set out for him. He would, after a while, close one eye, start swaying, fall down all in a heap, and begin snoring through his beak. By the time we returned from our nautical diversion, he would be gone, only to be back the next day. The ASPCA's jurisdiction did not extend as far as Friedrichstadt, and for all I know, they may approve of alcoholic geese. They could certainly not have objected to our seal encounters, however.

Just beyond the dune "island" and out in the North Sea, there were a number of sandy ridges exposed at low tide which one could wade to. We originally did so to look for sea gull eggs, a delicacy to stay away from. They not only look unappetizing, but taste of fish; unless you are a sushi addict, forget it. Those same ridges, however, were a Disneyland for seals; whole tribes of them were all over. Seals are both fast and shy, and so, on our first appearance, all of them took to the water. Seals are, however, also intensely curious and arguably not too bright. One of us began lying in the shallows (no big deal in June) and imitating a seal, by flapping his hands together and making barking noises. The more he did it, the more seals popped their heads up, and the longer he did it, the closer they came to have a better look. By this time there were three or four of us playing seal, and within ten minutes or so we were all side-by-side-by-seal, flapping and barking together. The moment we stopped, they stopped; if we got up, they took off back into the water. It was very damp, very friendly, and very smelly (seals have awesome halitosis), and one of the nicest memories I have of Friedrichstadt.

By this time, Germans did our cooking and everything else. Everyone had at least a couple of mechanics to look after whatever vehicle he claimed to be his, as well as two or three maids, and half-a-dozen people hanging about "just in case." All these people, in turn, had "delegates," who also got involved in the act, which was simply to make sure that we had food and cigarettes and they did not. Their food supply was very tight, and there were no cigarettes at all. Ten cigarettes would get you a mechanic for a week or take care of your laundry for a month. For serious entertainment, there was Hamburg, about an hour's ride away; some of us made it back in about half an hour, but that was probably because, by then, we only saw the road half of the time. Despite the terrible bombings, Hamburg, like Berlin, had enormous resilience, and people were picking themselves off the floor, almost literally in many cases, and carrying on.

One of my earliest recollections of Hamburg in May 1945 is of an unforgettable performance of *Beggar's Opera*. The actors were only adequate, but the setting was spellbinding. The stage of the theater had survived, as had the roof over perhaps ten or fifteen rows of seats. Everything else had collapsed, but enough space had been cleared in the rubble to accommodate several rows of trestle benches, which stood under the open sky. The walls of the building stood to a height of about ten feet, but everything behind the stage had been wiped out. There was the ever-present smell of brick dust, smoke, and decaying matter, the actors were wearing their own clothes or what was left of them, two jeeps (lent by us) provided the stage lights, admission price was cigarettes or food thrown into a bucket passed around by the actors, the sky was full of stars, and I shall never forget it.

The Germans in Hamburg were defeated, hungry, and occasionally desperate, but under very little restraint. Curfew was lax and laxly observed, and there was very little *vae victis* (woe to the vanquished) spirit about. The policy, at least in the initial months, was to ignore Germans altogether and let them fend for themselves, while we were living lushly in tightly guarded enclaves. The Russians, in their areas, kept on hunting and witch-hunting Germans from the moment the fighting stopped, but, aside from seeking specific people on various "proscribed" lists, and even doing that rather cursorily, the British treated the Germans as "nonpersons."

The hub of our entertainment universe was the Atlantic Hotel, miraculously standing almost undamaged, and still living on its former reputation as the city's most glamorous hotel. In the summer of 1945, it was the navel of our world; the staff, many of them prewar employees, seemed numberless, and the possibilities and facilities limitless. It was the largest, most raucous, and probably least reputable officers' club in any of the four occupation zones for the remainder of the 1940s, which did its later reputation little good; it was wild.

Poet Philip Larkin wrote the endearing phrase: "Sex was invented in '63, just a little late for me"; he should have been in the Atlantic way back when. Having accumulated whatever could be found in the quarters of the local High Command and Nazi hierarchy, supplemented by what could be bartered, bought, or stolen, the Atlantic kitchen ran three separate restaurants, any one of which would today have a Michelin rating. Meals were officially settled by paying "scrip money," an inane attempt to discourage us from "free economy" endeavors. Instead of wasting your pay on such nonsense, the thing to do was to find the nearest black marketeer (the Atlantic Hotel porter was usually the closest) and buy the necessary scrip for two or three cigarettes. The Atlantic porters did not, of course, only deal in scrip and cigarettes; they dealt in cars, jewelry, paintings, theater tickets, houses of any kind of repute, women of all or none,

Russian cossacks, Chinese laundries—they were awesome. I am convinced they retired very rich, and they richly deserved to.

We were thus just getting used to being lords of the Western Marshes and members of the "British Army of the Rhine" (one of Churchill's more orotund fancies), when Third RTR received orders to move to Suechteln. Once more, I was dispatched to find out where and what Suechteln was. It turned out to be a couple of hundred miles south of Friedrichstadt, on the outskirts of Krefeld (my wife's native city), and it was the largest mental institution in Germany, as I believe it still is. It was an immense, walled estate covering several hundred acres, with substantial three-storey brick houses dotted among lawns and trees, and a whole jigsaw puzzle of paths and roads leading through it.

I was informed by the Allied military governor in Krefeld, the first of that species whom I had met, that Third RTR had been allocated the western part of the estate, the remainder still being inhabited "by the originals," as he quaintly put it. My stay in Suechteln was brief, but for the week or two during which I was still a member of Third RTR, there never was a time of day when the fence dividing the two parts of the estate was not crowded with "originals" looking us over. Compared to our chaps, who were once again engaged in polishing bolts on tank tracks, the behavior of the originals seemed awfully normal to me.

By the time the regiment arrived a couple of days later (tanks get moved by flatbed transporters; left to move by themselves for such long distances, they throw tracks and wreck roads), I had mobilized the usual hordes of Germans to make those empty houses livable and, in the process, had discovered a complete German film unit parked outside Krefeld with no place to go. They had every imaginable variety of projector and the personnel to cope with it; best of all, they had a whole film library of "super productions," admittedly in German, but also in color and with music. For an outlay of fifty cigarettes and the promise of three meals a day, they attached themselves to Third RTR, who would hence be able to see a different movie nightly for three months without "repeats."

While in Suechteln we were briefly reminded what actual soldiering could be like. Our nearest neighbors were a Gurkha battalion, part of the famed Fourth Indian Division, whom Third RTR knew from its desert days. The Gurkhas have been written about endlessly and for good reason; they have won more gallantry awards in two world wars than all other British and Empire troops combined. They looked just as they had been described to me: small, dark, bullet-headed, manically cheerful, impeccably neat, loving everything military. The all wore khukris, a heavy boomerang-shaped knife, somewhat like a bowie, and for which all Gurkhas are famous. We were having drinks in their mess and we asked them about the often-heard tales that Gurkhas were able to decapitate an ox with one khukri slash and that they could be invisible and inaudible when they chose to be. The first query was quickly settled. A moon-faced, smiling Gurkha sergeant was called in, a very quick exchange in Gurkhali (I assumed) ensued, whereupon the sergeant went to a nearby oaken table, which had legs about four inches thick, drew his khukri, bent lightly at the knees, and, with a single casual backhand swipe, sliced one table leg right off. He then saluted smartly, smiled broadly, and marched out.

The other proof came the following night. There was a bet between us and the Gurkha officers that the Gurkhas could not launch a night attack with fifty men on Third RTR standing to at full alert and be able to get at us without our noticing it. The entire fighting strength of Third RTR, about 350 men, were dispersed in the open throughout the park; they could hide, but not inside tanks or houses. The Gurkhas, in turn, would put a white chalk mark where otherwise they would have used their khukris—the decapitation part would be dispensed with. There would be no lights anywhere, the exercise would start at midnight and end at 3 A.M. If, during that time, any of us heard or saw a Gurkha, we would challenge him, which would rule him "dead" and out of the game. It came midnight and all of us were listening like wolves. We did hear noises and did issue challenges, but every time we looked at whom we had found, it turned out to be one of our own guys blundering about. Came 3 A.M., the lights went on and not a Gurkha anywhere, any more than there apparently had been during those three hours. Except that every one of us had at least one chalk mark on him somewhere, most of us several, and some of them were on the chest! None of us would have survived the night. That's why it's safer in tanks.

We had been settled in Suechteln for about ten days when, from one hour to the next, in typically random and inexplicable army fashion, I left Suechteln, Third RTR and, in many ways, all things military, and entered upon the last and final stage of that seven-year metamorphosis. For the next twenty-six months, I was to explore just about all facets of Charles V's great statement: "To have another language is to have another life." We did not have the same thing in mind though.

## PART V

---

# BEHIND THE SCENES
# AND IN THE WINGS

I T STARTED JUST as casually as just about everything had since May 1940.

## 1

Teddy Mitford called me in and said, "Well, Mark, we're losing you. Jeep will take you to Oynhausen to report to Colonel Newman. Odd bird; met him once in the desert; don't know what to make of him. Speaks a lot of languages, I gather. You're his now; sorry about it. Well, we had some good times together. Keep in touch." We shook hands, I saluted—and I have not seen Teddy Mitford again, nor have I kept in touch with either him or 3rd RTR. It is quite baffling to me. I was proud to be part of 3rd RTR and still am; we had some good and some memorable times together, and I became fond of a number of people I served with. And yet I just wandered out of that phase of my life and the people in it, just as I did from the Pioneers and from internment.

I knew nothing about Colonel Newman—"the odd bird"—and all I knew about Bad Oynhausen was that it was in the center of the British Zone and housed the headquarters of the entire British Occupation apparatus. Why Newman had me transferred to his unit, and how or when he had ever heard of me before, are mysteries to this day. If it had to do with Himmler, then the connection is as hidden as his grave. It took me a while to locate Newman. Accessibility is no virtue in the army; it just leads to being involved in situations you would rather avoid; in organizations, where the *raison d'être* is both dubious and tenuous, anonymity is vital.

I finally located Newman and it was immediately apparent that he was a professional survivor and quite dramatically odd. I do not know how many languages he spoke, but he doubtlessly had the same Viennese accent in all of them. I had seen uniformed midgets before, but never one surrounded by four Great Danes. He knew all about me, back to my school days in Berlin, so we wasted no time on that; instead he outlined the little empire he controlled. He had nineteen "interrogation teams" operating in the British sectors of Germany and Austria and in Berlin, each consisting of three highly trained bilingual interrogation officers, who dealt with high-level prisoners on even loftier subjects. He made it sound as if Hitler might barely qualify for the interrogations he had in mind. He had a vacancy in his Schleswig-Holstein teams and that is where he wanted me to go, right away, now, the jeep was outside. "Ich weiss dass ich mich auf Sie verlassen kann, Captain Lynton."†

The last I saw of Colonel Newman he was being dragged through the door by his four enormous dogs. Eutin, where I was now headed for, is the capital of what Germans optimistically refer to as "Holstein's Switzerland." It is not that, but it is very pretty and an idyllic change from the somber reclusiveness of the Diethmarschen, over in the west. Eutin, a small market town, nestled between wooded hills and a very attractive lake, seemed more attuned to Heidi than to Hitler, and is the somnolent, wholesome little place that you will always remember kindly and never want to return to. Newman's interrogation section had installed itself in one of the prettier houses around, a rambling, thatch-roofed chalet on top of a hill, with a large garden running down to the lakeside and a mooring for four boats with, of course, four motor boats duly moored there.

Aside from three interrogation officers, there was a sergeant to deal with confidential typing and files, and six staff personnel who supposedly cooked, cleaned, or drove and of course did nothing of the

---

†"I know that I can rely on you, Captain Lynton."

kind. They in turn had a floating entourage of about thirty locals, who in return for an agreed cigarette rate, did it all for them. This was to be my home for the next eight months, though I spent a good deal of time away from it. Major Tom Higgins headed the section, a jovial, even-tempered, and most pleasant man who was an effective inter- rogator, despite the fact that his German was distinctly rocky. He was such a kindly soul that I think people just liked to confide in him and overlooked the fact that they did not understand his questions. My other colleague was Captain Wilfred Dewhurst, clearly handicapped by being burdened with such a lamentable first name, and also resentful of having a working-class background and lack of public- school education. Wilfred looked like the poor girl's Errol Flynn and behaved in a ludicrously affected fashion in public; in private, he turned out to be both bright and companionable. He spoke magnifi- cent German and was a fine, though somewhat predictable interroga- tor. I found out in due course that good interrogations involve frequent changes of pace, mood, and direction, and Wilfred was too uptight for that. He was good, though, in a no-nonsense way, and reveled in being referred to by his victims as "ein Englischer Nazi." Both Tom and Wilfred had been Intelligence officers since they had joined the army years ago, but were wholly unable to tell me just how you train to become such an animal. Being an Intelligence officer, I found, is mostly on-the-job training and a self-made endeavor—with the attendant risks of unskilled labor!

For the next three months I interrogated people in the Eutin area, in Berlin, Hamburg, Kiel, and even London; I must have spent ten hours a day doing just that. This really is an occupation where you learn by doing, but if you do not intend to run around so much and put in that many hours, here are a few ground rules I picked up:

☐ Silence is a great interrogation tool. Look at your man and say nothing; let him start talking. If he stops, keep quiet, let him start again. It does not always work and before getting into a trappist séance, you had better say something—but give it a try.

☐ Always give the impression that you already know most of what he is telling you; do not ever look or act surprised.

□ The more startling the information you get, the less you should react immediately. Just let it go by, let him talk of something else, come back to it later, and on a "just by the way" basis.

□ Take your time, set your own pace, do not have outside interruptions (unless they suit you, in which case, stage them).

□ Always ask open-ended, oblique, "laundry list" questions; do not tip your hand as to what you are looking for. "Are you a war criminal?" will not elicit a very informative response.

□ Keep control of your interrogation pattern; make up your mind whether and when you want to cajole or bully, be empathetic, or be remote, and when and whether you want to switch moods. Do not lose your thread or your temper (unless it suits your pattern).

□ Almost all interrogations are "jigsaws"; he will not tell the whole story in sequence, and sometimes he really only knows parts of it. Try and get a grasp of the general outline as soon as you can and note the missing parts. Keep on fishing for them as the interrogation progresses.

□ Above all, listen! Listen to what is being said, how it is being said, what is not being said.

If you remember all this and, above all, that flexibility is the key and that you might have to improvise at any moment, interrogation is a cinch—and fun to boot.

Interrogations with a set deadline are usually frustrating; you can get people to "confess by 6 P.M.," but it is no fun for either side, and you can never be sure that you did not miss some interesting bits of information along the way. I never used or witnessed any "tricks," such as bright lights, withholding food or water, let alone drugs or torture. I do not know whether that approach works, but I rather doubt it. Threats can be useful in some cases, but suppose you make good on them and the guy still does not talk, then what have you got left? If he dies or even faints on you, he is not going to supply many answers, and if he is sufficiently terrorized to tell you what you want to hear, how do you know whether it is really true?

Once in Copenhagen I did some "heavy breathing" stuff, out of sheer hooliganism; no one got hurt—and I did not get any answers either.

What does work, though I only did it once, is continuous interrogation. You get a team of three or four interrogators, who know each other and each other's methods well enough so they can establish an uninterrupted "pattern," and then get them to interrogate whoever it is around the clock, each interrogator taking a six- or eight-hour turn, while the victim being interrogated gets no rest or sleep.

You will break anyone within forty-eight hours; you will not feel that chipper yourself at the end of it.

All of these useful household hints of course only apply if you are interrogating someone whom you are just seeing for a few hours.

If he is in jail or detention, and you can pester him round the clock, there are some additional techniques, and we learned a good deal from the Russians how to adapt those. I had no occasion to practice these techniques myself and if you have read Koestler's *Darkness at Noon,* you know all about them. Essentially, it works on the basis of total isolation, where a prisoner sees or talks to no one but you. This sets up a dependency relationship, which you foster by appearing supportive. After several sessions in that mood, you will inexplicably switch to being confrontational, and from then on you alternate between moods in a stick-and-carrot pattern which—if you follow the instructions on the back of the envelope—should bring about almost Pavlovian responses. I have seen it done, and I have seen it work, but not always. It will not work with idiots, who do not realize what is going on, with psychopaths, who are out of touch with what is going on, or with that wholly unmanageable category of people who can discipline themselves to "switch off" altogether. Fakhirs and gurus are virtually interrogation-proof, but there were not too many of them around in Germany in 1945.

## 2

My only participation in continuous interrogation involved the most loathsome and enigmatic figure I met in all those months. Sometime in July one of the locals wandered in to trade information for some cigarettes, which had become a regular habit between Eutiners and our outfit. He mentioned quite casually that someone with an SS tattoo on his arm was working on a farm, a few miles up the road. He had talked to him and seen the tattoo in his armpit; name of Hasch or Hoess, the man had said. He got his couple of cigarettes and walked off; we routinely checked the name against our "wanted" lists and the only name we found was Hoess, Rudolf, SS Standartenfuhrer, Camp Commandant, Auschwitz—we were at that farm in about sixty seconds.

We found our man shovelling manure in the yard, carrying no guns, no cyanide, no documents, nothing. He admitted to being called Hoess, but claimed to have come with a bunch of refugees from Silesia and to have been a city employee somewhere. We took him back to Eutin and, at first quite by accident, fell into a continuous interrogation pattern. He seemed much too colorless and meek to have been what we thought he might have been, and yet there were occasional flashes of arrogance which did not fit with a low-level city employee. So we kept on plugging away, asking the same question over and over, going over his story again and again, each of us taking turns every two or three hours. When we had first taken him, we had accused him of being the Auschwitz Hoess, and he had of course disclaimed even knowing what Auschwitz might be. We kept on throwing that one up, and he kept throwing it out. I really do not know why we kept at it; I do not recall any hunch or hint—I guess we were just being obstinate and not getting enough rest, besides.

However, he was not getting any at all, and after about fourteen hours of this, he broke during Wilfred's "shift" and suddenly said, "I am Hoess. What do you want to know?"

Of course we wanted to know everything, and once he started, it was like opening a faucet. Hoess was much too big a catch to be dealt with by the likes of us, and we had alerted Oynhausen and Intelligence HQ right away, but since it took them a few hours to come up and collect him, there was plenty of time for him to talk to us. He was articulate, polite, cooperative, diffident, and quiet-spoken, and listening to him was one of the most eerily horrifying experiences of my life.

He told us he would get up in the morning, have breakfast with his wife, stroll through his little garden, and then set off to the camp gates, a few hundred yards away. He would spend all day in his office making sure that all details were taken care of to ensure that several thousand people would be gassed and incinerated in an orderly and efficient manner. He would interrupt the day to walk back to his house, have lunch with his wife, have another look at his garden, and then return. Except on "emergency days," he would stop promptly at six, go home, and take a nap before dinner. How many were disposed of in that way? On average maybe six to seven thousand a day, but on emergency days, they had managed up to ten to twelve thousand. He never talked of killing, he always spoke of "disposing" and this was not done to people, but to "items;" it was absolutely unbelievable!

Had he ever been personally present? Not often, he found the sight harrowing. Had he ever thought that he was doing wrong? He had never thought about it in such terms. How did he think about it? That he had been given orders and was carrying them out. Did that involve any personal feelings? He felt satisfied at having done an efficient job and at having been appreciated by his superiors. Was that all? No, he often felt tired, even depressed; it was a real pressure job, particularly on emergency days.

And so it went, in an amiable monotone, coming from a pudgy, meek, forgettable little man, the very epitome of Hannah Arendt's "Banality of Evil." By the time they came to collect him, we were almost as disconnected as he and were beginning to believe that the garden involvement was just as important as "disposing of items." He was eventually handed over to the Poles, who hanged him; I doubt that he ever understood why.

Very few encounters in those days, however, were that ghastly, though some had distinct Grand Guignol overtones. There was an extraordinary Royal Navy commander, all red beard and Francis Drake, who marched through the door one morning dressed like the Hollywood version of a Serbian goatherd, and carrying enough armaments to load a truck. After he revealed his true identity, he invited us to look "at the people out in courtyard," who turned out to be another dozen mountain bandits, festooned with lethal toys. Our friend was evidently multilingual and had been parachuted into

France several times, and notably so in spring 1944, to get a bunch of characters together, who would join him "in making a little trouble." This he had done and the survivors were out there, some French, several Poles and Czechs, some Spanish Republicans; all they had in common was that they were or had become competent assassins. The "little trouble" they had been making had nothing to do with sabotage or information gathering; they were not equipped for that and "anyway my boys wouldn't be interested." Stabbing an Ortskommandant here, strangling some SS type there, drowning a collaborator; what he was telling us was that this happy band of Robin Hoods had spent the past fifteen months murdering their way through Europe. He was now heading back to the navy (which cannot have viewed that prospect with unalloyed joy) but felt responsible for the boys, whose skills did not extend beyond killing and who were disinclined to learn new ones. So here was his proposal; if we could provide him with a list of "unwanted personnel," regardless of nationality, rank, or occupation, he would pass it to his boys, and they would take care of them for us. He seemed genuinely disappointed when we declined such a sporting offer, but appeared considerably cheered by our suggestion that perhaps the Russians or the French might be able to oblige him. He and his merry men marched out of the courtyard and our lives, presumably on their way to proposition de Lattre.

I spent most of my time in a nearby school, which we had converted into an interrogation center, a somewhat extended variation of a dentist office, complete with waiting room and back issues of *Yank* and *Men Only* (presumably to reveal the higher levels of Anglo-Saxon life). We each had our own "office" and the army kept the waiting room filled by the lorry load, simply by emptying all the camps in the area and sluicing them through us. Anyone found wandering about in uniform had been shovelled into a nearby catchment camp; no one ever bothered to establish a head count, let alone identities, and if the Germans had not been so tired and dispirited, they could simply have walked out of any of them. The idea now was to have a sampling of the inmates interrogated, however briefly, and anyone to whom we gave a clean bill of health, was simply told to go home. If we uncovered anything villainous or merely interesting, we sent that man to a large nearby camp where several thousand POW's were kept under guard, and with some semblance of administration. After spending most of the day sorting out and discarding a lot of chaff, we were, later in the afternoon, supposed to devote ourselves to those wheat kernels and see who and what we could come up with. That was the theory, and like most theories, it did not really work, but we did see a great many people and we did uncover things here and there.

Every once in a while, we would come across a truly big fish, and such a catch would be forwarded to "London Cage," to be dealt with by real experts—or so I was led to believe. The job really only dealt with identification of individuals who had committed crimes or who had been centrally involved in events that someone was interested in learning about from the German viewpoint. It was in that connection that some never-identified administrative deity elevated me briefly and inexplicably to an interrogational summit meeting. Tom Higgins got orders to detach me for an urgent assignment at "London Cage," with the promise that I would be back within the week—a military promise for once kept.

Off I went, by truck, overnight camp, and boat, back to London and to one of those vast and splendid Victorian monstrosities in Kensington Gardens, temporarily borrowed from some redundant embassy and now representing "London Cage," where the crème de la crème of VIP prisoners were being kept.

Having gone through the usual identification routine of name, rank, serial number, and having signed the Official Secrets Act of 1911—a wonderfully arcane and encompassing document, which in essence forbids you to talk about anything, including the weather, for the rest of your life—I was first interviewed by an equally strange Intelligence colonel.

Another word about the Secrets Act. They kept having us sign it periodically, rather like booster flu shots, and technically I am still bound by it till the Second Coming, and probably beyond. Well, if this be treason, make the most of it; I happen to believe these revelations will not imperil the empire or what is left of it. If I am wrong, come visit me in jail.

My interviewer turned out to be the military version of T. H. White's Merlin, a wonderfully distracted university don, who during our brief interview kept on setting fire to himself attempting to light his pipe. In between beating out sparks and grunting disconsolately, he suddenly said in accent-free German, "You are here to interrogate Field Marshall von Rundstedt on issues relating to the Ardennes offensive," thrust a sheet of paper at me, and disappeared. The paper was a list of very detailed queries covering the planning and development of the offensive. It is still a mystery to me why this could not have been handled locally, or why I was picked to do it. Mysteries are occupational hazards among the military, and the explanation is almost invariably that someone goofed and no one else cared.

I had hardly installed myself behind a bare desk with my sheet of questions, and found that there was just one extra straight-backed chair completing the furnishings, when the door opened and there stood Rundstedt. Everybody knew about him then, of course. Coming from generations of East Prussian Junkers, he was Hitler's oldest and (except for von Manstein, whom I met exactly a week later) most brilliant field marshall. None of that, however, had prepared me for the man himself. He was tall, ramrod straight, with a thick body and an infinitely wrinkled face (Rundstedt must have been in his seventies); his monocle and boots gleamed; his uniform and cap were a symphony of scarlet, grey, and gold thread with a Knight's Cross with Oak Leaves and rows of ribbons. Had Eric von Stroheim seen him, he would have turned in his Actor's Equity card. But what struck me most was the aura of total and absolute command; he was Field Marshall Gerd von Rundstedt, treating all around him with rigid courtesy and icy disdain. He looked at me for a moment with the hooded eyes of a very old turtle, and there was no question as to who was in charge here. He stalked into the room, leaning heavily on a cane, sat on the chair with his back not touching at any point, placed his cap on his knees, and said, "Ich stehe zu Ihrer Verfuegung. Bitte stellen Sie Ihre Fragen."†

In the three days following, the routine never varied. Rundstedt would give explicit comments in his clipped command voice, never

---

† "I am at your disposal. Please ask your questions."

changing in pitch or intonation; he would wait patiently for me to make notes, and he never evaded any issue or question. He never altered his ramrod stance, never smiled, never seemed to move a muscle. He was not friendly or unfriendly—he was the senior marshall of the German army and I was a captain whose name he neither knew nor cared to know. I just did not exist, except as a voice. The session would last from nine till noon, then he would be fetched to have a meal somewhere, and I would have mine in the canteen. Since in those days we really thought that tampering with the Official Secrets Act was a shortcut to the thumbscrews, no one in the canteen ever discussed what he was doing. At two in the afternoon, we would start again, Rundstedt making the identical entry, with that long iron-hard look, then sitting straight as a poker and stating, "Ich stehe zur Verfuegung," and we would go on till five. The first day I suggested a tea break to him and ran into that gun-barrel look. "Bitte bleiben Sie bei'm Thema,"† he said; so I did not try that again.

At five he was taken back to his quarters (which I later gathered was very comfortable; people of his rank were housed in mini-flats, complete with batmen; German batmen I assume, no one else could have coped with those boots), and I had the rest of the day off to roam around London and hang out at Le Petit Club.

The Rundstedt interviews went on in exactly the same manner for three days, at the end of which I had worked my way through the list of questions. I rang for his escort, stood up, saluted, and said, "Danke, Herr General Feldmarschall," and he got up, put on his cap, gave me another of his long, heavy-lidded stares, saluted, turned, and that was it.

I got back to Eutin well in time for the Manstein interlude. Manstein, generally acknowledged as the ablest of Hitler's dozen or so field marshalls, had no involvement with war crimes or even with being a Nazi, but he was clearly a VIP of the first rank, and as such fair game to be at least interrogated. Thus, when yet another of our cigarette-craving Eutiners told us that Manstein was hiding in a nearby village, a whole posse of jeeps and locally stationed infantry

---

†"Please, stick to the subject."

accompanied us to make sure we got him. To make doubly sure, we intended to catch him in bed and by surprise, and that we did. One moment we were creeping around the farmhouse in question just around dawn, and the next, we were confronted by a furious little gnome in a long white nightshirt, his sharp bird-like features brick-red with rage. He was brandishing a field marshall's baton, a gorgeous concoction of gold, ivory, and diamonds, and was making furious enquiries about what the hell we were doing waking people up at this time of day. He was not concerned about being arrested; he just thought we were being impolite, and he was, of course, quite right. So we apologized, and he calmed down and, unlike Rundstedt, turned out to be quite a jovial little fellow. He had a hair-trigger temper, though; while he was shaving with an open razor, I chose to hover very close by, just to make sure he did not do anything rash. I apparently got in his way or his light, because he stopped in mid-stroke and I have not been so verbally trampled since Sandhurst days. We finally had him calmed down again, dressed, and jeeped off the army headquarters—where they stole his baton.

I did not get back to Eutin right away, being instructed to stay on, "since we have you down here anyway," and thus got involved in another truly engrossing interrogation. Colonel von Harling, a handsome, elegant, urbane man, fluent in several languages, and married to a great German heiress, had surrendered to the British, having been chief of Intelligence of the German armies operating in the Balkans for almost four years. He was the one who told me about General Gehlen and his organization and the structure of German Intelligence in general.

My specific brief, supposedly a direct request from Whitehall, was to find out exactly what Marshal Tito and Draza Mihajlović had done during the fighting in Yugoslavia. When the Germans overran that country in 1941, Mihajlović and his chetnik troops had offered bitter resistance, and had been supported by the British with parachute drops and supplies. A year or so later, Tito and his partisans became prominent in fighting the Germans, and rumors started filtering out that Tito was not only fighting them, but also Mihajlović. Some time after that, there were more rumors that Mihajlović had actually allied himself to the Germans to fight Tito. After 1942, the lion's share of

Allied support had gone to Tito, but some aid had been given to Mihajlović almost right up to the end, and the Allies were genuinely confused as to what the respective positions of these two men were.

Harling made the situation perfectly clear. I wrote a fifty-page report at the time, classified "top secret" then. I have little doubt that Harling's comments clarified the Allied position towards Tito and brought about their concurrence in his trying and executing Mihajlović. A number of matters mentioned by Harling were also mentioned at Mihajlović's trial, where he used that memorable phrase that he had been "a leaf adrift in the storm of events." According to Harling, the Germans had first fought Mihajlović and subsequently both him and Tito. From the start, Tito and his partisans had been tougher opponents, but the Germans had had trouble fighting both. Mihajlović had made the first move, proposing a truce, which was then followed by an alliance with the Germans, both for the purpose of being able to fight Tito. He had made it clear to the Germans that, as a convinced royalist, he feared Tito and his Communists more than he did the Germans. His reasoning was that the Germans, already hard-pressed on other fronts, would ultimately have to withdraw from Yugoslavia, whereas Tito, if established, could not be dislodged again. Harling, who had personally conducted these negotiations, had agreed to the alliance, since the German High Command felt that it would be too costly to fight two separate resistance organizations at the same time. Thus Mihajlović had indeed been fighting on the German side and against Tito. His effectiveness and impact had progressively lessened, and aside from not having to fight him, the Germans had derived little benefit from the alliance. As Harling pointed out repeatedly, Mihajlović's reasoning had of course been quite correct. The Germans had had to leave the country, and Tito was unshakably entrenched. There was, however, not a shadow of doubt that, in the eyes of the Allies and of Tito, Mihajlović had committed treason. His trials and subsequent execution took place later that year and, legally speaking, were clearly valid.

Harling also gave me extensive information on dates, locations, and troop dispositions, and altogether re-created the entire Yugoslav scene, as perceived through German eyes, from 1941 to 1945. In terms of fact-finding and "history behind the scenes," it was far and away the most interesting interrogation I had conducted; Rundstedt was awesome, Manstein was funny, Himmler sensational, and my later political embroglios fascinating, but the Harling encounter was unique in explaining such a finite and complete episode of a particular time and place.

Harling and I spent two days together, the most civilized multilingual interrogation I can recall, a conversation really, and we established real personal rapport. When I left, he invited me to visit him at his hunting lodge near Augsburg, after he was released. He was freed soon after, but we did not meet again; we did however correspond with each other for several years afterwards.

Although the Intelligence Corps has its own badges and insignia, people like myself, merely temporarily attached and neither feeling nor really being part of it, never wore them. Until I left the army, I wore only the badges and insignia of Third RTR and my paratrooper wings.

## 3

After these dramatic intermezzi, Eutin was bucolic and restful; I interrogated my twenty or so bodies a day, anyone from local officials to senior German Army (Wehrmacht) officers. No one ever seemed to doubt that my fluency in German was solely due to the versatility of talents of the British Secret Service; the purity of my Anglo-Saxon origins was never in question.

I had a close call once, when, having requested the British Army headquarters at Oynhausen for a "temporary," to allow us more time to use all those motor boats, they sent us Sergeant McCullough, who turned out to be a guy named Polatschek, whom I knew from Pioneer days.

Polatschek was a Jewish thug from Vienna, where he had thrived as a truck driver by day and a pimp by night before he fled to England when the Nazis came. He had then led a boisterous and violent existence as a bouncer in various Soho night spots before ending up in the Pioneers, where I had met and avoided him. He was very much Commando material, which he joined as soon as that was possible, and where he performed blood-chilling and commendable deeds. He was a good assassin, but the thought that he qualified for Intelligence of any kind had never occurred to me, nor had the possibility that he, too, had changed his name. The news that Sergeant McCullough would be ours for a week rang no bell. It rang when he arrived. There I was, an amalgam of Ronald Coleman and Lord Kitchener, acting infinitely British, coaxing some information out of a senior general passing through our office, and there he was standing in the doorway.

Recognition was instantaneous, except that I said, "At ease, Sergeant," and he said, "oy veh, Loewenstein!" It puzzled the general, interfered with my leisure plans, and got Polatschek sent back to Oynhausen the same day.

Among the array of generals I dealt with at the time, the oldest was a gnarled gnome, with no hair and a nose like a billhook, who came in a wheelchair and with the name of von Lettow-Vorbeck. I had learned about him when at school in Berlin. He was a legendary figure who, in World War I, had first conquered and then mislaid a handful of African colonies for Germany, all of it with just a few native bearers and some leftover equipment from the Napoleonic wars. He now lived on a small estate outside of Eutin, in his high eighties, and I have no idea why he was ever brought in for interrogation since his interest in the world in general ceased the day Kaiser Wilhelm abdicated. We spent half an hour or so in idle and baffled conversation, during which he repeatedly alluded to "S.M.," culminating in the mystifying suggestion that we both be aware of the fact that that very day was S.M.'s birthday. Since he appeared amiably dotty in other respects, it was not until some days later, when I visited him at his place, that I caught on that "S.M." stood for Seine Majestaet, the correct pre-1918 address when referring to the emperor in conversation. I did occasionally visit the old boy on his farm afterwards; he knew some awesome African tales, and his capacity for liquor was impressive. The more he drank, the wilder the stories became. He should have written scripts for Tarzan.

Since the Intelligence Corps declared itself exempt from non-fraternization restrictions (as opposed to everyone else in the British

222 / ACCIDENTAL JOURNEY

Zone who just acted that way), our contacts with Germans were numerous and constant. Tom Higgins had the interesting distinction of having a private dentist, which went one better on the array of private butlers, chauffeurs, gardeners, cooks, and tailors whom all of us had. Tom's teeth called for no particular care, but by being "Major Higgins' Own," the dentist safeguarded his equipment from others' attention (everybody was "liberating" just about everything in those days) and, being a well-connected night owl, in return produced a succession of entertainers, dance bands, and stand-up comics, mostly from the Hamburg area, all of them well beneath borscht-circuit level, and all of them ready to sell their own and everyone else's grandmother for a meal and two cigarettes. I do not recall any of this bedraggled crew except one pianist, whose performance left no impression whatever, but who was accompanied by his wife, who never said a word all night and was arguably the most beautiful woman any of us had ever seen. This view was evidently shared by Hollywood and Robert Taylor. Two or three years later, I saw her picture in the papers as Mrs. Robert T., and subsequently even saw her in a movie as Ursula Thiess. I have no idea how she ever got from Eutin to Hollywood, but with looks like that, anything goes.

The German army was supposedly the most mechanized force in military history, but it still had a remarkable number of horses, and an entire cavalry regiment had been rounded up in a prisoners' compound just a few miles from Eutin. This led to our thinking that in return for teaching us how to ride, some of the senior Feldwebels would be only too happy to be let out of camp and have access to beds and limitless food. So we got three very competent-looking NCO's and assorted nags from the camp, and the lessons started the next day. I do not know how many ways there are to mount a horse, but I believe I know all the ways to come off one in a hurry. After a few days Tom and Wilfred, though no John Waynes, appeared to catch on to at least the rudiments, while I strained to scramble on, and came off with considerably greater velocity. My sergeant-instructor clearly enjoyed the food and facilities, but also had respect for horses and himself. After a week of this debacle, he respectfully but firmly asked to be returned to camp. I have not been near a horse since.

The most prized possession throughout my time with Intelligence was a small plastic card, indicating my name and showing a thumb print (a fool-proof method, on the assumption that everyone carried a print identification kit with him at all times), and blandly stating that the holder of this card was entitled to all assistance by all members of the British Armed Forces or Civilian Government throughout Germany and Austria, for whatever purpose and without any questions asked. All requests to be met immediately, and any question arising to be subsequently submitted in writing to the Home Office, department such-and-such (all British Intelligence activities fall under Home Office for budgetary purposes, but are answerable only to the Prime Minister's Office). I do not know how many of these cards were issued; in more than two years, I came across fewer than twenty people who had one. I have no idea at all why I should have been entitled to such a Walter Mitty document. I had occasional wild and wonderful fantasies of getting the RAF to bomb Monty's headquarters or of declaring Hamburg under curfew at high noon, just for the hell of it. In actual fact I used the card very sparingly. Once in a while I would take precedence over an apoplectic major general on an RAF transport to London. Fabulous potential, though.

When not dining *chez nous* (no hardship, since we had found a couple of cooks who had been that at the Hotel Adlon in Berlin; they even did things to Spam!), we had the choice of Hamburg or Ploen. Hamburg was a good two hours' by jeep, and aside from the babylonian Atlantic, there was now also the officer's club at the Reemtsma villa, a fabulous Bauhaus-inspired spread of cantilevered glass and marble with an immense indoor/outdoor pool, the first of its kind anyone of us had ever seen. Members of the Reemtsma family were tobacco tycoons of longstanding and while I doubt that they had committed any specific crime, they probably had employed "slave labor" like everyone else in Germany, and the house was just too magnificent not to be requisitioned.

The Ploen facility was very different. Built in the late nineteenth century, it was a heap of towers, turrets, and crenelated walls, all perched on a rock face overlooking a little torrent, and was quite ludicrously Wagnerian. It had been, for some sixty years, a very exclusive naval cadet academy, though it clearly had more potential as a mountaineering establishment. Most of its inmates had been massacred in the final weeks of the war, when Hitler increasingly relied on fanatical teenagers to do the fighting. The noncombatant staff, however, all aged sailors, was still on hand and, like their counterparts everywhere, served anyone in uniform with unwavering and wooden efficiency. A change of uniform or language was of no concern to such people; a uniform meant authority and no other meaning counted. Just as it is said of Wagnerian music that it is not as bad as it sounds, so Ploen was actually a most attractive officers' club to visit; it was close by, wonderfully spacious, hardly known to most other units in the area, and therefore almost always empty, and the food was spectacular. My months in Eutin were probably the most bucolic and orderly period during the entire years of this story and, probably for that reason, did not last long.

Looking back, it seems astonishing that we spent so much time on so many people to such little effect; even by military standards, it was largely a wheel-spinning exercise. I must have interrogated hundreds, filled out scores of reports, and sent dozens off for detention or further questioning. To the extent that I ever heard about them again, they ended up either as captains of industry or members of the Bundestag.

In mid-summer, I was detached for a couple of weeks to go to Berlin and be on stand-by for a bunch of people led by Hugh Trevor-Roper who were reconstituting Hitler's last days and who had done what to whom. Trevor-Roper wrote a book about it, and it is pretty ancient history by now. Presumably I would have come into play if they had inadvertently dug someone up who was still alive and who might have been worth interrogating. Predictably that did not occur, and I had a fine time just hanging out in Berlin. The entertainment value of Berlin in the summer of 1945 has become legend; the four Allied powers were ostensibly still on excellent terms and clearly wanted to outdo each other in displaying both cultural versatility and sheer entertainment. There have never been so many dinners, garden parties, and cocktail receptions studded with every star you had ever heard of, from Maurice Chevalier to Fred Astaire, from Laurence Olivier to the Bolshoi ballet, each night and every night. In a couple of weeks I saw more famous performers and performances than I did in the next couple of decades; of all of them, the Red Army Choir and

Dancers will live longest in my memory. Those whirling leaps in scarlet boots!

## 4

I got back to Eutin in time to pack and take charge of a newly formed Interrogation Section—five sergeants, three trucks, and me—to move north to Denmark to "sort out things," which took the next five months and was sheer bliss. Denmark, in May 1945, had been bursting with German troops, not merely those already there, but units retreating from Russia, Poland, Norway, and even some that had gone north, ahead of the British advance. The vast majority had been moved back to Germany, but the Danes had held on to several thousand men, whom they knew or suspected to be of interest to the Allies, for reasons ranging from war crimes to military intelligence. They had now requested to have some interrogators sent up to sort this whole lot out. Most units had been detained in Copenhagen, but some were still held in various locations in the countryside. There never was any doubt that we could have done the job in five weeks, rather than in five months. It is equally certain that it would have been crazy to have done so. Denmark and its attractions had become a byword throughout the British Zone, so much so that virtually the only definite instruction I received from anyone was to reply affirmatively to any enquiry from anywhere as to the whereabouts of any British Intelligence officer. If I received such call, I was to indicate that the officer was being expected or, if I wanted variety, that he had just left. During the next five months I received scores of such calls; I never saw a single one of my colleagues.

From the first moment, we liked everything about Denmark, even if it had not been for Danish girls, but there, of course, they were. Not all of them were blonde, but most were; not all of them were pretty, but enough, and some of them were just lovely. It was like stepping into an Andersen fairy tale—everything was neat, clean, whole, toy-like, and friendly.

Finding Intelligence HQ in Copenhagen was not difficult; the Danes are not secretive people and every tram conductor knew.

Colonel Bjoerling, its head (and later to become quite a good friend; he came to visit in Kiel often), was a certified hero of the Danish resistance, a redoubtable bridge player, and a delightful man, who knew everyone in Copenhagen and half of the population of Denmark. He looked and acted like a distracted academician, but was tough, whip-smart, and knowledgeable about his trade.

Bjoerling explained about the various camp locations, the arrangements for interrogation offices, transport, and living expenses (they used real money in that country!), and was about to allocate accommodations for my sergeants, who had been chatting up the local population downstairs. However, one of the sergeants came up to indicate that it would not be necessary for us to worry about them since they had found accommodations of their own. And so they had; for the next five months, I merely told them once a week where I expected them to be and when. What happened the rest of the time and with whom was no concern of mine. My own accommodation had been arranged in the Hotel Angleterre, a grand but somewhat antiseptic alternative. It was, and still is, a lovely hotel; I lived there for five months in comfort and splendor, and not always alone, either.

However, not all my free time in Denmark was spent as a pillow acrobat; Danes are hugely hospitable, and a British officer being very much a display item in those days, there was an endless and snowballing round of dinners, cocktails, cook-outs, and parties, and I regularly returned to Copenhagen for the next ten years to visit with the friends I had made. Aside from a lasting affection for all things Danish, I have been a particular fan of Scandinavian furniture, Tuborg beer, indoor plants, aquavit, open-faced sandwiches, Tivoli Gardens, and Georg Jensen ever since.

My mentor and almost constant companion was a Danish Intelligence sergeant, assigned to me by Bjoerling by way of general nursemaid (and doubtless to keep him informed about my activities; Intelligence people may like each other, but they do not trust each other). Per was a huge, prematurely gray mountain of a man who came from Greenland, where he divided his time between being a trapper and a general-purpose handyman for assorted polar expeditions. I could never figure out where he learned his excellent English, since he had never been outside Greenland before the war.

Listening to his explanations was enlightening, but unlikely, as were his explanations as to what he did or how he did it. He was the most resourceful man since Jules Verne's Passepartout and the greatest liar since Baron Muenchhausen. He looked like King Kong, could charm birds out of a tree, and was adored by women as much as he adored them.

In between all the feasting, there was work to be done. We had several thousand people to screen, and my sergeants and I settled down to a nine-to-five routine. Add the workload to the nightly revels, and the suggestion by some Oynhausen colleagues that we had to come back after five months because we were just plain worn out may not merely have been based on envy.

We set up interrogation headquarters in the Citadel, a forbidding Vaubanesque pile in the middle of Copenhagen, and daily processed truckloads of "suspects." Contrary to what our Danish friends may have believed, the overwhelming majority had nothing to hide and nothing to tell, and it became so dull a routine, that we resorted to heartless little schemes to liven things up. One of our favorites was playing "British Gestapo." We would put two or three people waiting to be interrogated into one bare room, and three of us would be in the room next door. One would do nothing except moan and scream whenever he felt like it, whereas the other two would howl away, "You're lying! Confess, Nazischwein!" and similar B-movie stuff. After a few minutes of that, one of us would yell, "That's enough! No point wasting our time; finish him off!" and would fire a few rounds into the wall. Since we had found a whole storeroom full of ketchup (which had given us the idea in the first place), we would smear quite a bit of that around the room, and if the "victim" felt so inclined, he would make a few dying noises meanwhile. We would end up simulating dragging out a deadweight, accompanied by suitable comments, "If I'd known that the bastard was so heavy, I'd have shot him outside," or a similarly encouraging *bon mot*. We did not believe that our listeners would be able to follow the script verbatim, but they would get the general gist. That whole performance would take less than five minutes, after which time the first suspect would be rushed through the room, barely able to make out the bullet holes and the ketchup and smell the cordite in the air, and then placed in the third room beyond, where he would actually face one of us about to interrogate him. By this time, he would be distinctly rattled, and we would have broken the monotony. It was a despicable thing to do, but it made for a change and no lasting damage was done, except to the walls.

Once in a while there was someone interesting to interrogate and the most intriguing by far was Dr. Werner Best, SS Obergruppen-fuehrer†, and the German plenipotentiary in Denmark throughout the Occupation. It was already widely known that Best was not only the most moderate among the German *gauleiters*, or viceroys, in various parts of Europe, but that he was a man of considerable culture and interests, insightful and sensitive, with a Hamlet-like streak of introversion and indecision. No one could ever quite explain how a man of his caliber and contradictions had risen in the SS hierarchy. He had been an early and convinced Hitler supporter but appeared to have grown disillusioned well before the outbreak of the war, yet had never been resolute enough to get off the bandwagon. Being named Gauleiter for Denmark certainly appealed to his ego, but he also seemed genuinely convinced that he could further understanding between the two countries.

Best took an extraordinarily tolerant attitude towards Danish resistance in general and the Danes' superb protection of their Jewish compatriots in particular (the Danes saved every one of them; no other country did that!). It was significant that someone like Best had been sent to Denmark, which, like Holland and France, had originally been designated by Hitler as a country with which he expected an accommodation, as opposed to Poland and Russia, which he intended to destroy and resettle. As the war progressed, opposition within those countries grew of course to a point where Hitler gave up any thought of cooperation, just as he had had to do from the first day on which German troops invaded Norway. I had some long sessions with Best, during which not many matters relevant to Denmark came up, but we talked at great length about his views of Nazi philosophy, where it had gone wrong, and

---

†A rank comparable to that of a U.S. Army four-star general.

how it related to Germany and to himself. He was well aware of what happened to the Jews and to others whom Hitler wanted to exterminate. He deplored it, and I believed him. We talked a good deal about art, literature, and other matters. He was an interesting, confused, tortured person and, in my view, deserved to be one of the few survivors among the top Nazi echelons. He subsequently served a few years in a Danish prison and then became a businessman in Germany.

We went on occasional field trips to interrogate at local camps and became very familiar with Denmark. Aarhus was the first and only place where I was ceremonially piped aboard a warship—only a German warship, admittedly, but a full-fledged light cruiser, moored in Aarhus harbor with its full complement of crew and some Danish sentries patrolling along the dock. Neither side intended the slightest bit of trouble. This, incidentally, was true all over Denmark. The Danes obviously had resented the occupation, and the Germans were clearly apprehensive of how their former victims would react. However, they had behaved less brutally in Denmark than anywhere else in Occupied Europe, and the Danes are not passionate haters, so both sides were behaving in quite a genteel fashion. In the case of the cruiser, there was a procedural snag. The captain was quite ready to surrender and had, in practical terms, done so weeks ago when he moored his ship in Aarhus. He seemed to feel strongly, however, that some official transaction should be involved and there had, so far, been no one to surrender to. The Danes had not been signatories to the Rheims and Berlin surrender documents, and the compromise solution to surrender directly to the Danish navy did not work, because it no longer existed. Within minutes of arriving in Aarhus, a small town where news travels fast, I had a written request by Kapitaen z/See Lorenz to be so good as to come to the harbor, "um mein Schiff in Empfang zu nehmen,"† a rather happy phrase, which conjured up visions of my writing out a receipt stamped "received with thanks" and having the vessel gift-wrapped.

---

†"to collect my ship"

I duly drove to the harbor to find the entire ship's company drawn up in formation along the decks, and as soon as I set foot on the ladder (or whatever the nautical parlance is), some very senior-looking sailors (could they be bo'suns or is that a fish?) started those shrill off-key whistles. As an observant movie fan, I knew that coming on deck, you turn to the rear end of the ship (stern? fantail? anyway, back there) and salute the flag, and so I did. I do not remember whether there was a flag, but I was clearly keeping to the script. There followed a flurry of formal handshakes, first with the captain, and then with a dizzying number of officers, all lined up in order of seniority, and finally I was asked to sign some very fancy surrender document, which the captain had had plenty of time to dream up in all the weeks he had been waiting. It was all a good deal friendlier and cozier than MacArthur on the *Missouri,* and just as kitschy.

After that, no one seemed to know quite what to do with that splendid bit of paper, so, in the end, the captain locked it up in the ship's safe, and it is probably still there. Since everything was now shipshape and Bristol-fashion, or whatever, and every conceivable etiquette had been observed, I got piped off the ship again in fine style and went back to my drab interrogation routine.

We were in Denmark for five vastly enjoyable months.

## 5

When I returned to Germany after those months in Denmark, I became suddenly and overwhelmingly conscious of the devastation of German cities, and particularly Hamburg. Nothing had changed since I had seen it last. The vast pyramids of debris were still there, the skeletal bits of masonry here and there, and the pervading, indefinable smell made up of burnt matter, wood smoke, burst drains, unwashed bodies, and brick dust that I would recognize instantly even now. What had changed was the weather. In the summer there had been sun and even leaves here and there, and a semblance of life going on, even of picking up a little. Now there was snow on the ground and in the air, the wind was whistling through those burnt-out masonry canyons, and people were moving about slowly, painfully, wrapped in shapeless covers, muffled up in anything that might keep them warm, dragging little handcarts or sleighs heaped with bits of timber, wooden crates, paper, anything that might burn and give off a little heat. People were beginning to die: of hunger, of cold, of "just giving up," and the corpses, too, were being pulled around on these little carts, very much like the pictures one had seen of the Leningrad siege.

To visit Germans in their homes was almost invariably a sadly grotesque experience. As likely as not you would enter a house where two or three floors had simply disappeared, and, clambering over mounds of rubble, you would reach a staircase that literally stood in the middle of nowhere, like a theatrical prop. Balancing upwards, you would end up on a landing that once led to the fourth floor. It would appear to sway at every step, but if you were determined, you would end up in front of an apartment door, surrounded by split and peeling masonry, and behind it, your "hosts" would inhabit anywhere from three to four spaces, boxes, cubicles, whatever; they certainly were not rooms! They had walls after a fashion, cracked and askew, and a good deal of furniture; frequently so much that it seemed more like being in a storage room.

Gas, electricity, and water were supplied so intermittently and unpredictably that no one counted on them. Instead wherever you looked, you saw bits of candles, buckets of water, and sterno stoves, and at least one of these emergency alternatives was always in use. None of the places had any windows; they had all been blown out years ago during bombing attacks. Instead, thick tar paper had been nailed over empty embrasures and held in place by wooden cross beams. There was never much light in these apartments; some of it might actually filter in through a crack in one of the walls, or, an absolutely eerie experience, you would open a door and it would literally lead into thin air, the rest of the floor having been blown off. Your host would almost invariably have built a waist-high railing as a kind of makeshift balcony and to reduce the accident rate. What heat there might be came from small wood-burning stoves tucked away among the welter of salvaged furniture, usually with the pipe running out through some convenient crack in the wall. There was also a natural, though unfortunate, reluctance to take off any clothes or to wash; there was no soap, there was no room, and there was no point. As the old saying goes: "Es sind schon viele erfroren, es ist noch keiner erstunken."†

I frequently spent the night in such places since there was a strictly enforced curfew at 10 P.M., and though this did not affect Allied personnel, a lot of the guards wandering around considered shooting much more fun than asking questions, so your time-frame in identifying yourself was restricted. Thus I would spend the night talking and listening to a cross section of Hamburg; university professors, Luftwaffe officers, ex-party officials, cabaret artists, petty thieves, survivors. During that winter people sought each other's company, and by meeting one, you were likely to be handed on through a widening circle and, within a matter of weeks, you knew a great number of people. Obviously I would provide as much liquor, food, and cigarettes as I could carry and, in turn, learned a great deal about Germany and Germans, before, during, and after Hitler.

I found it a fascinating winter, though naturally I was in a tiny minority. Aside from quick excursions into lechery, severely inhibited by that lack of soap, the average "occupier" had no interest in any contact with Germans, quite aside from the fact that they spoke no common language. Even those few people, like myself, who had previously lived in the country and were now back with the British, had too many traumatic memories of Germans to feel comfortable with them, except perhaps across an interrogation table. I never had such qualms and this led to some very varied and revealing talks and insights that winter. Despite being a German Jew, and thus only providentially having escaped the Holocaust, I have never equated all Germans with being Nazis, and I therefore did not feel uncomfortable among Germans in 1945, or ever since.

The overwhelming majority of my co-victors looked upon Hamburg as the Atlantic Hotel surrounded by a sea of rubble, and the Atlantic was, by any standard, a place of Homeric debauch. It is a universal military principle that the taste and aptitude for orgiastic indulgence increases in direct proportion to the individual's remote-

†"Many have frozen to death, no one has yet been stunk to death."

ness from any combat zone. Fighting soldiers take their pleasures quickly, raucously, and haphazardly, but when it comes to stamina and savoring endless extravaganzas, you should stick with paymasters, ordinance officers, supply personnel, or the quartermaster corps. All the rear echelons in the world were in the Atlantic Hotel that winter. I looked in once in a while, but it was not fun any more.

When I returned from Denmark, I discovered that the entire Interrogation Team operation had evaporated; quite possibly because Newman had dreamt up and sold someone a more interesting gimmick—that there were no more people to interrogate seemed too easy an answer. Tom and Wilfred had returned to Oynhausen and been redeployed in some administrative jobs. I was now under orders of 16 SHIO (Schleswig-Holstein Intelligence Office) and in charge of a Field Security Section based in Itzehoe, a small town as irritating and banal as its name, located halfway between Hamburg and Kiel, where 16 SHIO was located. There were five headquarter locations (the others being in Berlin, Hamburg, Hanover, and Duesseldorf) so the numbering was merely the usual case of pointless obfuscation. I spent less than three months in Itzehoe, and aside from my forays to Hamburg and some memorable visits to fellow FSS outfits, it was a total waste of time, though not a very taxing one.

A Field Security Section was supposed to look after a limitless number of undefined Intelligence activities within a specified area, usually covering about three hundred square miles, and at the time consisted generally of a captain, a lieutenant as his second-in-command, half a dozen Intelligence sergeants and corporals, a couple of wireless operators, and a couple of drivers—a dozen people in all—as well as some trucks and jeeps provided by the army. Typically, the FSS would then proceed to grab the largest and handsomest house in the area, at least a dozen Mercedes or similarly imposing vehicles, and about half a dozen German mechanics to look after them. They would be complemented by two or three first-rate local cooks to look after their inner needs, and an unspecified, usually migratory, number of "displaced persons," all female, all pretty, and all remarkably proficient in German, to look after their other requirements. So there you would have another twenty or twenty-five people as auxiliary members of the section. They, in turn, brought along friends and dependents, who would make occasional, vague and futile efforts to "help out," in return for which they would wolf down vast quantities of food and steal even more to sell on the black market. By the time you counted everybody, a Field Security Section might total close to a hundred people and operate with all the aspects, rights, and privileges of a minor German principality in the mid-eighteenth century.

The purpose of an FSS was to maintain its area in a state of bemused docility, by judiciously varied display of cajolery, arbitrariness, bribery, intuition, friendliness, blackmail, and terror, but above all omniscience. Military Government governed, Military Police directed traffic or arrested petty criminals, but FSS people made people disappear and reappear, knew things about you that your wife should not know (and quite likely knew your wife, which you should not know), and altogether behaved in the manner in which the "Secret Service" was expected to disport itself. Since that manner was the greatest secret of all, anything the FSS did was clearly part of it, and the more unpredictable the action, the greater the mystery and the awe of the locals. It sounds absurd and it was, but it worked.

Living in the splendid villa and park of some local nabob (these people were not necessarily in jail; just as likely they might now be squeezed in with the neighbors and be justifiably enraged; "oderint dum timeant"† was the motto of the times), a typical Itzehoe day would start with a smartly uniformed "butler" bringing in breakfast on a tray. The uniform for butlers was invariably an old Wehrmacht uniform with all insignias removed; the uniforms for maids were some black and white soubrette outfits, which made them look like a vaudeville road company. After checking with the "Operations Room" that no operations of any kind were pending or in progress (none ever seemed to be), I would repair to the main "salon" of the residence, where by 11 A.M., I would hold my daily audience. A number of Germans would invariably turn up, full of "wichtige Meldungen fuer die Herren vom Geheimdienst."‡ Almost invariably I had either heard that vital piece of news before (as likely as not from

---

†"Let them hate as long as they fear."
‡"Important news for the gentlemen of the Secret Service."

the same individual two days earlier) or, more likely, it was useless, except occasionally as an item of possible and eventual blackmail. All this would last for a couple of hours and was useful as a "public relations" exercise, since it accustomed some Germans to tell us everything at all times, and we, in exchange for a few cigarettes, would cement our reputation for omniscience.

So much for the business of the day. Now came the more taxing problem of having to decide between trying the latest "liberated" Mercedes, taking a boat out on the river, taking a nap, going hunting, getting bored, getting laid—all the updated multiple choices of an ancien régime marquis.

Evenings were usually spent visiting some neighboring FS section, ostensibly to "keep in touch," but primarily to get companionably smashed. Aside from not being all that notable, I find these outings difficult to recall not least because memory is the first faculty to go in those circumstances. I still marvel that, night after night, I used to drive miles and miles in an open jeep without recalling that I ever sat in it, let alone behind the wheel. Divine benevolence extends to boozers, as much as to babies.

From time to time several FS sections and their friends would get together to engineer debauches of biblical proportions, and the greatest and most debilitating of these often took place at FSS Sued-Diethmarschen, not too far from Friedrichstadt. The section was ensconced on a huge, rambling farm in the middle of an area famed for dunes, fens, and political assassinations. The Diethmarschen farmers, homicidal to a man, stood to the political right of Attila the Hun, and the entire population was already cheering for Hitler back in 1925. That the local FSS was now terrorizing them, they took in good part; they would have massacred them had the roles been reversed.

FSS Sued-Diethmarschen had two claims to popularity: they had accumulated the prettiest "displaced persons" in the entire region, and everyone held refreshingly polygamous notions about their presence. Their other, more startling, acquisition was a troupe of Chinese jugglers, remnants of the wreckage of a local circus. On ordinary days they acted as supernumerary "go-fers," silent, smiling, and small eaters, the ideal domestics, in fact. At parties, however, they would don their circus gear, and, though my perceptions may have been dimmed by circumstances then and since, I do not believe that I saw finer tumbling and juggling in China.

All those Mercedes, Horch, and Maybach cars that we accumulated, were black, large, and impressive (one belonging to a Hamburg Intelligence officer had reputedly been owned by Hitler; it was armorplated, weighed a ton, and moved like a tank), but they also tended to be fragile. All of them were at least six or seven years old, had seen war service, and even our superlative German mechanics could not prevent an occasional hiccup. I became the envy of my fellow-thieves when I managed to obtain one of the first batch of Volkswagens built after the war. The huge Wolfsburg plant had started operation again in spring 1946, and the first cars coming off the line were all painted drab olive green, but otherwise looked exactly like the beetle of the mid-1970s. I do not remember whom I bribed or threatened to get one, but I do know that I could still have driven it thirty years later. It was the most indestructible and reliable little car I ever owned, and we were inseparable till the day I left the army.

Before doing that, however, I left Itzehoe, just as suddenly and inexplicably as I had been posted there. I not only left that unmemorable spot behind, but the Field Security world as well, since I was ordered to report to 16 SHIO in Kiel, where I was to be stationed.

Thus, in the early spring of 1946, I started out on my last army assignment, infinitely the most varied and fascinating, which kept me wholly and happily involved for almost eighteen months, and which I have been thinking back on with equal pleasure and interest ever since.

## 6

Although the military presence in the four occupation zones was still massive, and would be for years to come, the British forces were being rapidly and almost entirely disengaged from any day-to-day running of occupied Germany. By spring 1946 they led a separate garrison existence, except for some isolated policing, in much the same manner as they still do. The actual running of the zone had been handed over to Military Government, a multitude of little local bosses, frequently made up of dusty remnants of the Colonial Civil Service, but by and large surprisingly effective. These people, whose jurisdiction rarely extended beyond the town they were allocated to, and never beyond an area greater than a large city borough, did not so much govern as manage, administer, and keep things running. I rarely came across anyone who spoke German or had ever been to Germany before, and only very few attempted to learn the language. However, I can only assume that running an empire for a couple of centuries creates some genetic aptitude for doing so; most of them were pragmatic, even-handed, unruffled, competent, and totally uninterested in who they were dealing with. Boches or Bazutos, it was all the same to them. They managed a town like they would a grocery store, unlike the Americans, who tended towards much more personal involvement, which frequently lessened their effectiveness. If they suspected any trouble or skulduggery, they would rely on the local Field Security Section to spot it in time, and on the nearest army unit to take steps, if it was serious enough to warrant that.

Political questions of the area were the responsibility of the Land Governor, to whom all the local chiefs reported, and who ranged from such faintly comic and mummified figures as Air Marshall Sir Charles Champion de Crespigny in Schleswig-Holstein to outstanding administrators like General Sir Brian Robertson, governor of Rhineland-Westphalia and subsequently of the entire British Zone. The split-up into separate Laender (Rhineland/Westphalia, Niedersachsen, Hamburg, Schleswig-Holstein, and the British sector of Berlin) was an immediate and deliberate postwar policy intended to break up the monolithic concept of a Prussia-dominated German state. The Americans similarly set up Bavaria, Hessen, Wuerttemberg-Baden, and so on, in their zone. The expressed and naive hope was that the Germans, disillusioned by defeats in two wars as a united Germany, would themselves turn to the pre-1870 concept of a loose federation of strongly parochially oriented, semi-independent provinces (laender). To nudge them in this direction, political activity at the local and provincial level was very much encouraged, and this was to be the task of the Land Governor, assisted by a staff of supposedly skilled political professionals, superficially disguised as army personnel. The federalist concept was still-born from the start, but the British and Americans clung to it for years, probably deluded by places such as Schleswig-Holstein, which historically has always had separatist tendencies and now clearly seemed anxious to emphasize its closeness to Denmark where there was food and peace, as opposed to flaunting their allegiances to Germany where there was neither. The Americans were doubtless misled by Bavaria's attitudes, which have not changed to this day, and which make Texas's self-esteem look like that of Rhode Island.

Although no politics beyond the Land level were permitted until well after I left Germany, I never met a single politician in all the months I dealt with them who did not rigidly separate Land issues, with which he was overtly involved, and federal issues with which he was covertly, constantly and intensely busy. It was Whitehall's and Washington's pious hope (which my colleagues and I never for a moment shared) that the Land concept would be the final form of the "new Germany." To any German politician his Land involvement was merely a "training wheels" exercise; his ultimate aim was always the Bundesrepublik, as it now stands.

The British and Americans thus ran their zones through a pragmatic, largely unmilitary Military Government, encouraging both an intensive and decentralized revival of political awareness, and generally keeping a deliberately low profile. The Russians and French, on the other hand, ran their zones as avowed conquerors, with iron fist and high visibility. The differing approaches were among the main factors of the rapid erosion of the "brothers-in-arms" euphoria; by spring 1946, the British were already deeply suspicious of the Russians and openly irritated by the French; and once in a while, we were beginning to wonder about the Yanks.

This then, in a rather ample nutshell, was the background against which I pursued two very full-time, though ostensibly unofficial, activities for the next eighteen months: the gathering and dissemination of political intelligence and having very close and very unauthorized peeks at what our erstwhile friends and allies were up to.

I may appear cursory in telling some of these tales, but I am under some constraints. For one thing, on the classic "need to know" basis, I was frequently unaware of who else was involved or what the ultimate intended purpose of what I was doing was. In addition I was very much a temporary amateur, often operating among long-time professionals. I am not suggesting that these by now geriatric spies are still operating, but since the Whitehall authorities only recently acknowledged that King Harry Rufus was gay, it would be churlish to upset them by gossiping about events a mere fifty years ago.

All this refers to my second hat; there was nothing remotely confidential about the "political intelligence" part.

Kiel, Germany's chief naval base, was and is a rather unattractive town, situated in very pretty surroundings, and had hardly been damaged at all. The war ended before the area was fought over and since the German navy operated almost entirely out of Norwegian and French harbors, it had not been bombed often. Compared to Hamburg, the place looked idyllic. The Kiel headquarters had about fifty operatives of one description or another, most of whom I barely got to know by sight. I joined half a dozen captains and majors in a vast and gothic architectural confection, which looked like an enormous dark-brown cuckoo clock, but which, in a gloomy, cinematic way, turned out to be both roomy and comfortable. These residential quarters of ours (SHIO offices were in a large, modern, nondescript barracks building a couple of miles down the road) were surrounded by a lovely fenced garden of about five acres, complete with ornamental lake, large enough to row on. It was certainly large enough to swim in, and we did, until one of my local politician friends inquired whether we had had the bottom dredged for bodies. We had not, we did not, and we did not swim there any more, either.

This became "home" for the next year and a half. I had a large airy bedroom with balcony and bathroom, and, given the surrounding architecture, could have posed for a Swiss travel folder, except for my astounding ex-German navy (Kriegsmarine) orderly, whose name escapes me but whose appearance is with me forever. He must have been nearly seven feet tall and was built in almost perfectly rhomboid shape, tiny feet and heron-like legs, widening to a very rotund middle, and then diminishing again to end in a totally bald, pin-sized head. He never slept, never talked, and you never had to tell him anything—because he was already busy doing it. Compared to him, Jeeves was a blundering oaf.

240 / ACCIDENTAL JOURNEY

Although most of our activities appeared sensitive to "un-authorized" eyes and ears, and some actually were, we were pretty lax about the people working for us. It never seemed to occur to us that any of our German employees might leak information to someone and, as far as I know, it never happened. The most likely reason was that, from idleness as much as for security reasons, there was surprisingly little in writing anywhere at 16 SHIO. Except for the fortnightly "Intelligence Report," commonly and accurately referred to as "Liars' Lullaby," and which both Stalin and Hitler could have read out aloud to each other for all we cared, just about all information was passed verbally. As time went on, even that diminished, and ultimately each of us virtually ran his own little intelligence fiefdom in his own head. Le Carré knows exactly what he is talking about.

The only security problem I recall involved my having taken over two large, police-trained Alsatian dogs, each the size of a bull calf. Large dogs were being adopted all over Germany, since their owners simply could not feed them. Mine were splendid animals, and, after a brief "re-orientation course," which involved a pair of my old pajamas and other dog voodoo, the police assured me that they were perfectly docile, which they were. However, the police omitted to tell me that they had trained the pair so that one would attack anyone entering a room and the other attack whoever was leaving it. To aggravate matters, they came from the same litter and looked alike. The only place where I could safely unleash them was in my bedroom so anyone wishing to enter would have to wait until I secured the hound who devoured arrivals, and the same individual would have to bide a wee before leaving, to give me time to tie up the animal who went for departures. It rapidly became very tiresome, so I returned them to the police with a liberal meat allowance (which the police probably ate instead).

There was the usual plethora of cooks, chauffeurs, chamber maids, orderlies, and mechanics, all displaying manic attachment to order, jollity, and fractured English—to be met on a dim rainy morning with, "Is good morning, ha ha!" sometimes made you wonder whether winning the war was worth it. There was the usual bulging car park, including some gargantuan Maybach 12-cylinder convertibles, which looked like Tiger tanks with chrome edges, and offered the comforts of a three-room flat. Aside from my little Volkswagen (the only one then running round in Schleswig-Holstein; showing off "downwards" can be the most fun of all), I recall an extraordinary Mercedes convertible with a hood about thirty feet long, all black, with silver compressor pipes sticking out like a surrealist octopus, the seating in red leather and four silver-spoked reserve wheels piled on the rear. That is the car we "flew" in from Helmstedt to Berlin, where it died for lack of spare parts. It was some car, while it lasted.

I was now part of the "political section" of 16 SHIO (a somewhat euphemistic designation; the other members trickled in six months later, and at peak strength there were three of us), and, as such, answerable directly to the Foreign Office, or to the personal delegate of that august body. There was a rather bewildering succession of these characters during the eighteen months that I had contacts with them. I forget the sequence and some of the names, but I do recall Chris Mayhew, Noel Annan, Abeu, Pakenham, and Kit Steele, though they probably did not drift in in that order. No one, except Annan and Steele, seemed to know which country they were in, and only Annan appeared to know what he was talking about. "Discreet direction" was Whitehall's leitmotiv in those days and these successive emissaries were long on discretion, but short on direction. Mayhew, heir to a Scottish brewing fortune, later had a long and maverick career in Parliament. Abeu, quite a fascinating man and reputedly a Harry Hopkins figure to the then Prime Minister Attlee, died in the late forties. Pakenham, now Earl of Longford and a member of that distinguished literary clan, has for many years courted headlines and derision by eternally crusading for causes, ranging from loving Germany to freeing child molesters. Annan, originally an Oxford don and now Lord Annan, had a distinguished career as an academic, writer, and critic, which included being head of the National Gallery and provost of King's College, Cambridge. Kit Steele never listened since he knew it all, and he let you know about it with unwavering pomposity. He was a most irritating man and predictably became England's first ambassador to the subsequent Federal Republic.

This then was the ever shifting stream of luminaries to whom I was supposedly answerable, but in reality my contacts were with unknown people back in Whitehall, whom I never met, but with whom I communicated by reports, cable, and phone, often half a dozen times a day, and, in a wholly anonymous manner, we got to know each other and our respective working methods very well.

The work, as such, was utterly engrossing and had a marvelously minuet-like quality about it; this is how it went. The British government wanted the Germans to be self-administering democrats at the Land level, passing their own laws, handling their own government problems, all along Benjamin Franklin's precept: "It's a republic, if you can keep it." However, there were of course endless caveats, such as that German political activities should have no federal tinge, nor infringe upon the rights and privileges of the occupying Allies, which were putty-like in stretch and lack of definition. The government trusted the German politicians to spot and sail around these reefs, since fortunately Captain Lynton happened to be in the area. The Germans knew Lynton as very hospitable (coffee, cigarettes, even Scotch!) always accessible, speaking astonishing German, which clearly pointed to long association with "ze seekrit zervis," and, for a mere captain, amazingly well informed about London's views and reactions. Much later, when I got to know some of these people really well, I tried once or twice to explain my identity and origins, only to be met with ironic smiles and a "we know ze seekrit zervis and its little stories" look. Being Loewenstein from Stuttgart, even if true, was just another cover to them.

Thus, rather than starting a debate on an issue, let alone pass a law that might have implications displeasing to the British, why not have a drink with Lynton and check it out, just get his personal reaction. Which they would do, and I would invariably ask for a day to think it over, and suggest another meeting for the day following. At the next meeting I would comment on what they had in mind to do, emphasizing this to be purely my personal opinion but, as it happened, it would invariably be sound and in keeping with London's view.

Now they knew that I knew that they knew that I had spent half the night on the phone with "my people" in London, getting their views and reactions, and that I was merely the non-canine version of "His Master's Voice," but that was the way we played it, and, of course, in reverse as well. Lynton would call and drop by, and express a purely personal opinion that he felt that a law or ordinance dealing with such-and-such a matter might well be on London's mind and what would the reaction be in the Land? Well, they would have a few drinks and kick it around, and if they, the German politicians, felt that it would not fly, that would be the end to it, and no more would be heard of it. But if they thought it might work, why then, by sheer coincidence, they would get a suggestion from the Land Governor to pass just such a law a short while later. Here too, they knew that I knew that they knew that I was sounding them out on direct instructions from London, since Whitehall was anxious to "tailor" its requests as much as possible. It was an absolutely fascinating way of doing business "by conduit," and quite foolproof, at least for a while. Throughout, I remained Captain Lynton, a lavish host, great linguist, with some shadowy connection to "ze seekrit zervis," and a remarkable guesser of pending events. The same pattern was repeated in the other provinces, each of which had an operative like myself, and all of us, never more than half a dozen in all, became quite well known to German politicians throughout the British Zone. We started to cross over into each other's areas, and, in my case, that led to dealing with some truly fascinating people—Schumacher in Hanover, Breuer and Reuter in Berlin, and Adenauer in Cologne—about all of whom more later. The happiest and least involved participants in this political minuet were the Land Governors. Thanks to us they were omniscient, and thanks to the response of the German politicians, they were all-wise; it fooled no one, but made them look and feel good.

"My" governor in Schleswig-Holstein was a really odd duck. Sir Charles Champion de Crespigny was a retired air-marshall and, judging by his looks and views, must have flown during the Thirty Years' War. His only qualification to be in this position might have been the fact that he was an Australian and someone in London had assumed that that made for some genetic aptitude for solving colonization problems. He stalked through life in mummified elegance and was one of the most handsome empty suits I ever met. He spoke no German whatever, which made his laudable desire to "mingle with the natives" a little difficult; hardly more so than mingling with us, since his Australian twang was almost impenetrable. A lonely man, was Crespigny. It did not however, deter him from acting benevolent and patriarchal in a glacially remote way.

The ultimate display of fine intentions gone awry occurred sometime in early 1947, when Crespigny got wind of the news that some Diethmarschen burgomaster, long retired, was about to celebrate his one hundredth birthday. He insisted on personally visiting this geriatric celebrity and requested my presence, to ensure that his wishes for continuing health and happiness for this ancient would be properly appreciated. So we all drove out in a cavalcade of staff cars to some obscure village in the Diethmarschen heartland, and finally located the celebrant, a wizened, senile, and demonstrably incontinent dwarf, huddled in a huge armchair and hovered over by his spinster daughter. Crespigny stalked into the room and delivered himself of a brief and noble address, to the utter incomprehension of the addressee. My attempts at suitably lofty translation produced no discernible response, and altogether the occasion had the warmth of a night spent on the north face of the Eiger. There being no point in extending this miasma of cross-purposes, we were about to retreat in good order, when the daughter indicated that her papa, who was making some snuffling noises, intended to respond to the honors done to him. This he did, by having the daughter hoist him carefully to a semi-upright position, whereupon he hung there, literally in suspended animation, clearly attempting to recall what the presence of officials, uniforms, flowers, and loud speeches called for. It finally occurred to him, whereupon he raised a trembling forearm and, in a quavering but quite clear voice, said, "Heil Hitler, Heil Hitler!" Crespigny, lost as usual in some aboriginal "walk-about" dream, never heard it, but the daughter turned ashen. She grabbed her father's arm, nearly tearing it off, flung him back into his chair, and hissed, "Nicht mehr, Vater, nicht mehr!" ("Not any longer, Father, not any longer!") It was one of the great moments of the era.

Shortly after arriving in Kiel, I was promoted to major. One of the constant and challenging mysteries about the army is that it consistently deals with contingencies that do not exist, while all the while landing supplies on the wrong side of the beach. Thus the "Political Section of the Intelligence Division" did not exist, for the simple reason that we invented both name and concept one evening, when the half dozen "political bodies," such as myself, came from the various provinces to meet in Hamburg to socialize and gossip. It struck us as a nifty little name, so some of us got into the habit of putting it at the end of our occasional reports. You can rely on the army when it comes to administrative provisions; to mislay an Army Corps is an occupational hazard, but it does not fool around with hierarchical ranking. Once it came to the notice of some clown in the War Office that there was a "Political Section" somewhere, the appropriate ranks were instantly allocated and the necessary directives issued; we all became majors overnight.

So there I was "Major Lynton, Third Royal Tank Regiment, secunded to the Political Section of the Intelligence Division, British Army of the Rhine."

# 7

Shortly before elevation to such eminence, and while still a mere captain, I spent a month in the United States, in the summer of 1946.

Army regulations not only excel in such obiter dicta as, "Electricity will move from plus to minus, as of December 10, 1944," a discovery previously only made by Colonel Hutton at Sandhurst, and which has eluded scientists to this day, but they also are such a jungle of jargon and contradictions that, given time and patience, you can point to authorization for anything you are up to—just like the Talmud.

I had not seen my family since the summer of 1939, seven years earlier, and while in touch since 1941, correspondence had been patchy and infrequent. It took no more than two savvy clerks, a few bottles of beer, and half an evening, to spot an obscure army regulation providing both free transportation and four weeks' furlough, and I set off, in June 1946, armed with a "courier letter" to the British Military Mission in New York. I had no idea whether such body existed, but was very familiar with the secrecy, complexity, and scope of my instructions, since I had drafted them myself. I got a lift from Kiel to London in Johnny Johnstone's Mosquito, one of the fabled planes of that era. Johnny was himself a legend, one of Britain's great air aces, and a casual acquaintance from equally casual encounters in the Atlantic bar. Why Johnstone flew to London that day I do not recall (probably to deliver nylons from some U.S. PX to various bare-legged girlfriends), but I do recall how he flew. I was sitting in the copilot's seat, and it was my first ride in a warplane; it will certainly be my last. Johnstone was kind enough to demonstrate the Mosquito's versatility both at speed and at roof level; I believed him much sooner than he thought.

He did, however, deposit me in flamboyant style right next to an American Airlines DC4 bound for La Guardia, to which my "courier letter" gave me automatic and free admission, and I set off on my first transatlantic air journey. By today's standards, it was both charming and wearisome. There were no more than forty passengers altogether, and given the frequent stops and a cruising speed that would hardly challenge a Toyota today, everyone got to know each other. Stewardesses were picked for looks and legs, which seemed a sensible compensation for the terrible food. Once in a while the pilot would request that passengers not hang around the pantry all at the same time, sipping drinks and chatting up the stewardesses, since it created weight distribution problems; those were the kind of days and planes. The tiresome part was that it took almost twenty-four hours, unpressurized and unheated planes made for low and bumpy altitudes and incipient frostbite, and all the refueling stops—at least three between London and La Guardia—made you feel like a flatulent yo-yo.

Everything about the United States was new, strange, and wonderful to me, not least being complimented by the immigration officer at being such a young, as well as heroic, lieutenant-general. I had no idea what he was talking about, but made suitably deprecating noises, which I happily repeated on numerous occasions in the weeks to follow. After a while I worked it out; New York had seen very few British officers in uniform up to that time, and people did not distinguish too closely between size and shapes of shoulder stars. Three British stars denoted a captain; three U.S. shoulder stars meant a lieutenant-general, so that was part of the puzzle solved. In both armies, decorations are worn in descending order of distinction, and in the second row of my motley lot, I (together with about 600,000 others) wore the ribbon of the European Theater 1944 Star, denoting mere presence. The colors of the ribbon, however, are very similar to those of the U.S. Distinguished Service Cross, which is not habitually worn low down in the decorative pecking order; so that explained the John Wayne imputation.

In addition, people during those weeks accosted me on the street and variably interpreted my green Third RTR shoulder flashes as denoting my participation in at least four assault landings with the marines, having led a Commando raid on Hirohito's palace, rescuing Macarthur's son from a boa constrictor, or some similarly awesome feat; in all, not bad for a lieutenant general of twenty-six! I cannot recall that many mistaken identities since Feydeau stopped writing farces. One of the better ones was being kissed at an A&P checkout counter, on the assumption I was an admiral in the Brazilian navy. Some situations were both extraordinary and memorable. Going down in a very sedate elevator in a Wall Street high-rise, I was stared at in solemn silence by the other passengers, and when we got to the ground floor, an elderly gentleman reached for my hand, shook it, and said, "Thank you," and then all the others in the elevator lined up behind him and shook my hand as well.

The pendant to that astonishing interlude was the speeding ticket caper, which O. Henry would have appreciated. My mother had incurred such a ticket some days before my arrival, not her first one either, and, on the advice of a canny legal friend, was pleading illness and asked me to appear before the judge on her behalf. It could do no harm.

I appeared in court on the due date and in full panoply—shiny leather belt, paratrooper wings, black beret, chest full of ribbons, green shoulder flashes—and was duly admired by a roomful of defendants, pickpockets, traffic offenders, prostitutes, and drifters, who, in a number of cases, were evidently well acquainted with each other and with the judge. The latter looked like a frostbitten rabbit, made Judge Jeffreys of the Bloody Assizes seem a social worker, and took on average about five minutes to hand out each of a volley of fines and jail sentences. In each case seemingly the maximum allowed by law, as I understood from whispers around me. In due course "Martha Louise Lowenstein" was called. I marched forward, took the oath in a clear voice, and pleaded guilty in equally ringing tones. The judge said, somewhat dazedly, "Are you Martha Louise Lowenstein?" whereupon I explained the circumstances of my presence, while he kept looking at me with myopic fascination. There was a silence, after which he enquired what kind of uniform this was. So I explained that, and there was another silence; by now the case had already taken longer than any other case that morning. Then the judge asked, "Have you been in any battles?" and I reassured him on that score. Then he wanted to know whether I had been involved in the "Battle of the Bulge," and I confirmed having been mixed up in that enterprise. There was another long silence. He looked at me with the solemnity of looking at Washington's tomb and said, "Men like you make it possible for people like me to sit here and do our jobs. People like me know what you men have done. Men like you do not get sentenced in this court. Case dismissed." The assembled villains actually clapped as I left the courtroom, and that is how my mother kept her license.

New York was hot, humid, only intermittently air-conditioned, and I fell in love with it and everything about it, and that love affair has lasted me all my life. The whole visit was one long blur of steaks, orange juice, and "catching up with each other." I put on twelve pounds in four weeks.

And yes, Virginia, there was a British Military Mission in New York!

Having been unable to locate such a body, I had checked with the embassy in Washington, only to be told that the mission had been disbanded in June 1945. I gave it no further thought, since I was perfectly able to draft a response to my "courier letter," should that ever be required. Then one day, idly looking over the occupancy board of the Cunard Building on Broadway, I spotted a reference to British Military Mission, so took the elevator to have a look. There they were, three English captains, by now having "Americanized" their uniforms by the addition of U.S. shirts, loafers, and caps, clearly anxious to know who had sent me. When reassured that no one had, they happily relaxed, and we had a few drinks, and I got their story. They had indeed been dissolved, but army administration being what it is, the paymaster-general had evidently not heard of it. Monthly pay kept on rolling in, and there was no reason to assume that it would ever stop. The disadvantage of no longer being in the loop for

promotion and possibly pay raises was amply made up by the likelihood that this might be a life-time sinecure. Provided no officious
type were to locate them and stir things up, there was no reason to
assume otherwise. I assured them that I was not that type, and we
parted with mutual expression of goodwill. They may be in the
Cunard Building to this day for all I know.

## 8

Looking back, I sincerely believe that some good things were
achieved in those eighteen months in terms of establishing parlia-
mentary and democratic procedures and attitudes in Germany, and
also in creating rapport between Germany and England. I am convinced that what we did then, including mistakes and misjudgments,
was an integral part of the political reconstruction of Germany and of
its political structure and attitudes today. Not central, not major, but
integral.

One of the fascinations of those years was constantly meeting
people who then, and even more later, were the Who's Who of
German politics. The democratic process in Germany had only lasted
for fifteen years before Hitler came to power, and had now been
interrupted for twelve, so there was not too much of a base to build
on. It was made more difficult by a particular element, which was then
novel to us, though it became increasingly familiar as nations have
emerged or re-emerged in the past forty years. The people the
Germans—and we—turned to, to revive the democratic process, were
literally almost all survivors. In some cases they had miraculously
survived years of concentration camps, in others, they had fled abroad
and had spent lean, Lenin-like years waiting for events to change. A
very few, notably Willy Brandt, Ernst Reuter, and Breuer, had spent
those years in relative comfort and safely; only Adenauer had not
spent them in exile. The rapidly emerging problem was that these
people tended to have a rigid, doctrinaire belief in the absolute truth
of their political dogma, and this was, of course, particularly true with
socialists and communists. They had survived the camps through a
messianic belief in the justice of their cause; it was one of the

mainstays of their survival. The unquestioning belief in the doctrine, however, had become so much a part of them, that they often seemed neither willing nor able to fit it to existing circumstances. In not facing practical facts, indeed in implying that we, as the occupying power, were opposing the ideologies they stood for, they made it difficult to establish a pragmatic, operating political structure that dealt with what simply had to be dealt with. Brecht's cynical truism, "Erst kommt das Fressen, dann kommt die Moral,"† was an exact summary of Germany in those years, and that meant predominantly playing it by ear, whereas the German politicians we were dealing with, insisted on playing it by the book.

The most impressive, flamboyant, mesmerizing, and difficult figure, by far, was Kurt Schumacher, the idol and messiah of the Socialists, who, had he lived, would have been the most redoubtable German politician of the postwar era. He had a long, narrow, bony head, with hardly any hair, the riveting dark eyes of a fanatic, an unsmiling slash of a mouth full of false teeth, a tall, totally emaciated body contained in a suit three sizes too small and twenty years too old. With a hypnotically compelling voice, he was the embodiment of a latter-day John Brown. He constantly and knowingly defied you to balk him, knowing that we neither would nor could. What can you say or do to someone who had been a hero in World War I, in which he lost an arm, and who had survived twelve years of concentration camps, during which he had lost a leg, all his teeth, and most of the bones in his face? There he stood, an empty sleeve pinned to that threadbare coat, a heavy wooden crutch tucked under the other shoulder, an empty trouser leg fastened above the knee, crippled, indestructible, raging, unforgiving—perhaps the most frightening man I ever met.

For the short period that he still lived—he died in 1947—he was "The Man," a demagogue, visionary, prophet, and an intensely dangerous politician. He was a good and sincere man and a dedicated Socialist; but he was also violent and embittered, conscious and endlessly resentful of the wrongs done to him and of the little time he

---

†"Grub first, then ethics."

had left. Thus he was rushing, pushing, bullying people to whom shrill and mesmerizing exhortations were not unfamiliar, and to which they were not unresponsive. It was a human tragedy and a political sigh of relief, when he died. There is no doubt that he would have been Germany's first chancellor had he lived. Rather surprisingly, our paths crossed quite often, and over eighteen months, we probably spent twenty hours alone together in various places. His private image was not different from his public one, except that he tended to whisper rather than scream. He was a broken, dying man, impossible to deal with, difficult to like (he would despise any sign of affection), but I admired him greatly.

After his death, the Socialists never found that kind of a messianic leadership again, neither with Brandt nor with Schmidt. Willy Brandt in those days played a very minor role. Oddly enough, his flight to Norway and his having assumed Norwegian citizenship was much resented by the same people who had no trouble acclaiming Breuer, who had gone to the United States and become a U.S. citizen, or Reuter who had spent the Hitler years in Turkey. They were the two big names among Socialists—Reuter as mayor of Berlin and Breuer as mayor of Hamburg. Only after Reuter's early death did Brandt emerge as his successor, and only after the Berlin airlift was he propelled into national and international prominence. The party itself, after Schumacher's death, turned to Erich Ollenhauer, a perfectly pleasant, but relentlessly mediocre party hack, whose lack of ability and charisma overcame even the British Labor Government's open favoritism towards Socialists. The emergence of the Christian Democratic Union (CDU) and Adenauer's leadership was largely due to the non-performance by Ollenhauer and his entourage.

Reuter, a comfortable, teddy-bear of a man, with a rumpled face and clothes to match, was a shrewd and wily politician, patient and highly effective behind the scenes. His avuncular appearance might have led people to believe him nice and ineffectual. I do not believe he was either. He was a superbly able pragmatist, as is his son, who today heads the entire Mercedes-Benz empire—hardly a Socialist's dream of the ultimate achievement. Reuter had not had a bad time, spending the war years advising the Turkish government on handling unions and related matters. Breuer had had an even better time, rising quite high in the New York union hierarchy. He was a solidly effective and factual man to deal with, smoother and more polished than Reuter, but far less Byzantine and subtle. One had spent years in New York and the other in Constantinople, and it showed. Reuter was more fun.

Breuer, on returning, faced the problem of being a U.S. citizen, which made it difficult for him to be a German mayor of Hamburg, and there was, of course, no German government which could endow him with citizenship. The simplest thing seemed to re-invent a citizenship of the Hanseatic town of Hamburg, a concept dormant since the decline of the Hanseatic League six hundred years earlier. That is exactly what my Hamburg colleagues and I did, and for several years Breuer was the first and last independent Hanseatic citizen in this century.

My personal favorite was Ernst Luedemann, the Socialist prime minister of Schleswig-Holstein, an old-timer who had been a Reichstags deputy before 1933. Tall, with a widow's peak of white hair and a white goatee, looking amiably Mephistophelean, he was a courtly and handsome man in his sixties. He was cynical, exquisitely mannered, amused and exasperated in equal parts by the foibles of his fellow men, and much too civilized and sophisticated to be an effective leader. He was, however, an excellent prime minister, simply because, reaching back into a vast reservoir of expertise in political guile, he could out-maneuver almost anyone around, in much the same way as an old-time Southern U.S. senator could, whom in many ways he resembled. He seemed to do so for amusement rather than out of a sense of purpose; and, of course, he splendidly looked the part.

What he liked to do best, and we did it on many a night, was to sit with some good wine and cigars and talk; politics, places, books, art, women. There were forty years of age and experience separating us, and we liked each other very much. We corresponded after I left Germany and until his death in the 1950s.

Luedemann was of course anathema to Schumacher, who could not abide his urbanity and lack of dedication, but was unable to persuade the Schleswig-Holstein Socialists to get rid of him despite the fact that Luedemann was a "carpet bagger" (he came from Silesia and had spent the Hitler years there, keeping a very low profile). His fellow Socialists in Kiel were well aware that Luedemann was very much persona grata with the Military Governor, who considered him eminently "clubbable," and therefore had no intention of ridding themselves of such an asset. Luedemann, in turn, considered Military Government a bunch of "harmless idiots" and treated them with exquisite condescension. Nothing he ever asked for was refused. Why should it have been? All his requests read very convincingly in both languages, since all of them were drafted jointly by the two of us.

Schleswig-Holstein was an easy show to run, but the real action was in Rhineland/Westphalia, just as it is nowadays. Since it was and is a Catholic area, the Socialists never had a dominant hold in that region, but it was not then Adenauer's fiefdom, as it became later. The British distrusted him, and he openly disliked them. He had been Cologne's lord mayor since the 1920s and had been a Francophile and anti-British even then. He had kept mostly out of sight during the Nazi years and had even been briefly jailed, but had survived unscathed and essentially undisturbed, and could hardly be termed a survivor. There was every practical reason for re-appointing him lord mayor in 1945 and that duly happened.

A couple of months later, however, some mindless British Military Government person, for reason never fully explained, not only had Adenauer dismissed but escorted from his office under armed escort. It earned the British Adenauer's undying animosity, and he was a good hater. More importantly, it turned him towards national politics. It is entirely possible that, without that asinine dismissal, he would have preferred to remain lord mayor of Cologne, as he had been for decades past. As it was, he turned his back on local and parochial politics, and began battling for leadership of the emerging CDU, eventually, and to this day, the major German political party. Adenauer was by then well into his seventies, an awesome figure, frozen-faced and of dark complexion (both due to some poor plastic surgery following a car accident in the 1920s), clever, ruthless, and autocratic, and notwithstanding his endearing Cologne dialect, a really unpleasant man. It was tough and challenging to deal with Schumacher, but it was also rewarding to confront such a personality. Dealing with

254 / Accidental Journey

Adenauer was, to me at least, dealing with a clever, sly, nasty old man. As he seemed to view me as a snotty, interfering juvenile, we came out about even. I did not have too many private contacts with Adenauer.

The purpose of meeting these august characters was similar to meeting with humble Landtag (a sort of House of Commons) members—to act as a conduit to and from London. Whitehall was pledged to let the Germans have political freedom of choice, except for extreme right-wing movements, which were of course banned. In practice, our instructions narrowed that spectrum considerably. Communists were to be discouraged whenever possible, while the Labor government in London clearly favored the German Socialists. It was therefore our brief to encourage democracy in general, but to be sure to pull in the reins if there should be too much of it. There was not much to be done in Rhineland/Westphalia from Labor's viewpoint. The dominant Catholic influence in the region had traditionally equated Socialism with blasphemy and unbelief, but London's hopes were on Arnold, the first Prime Minister of the Land. He, too, had spent many years in camps and had emerged as the leader of the reconstituted trade unions in the area. Although nominally a CDU man, he was leading the party and Rhineland/Westphalia into a distinctly left-wing direction, almost indistinguishable from the Socialists. Adenauer, then as later, led the right, conservative wing of the CDU, but Arnold had the crowds and the youth behind him. He was a hard-driving, capable, transparently honest, almost naive man whom I liked a lot. It is very possible that, in the long run, Adenauer, with his infinite guile and granitic patience, would have out-maneuvered him. As it was, Arnold died suddenly of a heart attack, still in his forties, and Adenauer took total control of the CDU and did not relinquish it for the next twenty years.

If Schumacher and Arnold had lived five years longer, we might have seen a very different Bundesrepublik, though not necessarily a more effective one. For one thing, the Franco-German alliance, a personal creation of Adenauer and de Gaulle, and one of the cornerstones of the present European structure, might never have emerged so clearly.

## 9

I was occasionally sent to attend Allied Military Government meetings either in Berlin or Vienna, where such gatherings were in almost continuous session, and a permanent group of quadripartite high ranking officers were arguing about how to run Germany and Austria. The policies and decisions to be made were neither very complex nor very numerous, since at that time, the needs and priorities in Germany did not involve issues of galactic impact, and those glittering people in Berlin and Vienna were largely addressing themselves to cures for which there was no disease.

They were, like all international conferences, incredibly time-consuming. By early 1946 it had become a virtual act of faith for the British and the U.S. delegations to oppose the Russian viewpoint, regardless of what it was, and of course the reverse applied. The French, with their incurable penchant towards individualism and mischief-making, were in their element and, by being unpredictably on one side or the other, were thoroughly unhelpful. All that would not have been such a waste of time had there not been the absurd stipulation, dating back to the euphoria of 1945, that all decisions had to be unanimous.

Delegates to permanent conferences are not unduly troubled by lack of results—which might curtail both the conference and their *raison d'être*—but what drove the British and Americans to booze and breakdowns was the Russian negotiating mode, a combination of Kafka and three-card monte. The minutes of the previous meeting are read out; the Russian delegate indicates that paragraph five is not acceptable. But it said in the minutes that he had agreed to it yesterday. Yes, he had. And now he did not? That is correct, now he did not. Would he care to explain why? No, he would not. So we have to look at paragraph five again? Yes, we have to. And so it went, almost day after day; the angrier and more frustrated the British and Americans got, the blander the Russians became. The French mostly found it amusing, which in a way it was. We once managed to intercept some confidential instructions to the Russian delegation in Berlin, dealing with negotiation techniques. They were urged to stonewall during weekdays and table major decisions and votes for

Fridays; the British and Americans being weekend-oriented crea-
tures, chances were that they would vote Stalin to be a U.S. senator
rather than miss a golf game.

I never found out what my colleagues and I were supposed to be
doing at these sessions, which we attended for a few days every couple
of months. We certainly were not expected to speak—being out-
ranked by at least four levels anywhere you look is a trifle inhibiting
anyway—and we were never told what to or whom to observe. It may
well have started as a "anything you can do, I can do better" routine,
since the Russians also had some majors and similar low-life just
sitting around and staring across the table. It was quite amusing, and I
can look back on an unblemished record of never having made any
contribution to any subject at anytime at all, except for that intercept, which was an accident and did no good, besides.

However, one of these visits involved one of life's great moments,
an event of Thurberesque splendor. It was in Vienna in early 1946
and with Austria slowly recovering from an extended spell of rape,
pillage, and systematic looting by the Russians (we said), by the
British and Americans (they said), or maybe the French. If you believe
in collective guilt and visceral anti-semitism (which I do not necessarily), anything that was done to Austria, was not enough. Schlagober or no Schlagober. Sacher torte, scenery, and charm do not make
up for Hitler, Eichmann, and Waldheim.

I was greeted in Vienna with the news that on the following day,
there would be horse racing, also accessible to civilians, evidently to
indicate that life had returned to normal. That normalcy would take
an equine aspect was no surprise: General Sir Ian McReady, the
British Commander of the Zone, was known throughout the army as
a horse racing nut. All the Allied dignitaries, as well as hordes of
Viennese, turned out to watch some scruffy-looking horses being
brutalized by some gentlemen jockeys, to everyone's boredom except
McReady who loved it. I was standing in the VIP box (not everybody
sits in the military hierarchy; the army fights for democracy, but does
not necessarily approve of it) flanked on either side by Americans,
Russians, and French, who looked respectively bored, inscrutable,
and disdainful. The most inscrutable was McReady's guest of honor,
Marshall Koniev (commanding the Russian Zone of Austria and just

as famous as his counterpart Zhukov in Berlin), who only showed signs of life at the announcement that the next race would be for the "McReady Cup," a small silver tankard, which McReady may have won at a monthly golf tournament. Koniev barked out some query to his interpreter, who, in turn, enquired how many more races there would be. Told that there would be another dozen (just enough to cover my horse racing requirements for a lifetime), Koniev snapped out some terse orders resulting in some of his guard troops hurling themselves into two jeeps and roaring off to Vienna, and the interpreter informing us that the tenth race would be for the "Koniev Cup." Nothing much happened for the next half hour, except for these undistinguished nags running in undistinguishable (at least to me) order, when suddenly the two jeeps came tearing back and a simply gigantic silver pot, the size of a small bathtub, was deposited in front of a beaming Koniev, who declared it to be "his" cup. It was not a very clean cup, with quite a bit of earth and leaves still in it, but it sure was huge.

When the race-meet mercifully ended, with Koniev in high good humor and McReady a mite miffed, I drove back to Vienna and discovered the story behind the cup, which both terrified and amused the Viennese for weeks afterwards. Evidently Koniev's instructions had merely been to find a cup considerably bigger than McReady's. His people had therefore raced back to the Hotel Imperial, which was the Russian headquarters at the time but which also had a large civilian Viennese staff to cope with running water, light bulbs, and other exigencies clearly beyond the awareness, let alone competence, of the Russian army. The two jeep loads had burst upon this milling crowd of civilians in the hotel lobby, had ordered every one aside, fired a few magazines into the ceiling to underline both the urgency and festiveness of the occasion, and then proceeded to uproot the largest potted rubber plant they could find. The Imperial has always been known for the quantity and size of its potted plants and the salvers containing them. Having secured this enormous oversize champagne bucket, the Russians then raced out again to the accompaniment of more random shots and general jollity and confusion. There may be some doubt whether the Koniev Cup was sterling silver; but who is to say that McReady's was?

## 10

I had known Wolfe Frank (né Wolfgang Frankenthaler) briefly in the Pioneers, and we had met again later at Sandhurst. He was recuperating in Kiel after a long weekend in Copenhagen, when he invited me to take a peek at the Nuremberg trials. Wolfe was an astonishingly handsome man, almost the twin of Maximilian Schell, and possessed of such charm that, since I have not heard of him either as prime minister of England or chairman of the Deutsche Bank, I must assume that he either married a succession of wildly wealthy women or became a con man in Saudi Arabia. He was not only charming, but bright and likeable and possessed almost unreal linguistic talents. I was not at all surprised to learn that he had been named chief interpreter at Nuremberg, anymore than it surprised me that he found me sumptuous accommodations in Nuremberg's premier hotel, at a time when visiting dignitaries had to make do with a camp bed in farm kitchens twenty miles out of town.

Hannah Arendt coined the concept "the Banality of Evil" after observing the Eichmann trial some fifteen years later, but it perfectly described the people sitting in the dock in Nuremberg, with one exception: Goering. In obvious ill health, bloated and pale-complexioned, in a dirty and ill-fitting uniform, handicapped by interminable (and not always accurate) translations into three "victor" languages, he nevertheless totally dominated the courtroom. He was sharp, aggressive, and contemptuous, even funny at times, in turn pathetic and clownish, center stage always, even when silent, which was not often. He reminded me of what I had read about Dimitroff during the Reichstag Fire trial in 1933. Since Goering presided over that trial, he may well have had him in mind as a role model.

Unlike Dimitroff, however, Goering never had any delusion about the outcome of his trial, and when he felt that he had clowned and bullied long enough (about a week after I saw him in the dock), he left the stage as contemptuously and flamboyantly as he had held it. It is a matter of record that he swallowed cyanide, and that, like all his fellow prisoners, he was carefully body-searched twice a day; there are only rumors as to how he obtained the capsule. The most outlandish and yet most likely theory, well in keeping with Goering's "be damned to you" attitude, is that he swallowed the capsule whole every day, recovered it from his own waste, reswallowed it, and kept on doing this until he decided that it was time to bite down on it. According to that theory, he must have had the capsule on him—or rather in him—when he was first brought to Nuremberg.

Even without Goering as a comparison, all the others were a drab and sorry lot; a bunch of middle-aged, middle-class nonentities, even Schacht with his air of frozen disdain, Speer acting like a startled spectator, or Hess with the mad, unfocused glare of a bird of prey. As for Streicher, Funk, Ribbentrop, Ley, Keitl, Frank, Jodl, Neurath, Kaltenbrunner, and Schirach, they turned high crime into a dehumanized bore. Unlike the Eichmann trial, which I attended many years later, the Nuremberg proceedings lacked both drama and humanity. There were too many people in the dock, too many judges, too many charges, too many technicalities. The vastness of the issues involved made them impersonal. Millions of nameless victims become a statistic, and it is impossible to identify with it. It was equally true at the Eichmann trial in Jerusalem, except when witnesses were called to speak of their own terrible memories and you would hear that "they took Mordecai and he was twelve and he is dead and Rebecca and she was eight and they shot her; and Sarah, who was nearly ten and she and little Simon went to Treblinka." At such shattering moments, and there were not many, John Donne's bell tolled unbearably for all of us. There were no such moments in Nuremberg.

Yet, since I attended a total of two days in court, I am not the definitive authority on the Nuremberg trials.

## 11

The final twelve months in my mini-Odyssey were mostly spent in and around the shadowy world of MI 6, shadowy partly by definition and intent, and also because there is a peculiar "now it's there, now it's not" aspect about such goings-on. There is, or was, nothing very complicated about the "division of labor" among British Intelligence institutions. On rare and brief occasions, such as the postwar years in

Germany, Military Intelligence gets entangled with ongoing professional Intelligence activities. For one thing, we might occasionally stumble onto something that would intrigue the pros, and for another we were there and on the ground, so we might as well make ourselves useful. We were mere water-carriers and the idea was for us to get out of the way as soon as possible.

The men who used people like me as gofers were sometimes MI 5, but mostly MI 6. MI 5, by far the larger and better-known organization, deals with "defensive" matters only. If someone plotted to remove Buckingham Palace brick by brick or kidnapped Princess Diana's hairdresser, those would be MI 5 matters, and there is quite some overlap between their activities and that of Scotland Yard Special Branch. MI 5, a thoroughly efficient outfit by and large, does not encourage publicity, but Rupert Murdoch invariably seems to know who is in charge there, and will tell his Sunday readers all about it.

In the ordinary course of events, MI 5 and MI 6 would feel about any association with Military Intelligence much as ordinary people would feel consorting with lepers, but those postwar years contacts were brief, and as everyone knows, leprosy only presents a problem with prolonged exposure. The nomenclature of MI 5 and MI 6 is absurd; that M stands for Military makes any of its members wince, and over the years, MI 6 became much happier being referred to as SIS (Secret Intelligence Service), until James Bond ruined it for them. MI 6 is the real glamor outfit, small, deeply secret (except to Rupert M. evidently), and deals exclusively with "offensive intelligence," thus it operates only outside England, just as MI 5 only operates within its borders. All Le Carré's people are MI 6 personnel, and since he was one of them, he knows exactly what he is talking about. "Moles" are the classically successful MI 6 operators, people so long and well established in their area of activity, that they have assumed a new identity and a new life. In recent years MI 6's halo has slipped badly and frequently, but in my time its reputation was unassailable, largely because it was uncheckable, and consistent rumors that MI 6 had infiltrated the German High Command and that, for years, some senior German staff officers were actually "moles," were widely and readily believed. I find the thought that Manstein's real name might have been Smith a little hard to credit.

I do not however disbelieve the mole concept, not least because it is now generally believed (though not by the British government) that Sir Geoffrey Hollis, now deceased but for many years head of the MI 6, was a Russian mole, and Burgess and McLean were not exactly digging above ground, either.

If I met any British mole while in Germany, I am not aware of it; chances are I did. The "need to know" concept and operating through various "cut-outs" is a way of life to such people, and while I am sure that they used some of us quite extensively, and while, in a few cases, I even got some insight as to the operation involved, I never really knew who pulled my little strings. I would be told by the head of 16 SHIO (one of my friends who later relinquished amateur status; or maybe he never had it?) that a chap named so-and-so would come round in the next few days and talk to me, and that I had been "cleared" for the assignment. Where the original orders and information came from, I do not know; the man I would be talking to would never be the same person twice. In turn, I would report what I had heard to someone designated to me, and that would always be a different person.

Nothing that was thus passed from Aix to Ghent ever seemed particularly earth-shattering to me, or even very "intelligent," but in those jigsaw puzzle situations you just do not know. Most of my activities consisted in meeting with, listening to, and paying off assorted links of assorted networks (I assumed), all vague and shadowy figures, whom I very rarely met more than once, and who collected their cigarettes or whatever, and disappeared back into the mists. The time and venue of these meetings varied, ranging from broad daylight in my office in Kiel, to midnight encounters at some scruffy farm in the Russian Zone. It was often wet and uncomfortable, usually dull, frequently scary though hardly ever dangerous. It rarely made any sense at my level. In turn, I would get involved in similar venues and at odd times of day, passing on what I had been told to equally transient and shadowy folk who hopefully understood more of the story than I did. Overall, it was more frustrating than glamorous and there were more chills than thrills. It was also faintly sinister, since this "Chinese Box" approach made effective control impossible and clearly encouraged not only private empire building, but empires that might be wholly out of step with declared intention and policies. To make the point, I had a weekly allocation of twenty thousand cigarettes and no one to render an account to. At current black market rates, that meant about ten million marks a year, and I was not exactly head of MI 6!

Although my "Political Section" colleagues and I were nowhere near as enamored of the German Socialists as the Labor government was (not least because we were not that crazy about the Labor government), we did comply with Whitehall instructions to be particularly supportive of them. MI 6, to my certain knowledge, actively supported the CDU and any party to the right of it with both money and information, and consistently and cheerfully undermined the policies of its own government. You do not believe that? Look at the CIA and Latin America. In neither case is it possible to determine whether this is someone's perception of what is in the best national interest or merely a megalomaniac and frivolous exercise of authority, which no one can control and for which no one is accountable.

Information gathering, as interpreted in those circles, made my previous involvement in this field look like finger painting to Manet. You want to know everything about everybody, simply because sooner or later you will find something which gives you a blackmail base; it is that simple. And everybody means everybody; Germans, fellow Allies, your own people, what they did, when, where, and with whom, and with photos (preferably genuine, but we had some nifty fakers around). A lot of cigarettes went that way, just accumulating first cabinets full and then cellars full of files. The most disillusioning part of it all was that it worked; I never met anyone who was "pressure proof." When threatened with blackmail, the Duke of Wellington said, "Publish and be damned!" Well, no one has said it since. . . .

"Operation Rusty" was typical of the skulduggery of those days. It started with General Gehlen, then head of German Intelligence, being captured in 1945 by the Americans who, of course, did not tell us about it. Gehlen disclosed to them that he still had an operating network reaching out towards Kronstadt and other Russian naval bases, which he was prepared to put at their disposal. Of course they did not tell us that, either. The arrangements they made with Gehlen were to release him, have him run his network, and let them have information about the Russian navy. By mid-1946, the Americans had some doubts about Gehlen, so they started penetrating his network by infiltrating some of their own people, also with the idea of eventually being able to run the network without Gehlen. We of course knew none of this, but some of those people who talk to some people like myself mentioned bits and pieces, which gave MI 6 some food for thought.

So "Operation Rusty" was set in motion, which involved infiltrating the Americans, who were busy infiltrating Gehlen and his people. In the end, Gehlen was in touch with half a dozen people whom he thought to be "his." In fact four of them were "turned" by the Americans, and three of those four were "turned" by us. What they had to say, they first told us, and then told the Americans, and then told Gehlen, who told the Americans, who did not tell us—follow me? Eventually the Americans closed down the operations, since they did not think the Russian navy worth watching (not the smartest CIA decision of the century), at which time we told them about "Operation Rusty" and that we could all have saved ourselves time and expense by acting like friends and allies. They did exactly what we would have done: listened with interest and made sure that next time we really would not know anything about it. The entire enterprise took just about a year from start to finish, and, for once, I was around long and often enough to follow the play and the cast of characters.

## 12

Sometime during "Operation Rusty," and as a change of diet and environment from skulking around derelict farms in the Magdeburg area, I spent a week in Paris. The center of Allied jollity there, and quite possibly in Europe, was the officers' club in the Faubourg St. Honoré, a quite unbelievable establishment, which gained instant credibility once you knew that it was the home of Baron Phillipe de Rothschild. Of all the lavish mansions that family owned in Paris (and that includes just about every *palais* in town), the Faubourg St. Honoré site was *non pareil*; it dwarfed the British Embassy next door, which was not exactly a hovel either. The baron had spent the war years in New York and, on his return, had turned his home into a temporary Officers' Club, all furnishings and staff supplied and paid for by him, and food and drink supplied by us (a double Scotch for one shilling may be the least believable occurrence of all those years). The unreality of it all was brought home to me when, propped against the bar, surrounded by Gobelins beyond price and breathtaking Persian rugs not quite hiding wonderful parquet floors, I was approached by a gray-haired, lean, superbly tailored gentleman, who inquired in impeccable English whether everything was to our liking. On my assurance that it was, he smiled and walked off, the only civilian among a host of uniforms of all nations. "Le patron," the barman informed us, "he comes around once in a while and has a look."

The time I did not spend with the Rothschilds, so to speak, I spent with my father's Michelin friends, telling them how and where I had won the war. Both their hospitality and gullibility were memorable, and, bloated by sympathy and soufflés, I promised to join the firm once I left the army. I had really not given any thought to what I might be doing once I was out of uniform. While the fighting was going on, it did not seem a critical issue, and once it was over, there was always tomorrow to think about it, since today nothing intelligent occurred to you. All I knew was that I was not going back to the law because I was reluctant to settle down to three more years of studying, which a final law degree would have entailed. All I have known ever since is that that was a foolish decision.

I had been cleared for and was at times involved in matters with an "Eyes only" rating (second only to the "destroy before reading" classification I suppose), but whether the War Office employed Chinese Field Marshalls or Masai tribesmen was a matter of indifference to the Home Office. As far as the Home Office was concerned, I remained a German national until they decided otherwise. They had stopped naturalization proceedings when the war broke out, and the five statutory years required for naturalization purposes clearly referred to peacetime years, since war is a state of mind and period of time in which the Home Office does not operate at all. So naturalization proceedings once again got under way in May 1945, and since I had only been in the country for three years by September 1939, I would not be due until 1947. I had been in British tanks? I could have been in the Tower of London for all they cared.

Thus on March 17, 1947, having been in British uniform for just over six years, an officer of His Majesty's for over three, and dealing with rather complex Intelligence matters for eighteen months, I swore the Oath of Allegiance and became a British subject in due form. It was frankly no longer as much of a thrill as it should have been.

That thrill came almost five months later. On August 5, 1947, "my number came up," and I was demobilized. It was six-and-a-half years almost to the day since I joined the army and seven years, two months, three weeks, and six days after coming off the punt in Cambridge, when my world had, if not altogether turned upside down, at least tilted a bit.

The occasion was heralded by a very impressive document issued to me (and, slightly differently worded, to probably a million others) under the facsimile of the secretary of War and it read:

> Sir,
>
> Now the time has come for your release from active military duty, I am commanded by the Army Council to express to you their thanks for the valuable service which you have rendered in the services of your country at a time of grave national emergency.
>
> At the end of the emergency you will relinquish your commission and at that time a notification will appear in the London Gazette granting you the honorary rank of Major in the Royal Armored Corps. Meanwhile you have permission to use the rank with effect from the date of your release.
>
> I am, Sir, your obedient servant.

I ought to know the text, the document stands framed right in front of me. Just as well that the Home Office got around to me when it did, otherwise the reference to "service of your country" might have been a bit ambiguous.

I was also informed that the army would pay for eighty-six days leave, by some complicated computation; it may not have been union wages, but it seemed reasonable to me at the time. More so than having to report to the north of Scotland to be demobilized, but then the army can foul things up right to the wire. It took about four hours less to get there than to cross Russia on the Trans-Siberian Railroad, and in half the comfort. The army's bounty included the issuance of a gray pinstriped suit, tailored along the lines of a horse blanket with apertures—the top would have fitted a giraffe, the bottom a hippopotamus—shoes that were too yellow and too small, a shirt that was too blue and too large, tie and socks, which I gave right back, and a hat, which I lost.

Thus equipped, I rejoined the ordinary world.

# EPILOGUE

I HAD ORIGINALLY intended to go to Oxford and was scheduled to sit for scholarship examinations there in January 1938. Since Cambridge held virtually similar examinations in December 1937, I had taken them by way of a trial-run and, to everyone's astonishment, most of all my own, had come out with a major scholarship. Since the "bird in hand" is a sound Anglo-Saxon maxim, and since I am indolent by nature, I passed on Oxford.

I loved Cambridge above all other places and do to this day. Still, had I gone to Oxford, I would not have been interned. Had I not been interned, I would certainly not have joined the Pioneers, perhaps I might not even have joined the army. Oliver Wendell Holmes once wrote, "It is required of a man that he should share the action and passion of his time, at peril of being judged not to have lived."

Maybe so, but in my view, it was still a pretty accidental journey!

**M**ark Lynton was born in Stuttgart, Germany, and holds a law degree from Cambridge University. He served for seven years in the British Army in World War II before embarking upon a forty-year career as a corporate executive. He is now a U.S. citizen and lives in Larchmont, New York.